Speaking Out

International Institute for Qualitative Methodology Series

Series Editor:
Lisa Given, *University of Alberta*

The International Institute for Qualitative Methodology, under the auspices of the Faculty of Nursing at the University of Alberta, was founded in 1998 to facilitate the development of qualitative research methods across a wide variety of academic disciplines through research, publications, conferences, and workshops. The series consists of volumes that have received the Dissertation Award of the Institute, then were revised for publication.

Speaking Out
Storytelling for Social Change

Linde Zingaro

Left
Coast
Press
Inc.

Walnut Creek, California

LEFT COAST PRESS, INC.
1630 North Main Street, #400
Walnut Creek, CA 94596
http://www.LCoastPress.com

ISBN 978-1-59874-420-0 hardcover
ISBN 978-1-59874-421-7 paperback

Library of Congress Cataloguing-in-Publication Data:

Zingaro, Linde.
Storytelling for social change / Linde Zingaro.
    p. cm.—(International institute for qualitative methodology series)
Includes bibliographical references and index.
ISBN 978-1-59874-420-0 (hardcover : alk. paper)—ISBN 978-1-59874-421-7 (pbk. : alk.
paper)
1. Storytelling. 2. Social change. I. Title.
GR72.3.Z56 2009
808.5'43—dc22 2009012992

Printed in the United States of America

∞™ The paper used in this publication meets the minimum requirements of American
National Standard for Information Sciences—Permanence of Paper for Printed Library
Materials, ANSI/NISO Z39.48–1992.

09 10 11 12 13 5 4 3 2 1

Text design art: Skycircle1, from "The Work of the Sacred" (2005), Linde Zingaro,
photographer

Chapter 8, p. 165: Thanks to Ferron and Nemesis Publishing for the item from Ferron's
Testimony.

Contents

For Janel, for Helen, for Sherry-Barry, for Tuck,
and for so many others,
voices lost.
And for all those who spoke out for them.

Acknowledgments

I first wish to acknowledge my debt to the speakers who talked with me about their work—Alma, Anise, Anne, Beth, Ellen, Katalina, Kate, Jacques, James, Mary, Ned, Renee, and Sally— whose wisdom and commitment have informed every page of this text. I am also very grateful for the academic assistance of many: for early support and inspiration by Donna Zapf and Mark Selman in Graduate Liberal Studies at Simon Fraser University, and by Allison Tom in Ed Studies at The University of British Columbia; for the interest and the scholarship of the professors and students I encountered in courses and in the Ph.D. program at UBC, and especially to my wonderful committee—Shauna Butterwick, Valerie Raoul, and Garry Grams. Profound thanks and appreciation to Lisa Givens and the International Institute of Qualitative Methodology, who selected my work for their 2008 Dissertation Award, and to Mitch Allen and Left Coast Press, Inc. for revision and publication.

For the development of the original thesis, I am grateful for the financial support of the Social Sciences and Humanities Research Council and the University Graduate Fellowships, a Graduate Research Grant from UBC, as well as travel grants from both the Faculty of Education and the Faculty of Graduate Studies at UBC. For the move to a more accessible version, I am indebted to Sandra Butler for mentorship and encouragement.

My greatest debts, however, are personal ones. I will never be able to repay what I owe to all those people over the years who have shared lives and stories with me, both in Canada and in Japan. My witnessing of their pains and joys, their strengths and struggles, and their witnessing of mine, have contributed to this work, as they have enriched my life and made meaning for me when nothing else could. My son and his partner, my grandchildren, and my dog forever ground me in the beauty of the real, and my friends and colleagues allow me, in our relationships, to work toward compassion and responsibility. My most profound and continual gratitude, however, is for the constancy, the integrity, the stalwart strength, generosity, and endurance with which my partner Liz Whynot has shared her wisdom and her life with me.

CHAPTER 1

Introduction: Disclosure Consequences

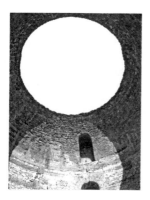

I can tell you anything. All you have to believe is the truth (Allison, 1995, p. 94)

On October 14, 2003, the *New York Times* reported that a man had committed suicide by walking in front of an eastbound New Jersey Transit commuter train. He had "publicly acknowledged that he had been sexually abused by his parish priest" and had been "instrumental in organizing New Jersey residents who had been abused by priests." He had become "an active speaker with the New York unit of the Survivors Network of those Abused by Priests . . . who was always available to break the silence . . . volunteering and making himself available for more and more speaking opportunities." People close to him said that they did not know why he might have killed himself. The parish priest who was advocating for the survivor's group is quoted as saying: "He didn't seem alienated . . . we don't know what triggered this death" (Smothers, 2003).

In his book *Why I Didn't Say Anything*, Sheldon Kennedy describes his painful situation after he had agreed to speak publicly about pressing charges against the hockey coach who had sexually abused him for much of his adolescence:

. . . in public, I had to play the role of the heroic survivor . . . I'd talked about my abuse, put my abuser in jail, received treatment, and inspired thousands of people—[but] why was I still such a mess? No one wanted to talk about that. . . . (Kennedy and Grainger, 2006, p. 155)

He describes his experience on a television interview show where he was introduced along with another man who had been sexually victimized:

Martin Kruze, the Toronto man who blew the whistle on the pedophilia ring that had been run out of Maple Leaf Gardens for decades. . . . Kruze had been abused by at least four Gardens ushers over a seven-year period, and after his story broke in the media, dozens of other victims came forward to press charges. . . . But what the viewers couldn't see was the struggle going on inside of me, a struggle that would come close to destroying me over the next eight years, and they couldn't see the struggle that was tearing Martin Kruze apart. A few months later, three days after the man who introduced Martin to the Gardens pedophilia ring was sentenced to two years less a day in jail, Martin committed suicide by throwing himself off the Bloor Street Viaduct in Toronto. (Kennedy, 2006, pp. 155/156)

For a chapter in a scholarly book, an Assistant Professor of Sociology produced an account of her experience of speaking on a CBS TV program after being invited to participate in a particular debate because of the relevance of some of her previously published academic papers. As "the daughter of a mother with mental retardation and a father who was diagnosed as a sexual psychopath" (Ronai, 1999, p. 142), she understood herself to be a credible speaker on the subject addressed in the program— "a researcher who *is* the phenomenon under consideration, including the areas of childhood sexual abuse, exotic dancing, and having a parent with mental retardation" (1999, p. 143). In this context she describes the thoughts and feelings that led her to a temptation to think of herself as a "victim of the news media." She provides what she calls a "layered" analysis of the experience of being asked questions that forced her into a position where her academic credibility was ignored or irrelevant, and where she found herself "inarticulate, trapped in a free fall" (1999, p. 150), not knowing what to say or do to avoid colluding with the construction of her as the "good victim" that her testimony was intended to support. "To fulfill the journalist's role as the culturally prescribed protector and bearer of truth, he needed me to be a concomitant, appropriate, culturally prescribed victim" (1999, p. 152). Her paper is an enactment of her refusal of this essentialized position, framed within an understanding of the social uses of victim discourse; it constitutes a public recuperation of her own agency in choosing to speak about her experience—however painful the process: "'Victim' is a moment in the dialectic of identity, one pose among many that constitute parts of who we all are as long as we engage in this discourse" (1999, p. 156).

These three texts —Smothers, Kennedy, and Ronai—are among the few public references to an emotional economy that operates beneath the surface of one of our present culture's most familiar social conventions: the offering up of "the real story" of trauma, pain, or humiliation, from someone who has "been there." Every day—in print, in cinema, on television, and very commonly on the internet, and in various Truth and Reconciliation processes—a particular kind of story is being told, and told again. In the first person, often with graphic detail, delivered with emotional intensity in a language of urgency and significance, individuals are speaking out about their personal suffering from some direct experience of trauma or injustice—as victims of natural disasters or of human-generated, social harms. Each of these stories is hard-won, and the telling of them is an important step in the person's struggle to make some kind of meaning out of seemingly inexplicable suffering, humiliation, or terror. With the best of intentions, many of these stories are advanced or encouraged in the context of an ideology of empowerment that equates speech with power, implying that the benefit of having one's story heard has enduring political, social, and therapeutic value to the speaker. However, these narratives enter a specific historical and epistemological environment, incorporated into discourses and regimes of meaning that are supported by particular conceptions of power, causality, and agency—and these frameworks determine not only the language available to describe experience but also the ultimate significance of the telling.

> Through rules of exclusion and classificatory divisions that operate as unconscious background assumptions, a discourse can be said to set out not what is true and what is false, but what can have truth-value at all, or in other words, what is statable. (Alcoff and Gray, 1993, p. 265)

The forms and conventions of these discourses also work to position the speaker of such a story in some way that allows the listener the possibility of a comfortable relationship to the information she provides. If the knowledge is too threatening or too different from the listener's experience, it must be attended by some expert reference—an explanation above and beyond the story—or the speaker is seen as not quite credible. A story without recognizable landmarks, or some measure of a familiar narrative trajectory, marks the teller as lying, or possibly exaggerating—as deranged, or at the very least, confused. This part of the process is not represented in the ideology of empowerment that is the primary support for such speaking out and has mixed potentials for the speaker. The need to represent something outside ordinary storied experience requires not only a powerful performance of the testimony of an eye-witness to an unimaginable event but also the receptivity of the audience to whom the testimony is offered—the interlocutor's willingness to be a witness to the truth of the performance and to the full subjectivity of the performer. It is in the context of this dialogic dependency, what Kelly Oliver calls "the paradox between the necessity and the impossibility of witnessing," that our sense of ourselves as valid social subject is denied or recognized:

> Subject positions and subjectivity are constituted through the possibility of witnessing in this double sense. The tension inherent in witnessing is the tension between subject positions, which are historically determined, and subjectivity, which is an infinite response-ability. (Oliver, 2001, pp. 86/87)

My investment in the various theoretical and practical implications of these concepts predates my attempts to write about them by some years. In 2000, I entered a postgraduate program because of a personal need to deepen and articulate my understanding of an experiential reality that links together many stories like the three painful accounts with which I began this text and countless others that I have witnessed in my practice and in the world. I wanted to explore the meaning and significance of a phenomenon that for many years in practice with vulnerable people, I have called "Disclosure Consequences": some of the different manifestations of the apparently inexplicable, often self-destructive suffering of a person *after* s/he has found the strength to speak out or tell about some experience of harm or humiliation.

I became painfully aware of this dynamic in the late 1970s, as a result of an incident in the first group home for street youth that I operated. At that time an increasing social awareness of the extent and consequences of family violence had contributed to many changes in welfare policy, including the provision of extensive training in the specifics of sexual abuse of children for child protection workers. Our staff had identified a young woman in the emergency shelter as needing to be taken into the care of what was then called the Ministry of Social Services, because we believed that she was unsafe at home. A newly trained social worker came to the house to interview her, in order to justify a court-ordered intervention. After about an hour with the girl, the worker came out of the office where they had spoken in private and went to the other room to phone back to her office to make arrangements for the child, very satisfied with her work. The child came out of the office, went directly into the kitchen, and—right in front of me as I was cooking—grabbed a large chopping knife and smashed the blade down onto the back of her hand, attempting to cut off her fingers. This explicit demonstration of the pain of disclosure has informed my practice ever since.

From this event, from some of my own experiences of disclosure, and by having been in a position to observe many other situations in which the self-punishment process has taken a little longer to come into effect after a disclosure, I came to believe that for some, telling a story of our experience of shame or helplessness holds the potential for this kind of response. I believe that this reflects an emotional logic, based on holding ourselves responsible for what has happened to us, which creates the need to provide some external evidence to match the internal experience of worthlessness that is the consequence of marginalization/victimization/oppression. For some people, this self-discrediting impulse involves getting drunk or using drugs; gambling, fighting, sabotaging their work or their important relationships; for some, the punishment requires self-mutilation, or even suicide. It is only within the limits of these processes of self-punishment that speaking out, treatment or therapy—the talking cure—is useful or even safe. The idea that it feels better to let it out is true only to a point, and that point must be identified and managed responsibly by the practitioner or helper—whether she is a researcher, therapist, social worker, health practitioner, or a teacher interested in experience as authority. I was gratified by the recognition of this dynamic again when I read the work of revered psychotherapist James Bugental, in which he describes a similar incident of over-disclosure from his early practice, from which, he says, he "learned the power and dangers of unmodulated catharsis and got a dramatic first view of the depths of the subjective" (Bugental, 1992, p. 62).

In the process of theorizing this practice-derived knowledge, I have found sources for the language that I needed in many different disciplines. The shift from the kind of "trauma talk" (Marecek, 1999, p. 82) that is commonly understood in anti-violence or social justice practice to the more academic terminologies of philosophy, psychology, and cultural studies has been useful to the extent that it has allowed me to describe finer distinctions within the range of ideas that inform the work that I continue to do. Melding those more abstract textual resources with the voices of practitioners who, like me, are exposing the experience of marginalization as a part of our professional identity, will, I hope, result in a mosaic—an image made up of unique and separate, even contradictory voices, concepts, and practices—an arrangement of individually shaped and colored elements that together make a meaning larger than that offered by any single piece, any solo voice.

The Price People Pay to Tell the Truth about Themselves

When I began with the conception of the academic study that is the basis for this work, I was motivated to produce material that would enter into dialogue with Gayatri Spivak's famous answer to the question of subaltern voice: "both that the oppressed can speak and that they cannot be heard outside colonizing regimes of meaning" (Lather, 2000, p. 156). My examination of the phenomenon of speaking out, as it has been variously articulated in the literature, had led me to the belief that some profound contradictions exist within/between the discourses that underline the epistemology of empowerment, and that these contradictions have contributed to a particular absence of certain knowledges or positions in the research. Part of what is missing, I believe, is any description of the lived experience of what it might cost the individual who is called on, or who holds herself responsible, to speak out in a public way about her own painful experience of some social issue.

In empowerment terms, and particularly in research where empowerment ideology is a commonly expressed justification for the interaction with marginalized individuals, the actual helping or empowering service that is on offer is precisely the facilitation of the individual (marginalized) person's ability to "tell her own story"—in effect, to leave the margin by being recognized as exercising voice. But if the person is perceived to be powerful enough to be allowed a voice—to be seen, or heard, as an individual, embraced as a creditable witness—then she is no longer marginal and cannot be seen to represent that class of persons who suffer the pains that she has learned to describe, because she is no longer voiceless, no longer the same as they are. Only a performance of pain, what Berlant calls the "traffic in affect," works as a believable witness account of subalternity:

> Subaltern pain is not considered universal (the privileged do not experience it, do not live expecting that at any moment their ordinarily loose selves might be codified into a single humiliated atom of subpersonhood). But subaltern pain is deemed, in this context, universally intelligible, constituting objective evidence of trauma reparable by the law and the law's more privileged subjects. . . . The universal value is here no longer a property of political personhood but a property of a rhetoric that claims to represent not the universal but the true self. . . . In this political model of identity, trauma stands as truth. (Berlant, 2001, p. 144)

In this truly tautological structure, a second-order, critical academic position allows first-hand reports of war, violence, and brutality to be subsumed under dismissive terminologies and distancing language at the same time that it requires researchers to attend to their "engagement with individual knowers" (Naples, 2003, p. 52). Some of the language used to analyze "trauma talk," and "survivor discourse" (Alcoff and Gray, 1993; Lamb, 1999; Naples, 2003), as well as the debates on the truth value of memory and testimonio (Campbell, 1997; Gardner, 2001; Haakon, 1999; Tierney, 2000), function to recreate, in macro terms, the specific conditions that are experienced in micro terms by the subjects of my study. The stance of interrogating the truth claims or the authenticity of an individual witness creates a distance, for the reader/listener, from the dangerous knowledge of larger structures of power and privilege. If this individual witness cannot be believed, if she can be reduced to a particular instance of either tragedy or heroism, or if her speech can be categorized or subsumed within a bounded discourse, then the content that she offers is once again banished to the condition of "impossible knowledge" (Haig-Brown, 2003) and can be theorized out of danger.

In the final analysis, although this particular trick of translation may indeed serve the need to produce new, and possibly useful, questions for the researcher (Foucault, 1977), such "local knowledge" (Geertz, 1973) as might be unearthed in this process can/must always be examined for the possibility of the presence of "unreliable witnesses" (Meiners, 2001). Researchers are reminded that, in the service of reality, they can't generalize from such narratives, life stories, or testimonials, because the story represents only one of many partial, positional, truths. In the end, the empowerment ideology implies a central paradox:

> There are particular problems in viewing reality as entirely personal and contextual . . . when the object is emancipation. If there are really no such things as "facts" about the way people are treated, then there is also no such thing as discrimination or oppression. . . . The enforced injustices of social inequities . . . (are driven) . . . into the personal cupboard of privately experienced suffering. (Oakley, 2000, p. 298)

Speaking into Relation

From the beginning of the process, I was concerned that my project could have the potential to reproduce the problem that I am trying to identify. My research required me to work with speaking subjects in the creation of a textual record of their/our experience. But I did not imagine that this process of re-membering would be painless. In fact, I expected that for some of my interlocutors, I might well be setting up the risk of falling into some version of the self-discrediting suffering of Disclosure Consequences. It was with this dynamic in mind that I determined the criteria on which to base a choice of research methods and orientations that would allow me to hear the spoken stories, to make room with respect for the silences, and to protect the storytellers (and me) from falling into the trap of a conventional way of understanding the situated knowledges they describe.

I believe that we do not in fact speak out at all—we speak *into* relation. Because this is true, both the role of the powerful/Knower and the role of the powerless/Abject are possible for every person who speaks into the space of relation, particularly in the public realm. In the end, no matter how well we can speak, or how carefully we construct a political action, much of the outcome is still to some degree dependent on the context of speaking and the positioning of the listener/interlocutor. Assuming that these informants are Knowers, I have been committed to producing a context in which my interactions with them could allow the exchanges between us to operate as performances of that power and could help us both to avoid the kinds of interactions that produce the Abject.

I was privileged to speak with informants chosen by a strategy of "purposive sampling—[whereby] the sample produces the knowledge necessary to understand the participant's location in structures and processes"

(Oakley, 2000, p. 63)—based on their previous self-identification as "speakers" in some public context. Because I have done the same kind of work for twenty-five years in the same city and have some reputation for advocacy and speaking out, I have a wide network of bordered colleagues, some of whom volunteered to be interviewed when I spoke about my project. Other participants, previously unknown to me, were encouraged to contact me by friends or colleagues who were aware of the study. Of course, any person with whom I have ever had any therapeutic or mentoring relationship was excluded.

While my participant cohort would appear to comprise people with a robust voice, in that they are self-defined as activists, and as having some power that therefore might sustain them as well as support others, I did not take for granted that in this investigation I was entitled to ignore ethical concerns for "vulnerable subjects" (Hollway and Jefferson, 2000). In fact, to the extent that I have been successful in eliciting the kinds of stories that could further my intentions, I asked for responses and subjective narratives of a very personal nature. These accounts could have had the potential, if even momentarily, to take the participants in this study back to the experience of stigma or voicelessness—back to describe their knowledge of a world that, by virtue of performing their activist roles, they have largely left behind. These are stories of travels within and across a territory that lies unexamined in the undefined space between the seemingly incommensurate experiences of victimization and power, between helplessness and agency, between silence and voice.

Where Silence Is NOT Consent

By remembering the social constructionist commitment to observe "the way language creates our worlds" (Gergen, 1999, p. 64), I have been concerned to resist contributing to the current conception of power that holds that agency, voice, or resistance is the necessary and constituent component of the Subject. For me, this position colludes with the implication that a lack of voice or representation is the mark of the failure of the agentic subject, the belief that one who remains (or falls) silent is not a fully real Subject in relation to my subjectivity but a representative of the essential Abject:

> The abject designates precisely those "unlivable" and "uninhabitable" zones of social life which are densely populated by those who do not enjoy the status of the subject, but whose living under the sign of the "unlivable" is required to circumscribe the domain of the subject. (Butler, 1993, p. 3)

The definition of agency that requires us to speak (and to be heard) in order to exist as credible social beings consigns whole worlds of experience to an arena of "impossible knowledge" (Haig-Brown, 2003) and ropes off wide areas of social life as unsayable. If we assume in our engagement with others that silence is the mark of the Abject, and yet continue to use only language that is coherent with the identification of agency as voice, then no matter how clearly we desire the outcome of empowerment for the other, we participate in the process of constructing a silent interlocutor as Abject. For example, in narrative reports of violence and abuse:

> What can and cannot be said is so constrained that women who tell stories about more than one occurrence of abuse begin to look like victim personalities, crazy, having an axe to grind, or all three. (Weis and Fine, 2000, p. 110)

I believe that some description of the costs and pains and joys of the movement to voice can be articulated, leaving room for what cannot be spoken, without creating yet another representation of the Abject. I hope that these descriptions help to map some specific implications of the epistemology of empowerment by voice, by illuminating some of the constraints imposed on our ability not only to speak but also to hear, and by outlining the shape of some of the edges of our competence to read certain locations, knowledges, and kinds of experience. I hope that, like painting the solid frame around an open window, coloring in these stories can allow us to recognize the structures that define experiences that lie outside the window. After that, we are into a different set of problems:

> Once we have encountered the limits of the sayable, we must acknowledge the existence of "unsayable things" and, by means of a language somehow formed on being silent, articulate that which cannot be grasped. (Budick and Iser, 1989, p. xii)

My original intent was to describe the experience of people living in a particular social location, using their direct knowledge of this bordered practice in a way that could shed light not only on others who share that space but also on the ideologies and systems that contain/constrain them. The language of voice and speaking out has framed much of my conversation with participants, not only in my original description of what the topic would be but also because the rhetoric of voice as power seemed to provide consistent meanings for all of our interactions. But as I began my research, I found that, although I was still interested in the same sites of knowledge for my source of data, I had narrowed the range of questions that I was prepared to ask, and had, if anything, increased my own ethical restrictions on the kinds of data I wished to analyze. I have returned to Spivak:

> To read for difference rather than the same; . . . to probe the price people pay to tell the truth about themselves; . . . and to situate interpretations as supplement rather than mimesis, both inadequate and necessary. Such lessons are endorsed toward a goal of what Gayatri Spivak terms a "knowledgeable Eurocentrism" rather than a naïve one in first-world dealings with third-world texts. (Lather, 2000, p. 153)

Assuming the self-conscious Eurocentrism of my location in the privileged position of a graduate student in a sophisticated Western university as
well as my own "multiple marginality" (Turner, 2002), my primary intention for this project was *to probe the price people pay to tell the truth about
themselves.* With this as my aim, I believed that my methodology must operate, as Lather suggests, "within/against the assumption of letting the voices
speak" (Lather, 2000, p. 158), and, importantly, that my representation
of the work must "assume the narrator as BOTH unreliable AND bearer
of knowledge" (Lather, p. 159). Attending to the contradictions of these
requirements, I begin by recognizing that

> . . . given the difficulties of speaking out of difference, to be both intelligible
> and yet not reinscribed into the very normative frameworks that constitute the
> difference is the (impossible) task of the subaltern. (Lather, 2000, p. 156)

I was not interested in engaging in the insider/outsider debate on
validity, although there are some responses recorded in the dialogues with
participants that address that issue. Rather, I am assuming a more "fluid"
location for the subjects of my research, whereby

> . . . our relationship to a community is never expressed in general terms but
> is constantly being negotiated in particular, everyday interactions; and these
> interactions are themselves enacted in shifting relationships among community
> residents. (Naples, 2003, p. 49)

This, it seems to me, is more in line with a social constructionist position
from which a report of identity or insiderness can be seen as the offering of
a truth claim, one that assumes a kind of knowledge, attained by experience
and/or location. This approach does not require me to determine the truth
of a truth-claim; in fact, "constructionist views function as an invitation to a
dance, a game, a form of life" (Gergen, 1994, p. 79). What it allowed me to
do was to disengage from the processes of interrogation that are such a significant feature of academic (critical) reading of any statement of experience
and to attend to a desire to represent an encounter with that unrecognizable
entity —"the political figure between domains, between forms, between
homes, between languages" (Said, 1993, p. 332).
I chose to resist the "aerial distance" (Martin, 1996) of the language of
trauma discourse and survivor discourse in the process of this study, except
for the purpose of identifying "the repertory of concepts and categories, the
systems of statements, and the narrative frameworks that speakers rely on
to make themselves intelligible" (Marecek, 1999, p. 161). But neither was
I interested in contributing to the trend to "excessive witnessing":

> . . . excess in the dual sense of too much horror leading to the impossibility,
> abolition, or futility of witnessing . . . but also in the sense of unreserved,

transgressive, savage obligation to tell the truth, a call born out of the pitiless awareness of the absurdities and injustices that excuse such horrors. (Zulaika, 2003, p. 89)

I hope this work articulates what people in this position feel when we choose to expose our stigmatized identity/knowledge—to come out from passing to disclose our (otherwise invisible and unmentionable) marginalized status—and how self-disclosure can affect us after the performance is over. It is the risk of the experience of social invalidation that the choice to speak defies and to which our chosen silence submits. This research has been undertaken to examine the perspective from within this intersection, from the place where an individual's contribution to our knowledge of the inexplicable enters the rhetorical space into which her story must fall.

... every life is always already partially scripted, partially contained within pre-existing narrative lines: a film that is already running colors and flavors even one's simplest utterances, and hence one's (observational and other) knowledge claims, one's testimonial moments. So the incredulity issue becomes an issue about stories, scripts and improvisations: about how some story lines pull people back from being able "freely and honestly" to speak the truth, tell it as it is, about even the simplest of everyday things. (Code, 1995, p. 73)

The data for this project derives from a series of interviews with a group of experienced helping professionals who could be described as "bordered." This means that, having gained some kind of credential or position of authority and responsibility recognized by dominant culture, they (and I) also identify ourselves as having lived through, or as living with, the same kinds of difficulties that our work is intended to ameliorate for others. As educators, counselors, health practitioners, researchers, and community activists, the women and men who volunteered to speak with me about their experience share this border. Like the inhabitants of Anzaldúa's *Borderlands*, they also share a conception of the border as a lived space, not a line of demarcation. Trauma, poverty, mental illness, racism, homophobia, transphobia, ethnic or religious discrimination—for each of us, the experience of one or more of these informs our daily practice with others, and intentional self-disclosure of our identification with these issues has become a rhetorical and political tool of practical use in our work.

I want this work to illustrate a view from the edge: from within the spaces inhabited by the apparently powerful activist who, by speaking of his/her own experience, is purposefully reentering/re-enacting a socially negated identity with political intent. For most inhabitants of this space, the action of speaking out is grounded on an ideology of empowerment and involves using the definitions for, and demonstrations of, the kinds of power that can be recognized by dominant society, while working to facilitate and valorize the knowledge and agency of the marginal. The fact that I locate myself in this exact position did not make this project any easier—it required a careful analysis of methodological options for the project.

Because of the need to revise a strictly academic project to allow a more accessible reading, the next two chapters represent a summary of four very theoretical sections of the original thesis and may be relevant to those readers, in particular, who are interested in qualitative research or a more theoretical engagement with the ideas. In order to provide an adequate explanation for the context of the interviews, and to offer a philosophical ground for many of the responses quoted in the text, the first chapter examines some of the implications of the empowerment ideology that operates as the justification for much social justice activism. After that, some of the familiar concepts supporting many individual and group efforts at voicing subordinate claims are presented in a kind of glossary, sketching an overview and critique of this language and an explanation of some of the terminologies that will be found later in the book.

The concerns specific to the choice of the vignette methodology for data-gathering in this context are discussed in the following chapter, along with a further description of the arts-based approach that was used for the representation of the material. The rest of the text may be more familiar to those people working or volunteering in helping roles, since it is a more direct engagement with the remarkable voices of the participants in the study. For some readers, this part of the work might feel a bit like meeting a mentor who has been on the front lines for many years, one who has a sincere desire to provide support for those who are just beginning a work life, hoping to contribute to social change. For others, perhaps those having had more experience in practice, it may provide some validation, encouragement, and a different look at the language—seeds for a continued conversation on the meanings of our work, for us, for our communities, and for the larger contexts in which we live.

The kind of conversation that I imagine is one that has, I believe, been interrupted in the last several years, first by our necessary response to various forces: the tendency to focus on specific techniques or evidence-based interventions and on the continual need to manage funding crises in our increasingly lean economies. But I also think that the gradual professionalization of the fields of helping that I am concerned with has also contributed to the depoliticizing of our commitments to one another and to the populations that we have pledged to serve. As we learn to adapt to the increase of expectations for performance that accompany our professionalized roles, we often become more isolated as people. Many of us have no time and no context for the kinds of exchange of knowledge and experience that slips through the cracks of formal training, of textbooks and policy manuals. Our need to understand ourselves as ethical, responsible, and capable of a real contribution to change is repeatedly pushed to the side by the daily demands of the work—relegated, with our need for self-care, to the occasional facilitated retreat or team-building exercise important enough to be supported by the organizations that use our skills. Such structured opportunities for connection may provide some comfort and even offer some skill-building, but they do little to actually address the inner struggles of those who, by virtue of our work, must daily confront the reality of suffering for a population, or even of a single individual, with care and compassion.

I have undertaken the research that provides the data for this study in the desire to illuminate a particular practice, engaged in by a significant number of people—a subset of those multitudes working in helping roles. Although not limited to a specific site or location in space, I contend that the performances that constitute this practice play an important role in society, grounded as they are in present discourses and ideologies and contained within a current understanding of the ways in which individuals and communities interact with each other. However well recognized it is as a convention in our culture, speaking out as a political act of advocacy for others is an action the mechanics of which have not often been brought into focus. Each speaker, and perhaps especially those bordered by their movement from some subaltern position to a situation of professional responsibility for others, seems to emerge full-grown and articulate, the result of some unimagined transformation that we have not been witness to and have not thought to define.

I have invited others who engage in this practice to discuss with me some of the skills, the satisfactions, and the successes of this kind of professional confession but also to help me to identify the risks and the failures that we have all inevitably experienced on the way to expert speaking. In uncovering the possible costs and losses of self-disclosure, this study is constructed neither as a call to discontinue the practice nor as a story of victimization. Rather, it is an attempt to identify the epistemology, the ethics, and the integrity that work to support such powerful and risky intentions and to recognize and celebrate the strength and the creativity of the many people who share this space. In the end, it is possible that the approach I have chosen will be viable only within the practice of what Lyotard calls paralogy[1]: "that which refines our sensitivity to differences and reinforces our tolerance for the incommensurable" (Fritzman, 1990, quoted in Lather, 1994).

CHAPTER 2

Ideology, Terminology, and Method

In social justice activism, perhaps more than in other professional settings, the ideology that supports our daily work is embedded in terminologies used in such a way as to become a kind of shorthand. For many of us, particularly those working under the pressure of the continually expanding need for care and community involvement, the concepts that ground the practice can be obscured, our concern for the welfare of others taken for granted as a positive in itself. This chapter begins with an attempt to address some of the assumptions and the critiques that inform and support the actions of so many, across disciplines and responsibilities. The last part of the chapter examines some of the terminologies commonly used in the fields where interactions are often enacted in the name of empowerment, and it outlines the relevance of these ideas, first in the context of the work we do in the service of others, and then for the methodological choices we must make in researching the voices of the margins.

If Empowerment Is the Solution, What Is the Problem?

For the purpose of this project, I address empowerment ideology as something not entirely rational—something that, like feminism, requires a conversion but that also includes historical cosmologies or explanations for its own existence and provides ethical guidelines that work toward the development of a moral philosophy. Perhaps most important, it supports or even demands active (activist) proselytizing. In fact, I contend that this ideology is largely defined by its moral justifications and its methodologies for the recruitment of new converts. The interviews that form the basis of this work were undertaken as an attempt to articulate an intellectual exploration of the implications of empowerment from a very specific position: not only that of a convert to empowerment ideology but that of someone who inhabits a complex borderland, having attained a kind of social power, or cultural capital, by working to empower others who share my historical powerlessness. Particularly because of my choice to make my own history visible by using self-disclosure as a part of my professional practice, I was aware that as I did my research, I was risking my own comfort. At the very least, what was at stake was whatever un-self-conscious ease I might retain in my practice and, at worst, my own disillusionment and loss of confidence in the meaning of my work.

In the choice of participants for my research, I presumed the possibility of a shared membership in a community based on this ideology: across the commonly acknowledged boundaries of race, class, gender, sexual orientation, and even of academic discipline, some recognizable solidarity exists. I have had to approach this project as a thought experiment by imagining myself as belonging to this larger culture, one joined, however loosely, to form a community of empowerment practitioners. As is true of any group bound together by an ideology, there are certain to be many experiences of difference and dissonance within the group, as well as varying levels of awareness and/or analysis of the possible biases and blindnesses inherent in such a taken-for-granted value system. I belong to this group, or I have a "self constituted by this community" (Bickford, 1996), and therefore I most likely share some of these values and possess my own particular biases and blindnesses as well. However, if, as a card-carrying member, I were not allowed to question or even to challenge the assumptions and the rules of the group, then the very ideology of this community would ensure its own dissolution, since the common practice of its membership rests on at least one primary value: that of the virtue of critical thinking.

So what is the "stuff" of membership in this community? What are the principles with which I must agree in order to establish my membership? What are the constraints, what are the limits to my dissent, what lines of resistance or transgression will guarantee my exclusion if I overstep? What is the language with which we communicate meanings particular to this community and within which I understand these limits and their social consequences? In order to distinguish the "figure" of any one of these characteristics, I must uncover what constitutes the "field" in which they all operate—I need to interrogate a number of the basic assumptions underlying the ideology and mark the differences across some of the territories where it is used.

The Power in Empowerment

Logically, if one is to work toward the empowerment of others, one must be in possession of, or have access to, something understood as power, which can somehow be transferred to those who are in need of it. The central problem for empowerment theories is embedded in this paradoxical situation: how can we have something, give it away, and still have it? How can we have something that has been used to harm or exploit others (even ourselves and others like us) and use it to improve their (our) lives instead? How can we tell if we are being harmful with what power we have? Much of the current debate about the nature and the ethical uses of power is conceived as dichotomized between "power over" (a person, group, or resource) and "power to" (effect change, produce or reproduce some social consequence or action):

> The dominant tradition of power analysis uses a strategic conception of power and, in so doing, effectively equates power with domination. . . . In this perspective, a politics of power necessarily becomes a politics of strategic success through appropriate resource mobilization. (Stewart, 2001, p. 6)

According to this view, "power refers to the transformative capacity of human action" (Giddens, 1993, p. 117). Foucault's argument makes a distinction between premodern sovereign power (repressive, coercive) and modern disciplinary power (inherently productive). The significance of disciplinary power is found in what he calls subjectivisation—the production and reproduction of subjectivity:

> There are two meanings of the word subject: subject to someone else by control and dependence, and tied to his own identity by a conscience or self-knowledge. Both meanings suggest a form of power which subjugates and makes subject to. (Foucault, 1982, p. 212)

Judith Butler expands this analysis to include the power of language and discourse:

> Power is not simply what we oppose but also, in a strong sense, what we depend on for our existence and what we harbor and preserve in the beings that we are. . . . Subjection consists precisely in this fundamental dependency on a discourse we never chose but that, paradoxically, initiates and sustains our agency. (Butler, 1997, p. 2)

Another important concept that contributes to the theories underpinning empowerment practice is Gramsci's idea of power as public consent to

social control. In this framework, as a coercive process legally enforced by
dominant cultural and state structures, hegemonic power is defined as

> the "spontaneous" consent given by the great masses of the population to
> the general direction imposed on social life by the dominant fundamental
> group. . . . (Gramsci, 1971, p. 12)

Following Hannah Arendt, Habermas articulates an alternative
model of power that has also contributed to empowerment ideology. He
emphasizes the value of social relations grounded in communicative action
in his conception of a struggle between the larger structures/systems of
domination and the sociocultural life-world:

> these struggles are not to be understood as strategic conflicts over desired
> goods; rather, the struggles concern the legitimacy of existing social norms and
> the introduction of new ones. . . . *They are above all struggles over normativity.*
> (Stewart, 2001, pp. 46, 47)

So is it a requirement for membership in the empowerment community
that I know about/understand/agree with these conceptions of power,
or is it that such a coming to know/understanding/agreeing may actually
constitute the original conversion to the ideology? If, at the same time, this
consciousness of power is "power/knowledge"—then the "stuff" that, by
its own definitions, makes the difference between those who have and those
who do not have power is also the stuff that makes those of us who have
power dangerous (potentially dominant or oppressive) to those of us who do
not have it/ know it/understand it. This may signal the entry of the second
of the self-contained opposites that seem to proliferate in empowerment
ideology. As soon as I know that I am recognized as having this power, as
soon as I understand how power works, I am responsible to resist it in myself.
My continued recognition by this community depends on my willingness to
work to assist others in attaining it, since "the idea of liberation itself, the
acknowledgment that the other is also a self, commands that one assert the
necessity of each person's freedom" (Khanna, 2001, p. 117). How do I go
about this?

> To empower implies the ability to exert power over, to make things happen.
> It is an action verb that suggests the ability to change the world, to overcome
> opposition. It has a transformatory sound, an implicit promise of change,
> often for the better. (Parpart et al., 2002, p. 5)

It is at the point of entering into praxis that there is a separation between
the various disciplines within which the concept of empowerment has been
taken up. Two of the most important areas of critique within empowerment
ideology are based on the contradictory conceptions of "power as property," which implies a need for rights or access to resources, and "power as

voice," which requires participation or representation. In the fields of social services, community development and health care, "proponents of empowerment tend to regard it as simply a quantifiable increase in the amount of power possessed by an individual or group" (Cruikshank, 1994). In that context, then, "power is thus transferred in the same way that property is, in the sense that to empower suggests to give power or to confer power" (Pease, 2002, p. 137). It is interesting that within the rules of professionalism for both health care and social service, identifying oneself with this ideology carries a specific benefit, that of valued membership in the community of empowerment practitioners. But, in the ideological framework of empowerment even those advantages that may accrue to the agent of empowerment are the focus of their own critique:

> The language of empowerment is increasingly becoming a part of the professional's legitimacy. To be empowering in human service work is to be self-legitimating. Baistow (1994/1995, p. 45) raises the question, however, whether empowerment can survive as a construct with critical potential whilst it also becomes another tool in the kitbag of the professional. (Pease, 2002, p. 137)

In this context, Nancy Fraser describes the administrative power inherent in the expert needs discourse, where professionals (even, or perhaps especially, empowerment professionals) are engaged in problem solving for their various constituencies by politicizing the issues that are seen to contribute to suffering and inequity. She describes the way that the expert power of the activist professional works to create the definitions, not only of the problem but also of the appropriate solutions:

> these discourses consist in a series of rewriting operations, procedures for translating politicized needs into administrable needs. Typically, the politicized need is redefined as the correlate of a bureaucratically administrable satisfaction—a "social service." (Fraser, 1989, p. 174)

The consequences of another paradox of empowerment ideology are lived out every day in many areas of social service, where social workers, health providers, and community support activists work to weave the safety net that is "our institutional form of publicly sponsored compassion" (Froggett, 2002). In many of these settings, the actions and best intentions of empowerment practice are based on the fundamentally individualistic assumption that all people can/should be able to be empowered—given voice, recognition in their own terms, and access to whatever benefits are available, even within an economy of scarcity. Historically, changes in policy on the delivery of service in both health and social services arenas have been driven by the social justice concept of an abstract right to access to the goods of the community, but in the present environment of political conservatism that exists in many Western countries, changes in the logics supporting public responsibility have, however, shifted the use of the rhetoric of empowerment to fit a paradigm that Froggett calls a "mixed welfare." Policy initiatives, such as Work to Welfare and Kith and Kin child protection services although initiated as fiscally driven strategies intended to avoid developing dependencies in those in need of support, are now described as empowering the client.

The result of this shift is the reconstruction of service systems, based on the neoconservative philosophical foundations of contractualism and consumerism, whereby access is available to those who ask—and only to those who *can* ask in a way that declares a recognizable or acceptable claim. In this regime, the passive voice is no voice at all. Power in these systems is constituted in such a way that it requires of us first the knowledge of what services are available to us and then the ability to say what we need, as well as the political skill to demonstrate persistent determination that those needs will be met. As a result, much of empowerment practice at the activist level is intended to prepare marginalized people to participate in this demand-driven "rights" environment, to self-advocate in this contested space of competing needs by developing active, autonomous consumer voices and by learning the language of entitlement.

> To achieve autonomy we must be capable of a pattern of deliberation in which we assess desires and values as well as our situations, including relationships, in order to exert the requisite control over our lives. (Furrow, 2005, p. 31)

But perhaps the most cogent critique of these constructs of empowerment comes out of the Ethics of Care, which presumes, at least by implication, that there will always be some people who will NOT be able to be empowered as individuals—that equality is not necessarily reciprocity and that, as a society, we must take into account, and take responsibility for, those who cannot care (or even advocate) for themselves. In a structure that acknowledges that some people will be unable to speak for themselves, the moral responsibility expected of care or dependency workers would be extended to include speaking out, not necessarily for the empowerment (or independence) of those vulnerable others, but for their right to be dependent.

> All of us are dependent in childhood; most of us are dependent in old age; and many of us are dependent for long periods of time (sometimes throughout a life) because of ill health. . . . Because dependency strongly affects our status as equal citizens (i.e., as persons who, as equals, share the benefits and burdens of social cooperation) and because it affects all of us at one time or another, it is not an issue that can be set aside, much less avoided. (Kittay, 1997, p. 221)

While the rights argument for social justice may be the primary justification for the development of any of these services, the ethics of care discourse shifts the focus to attend to recognition of the value of relationship and of a response to the needs of particular individuals in the many ways that they may differ from each other. The assessment of what may stand as appropriate delivery of service to vulnerable populations is changed, with the move away from the focus on some abstract universal model of the free and equal "reasonable man" as the implied definition of the democratic citizen. Does an ethics of care orientation change the meaning of empowerment?

Although the Ethics of Care position is grounded on the assumption that "a crucial resource for the resolution of moral problems is the ability to communicate among persons involved or affected" (Walker, 1992, p. 168), there is also a recognition that "this avenue of understanding is not always open" (p. 168). In the frame of empowerment ideology, the painful evidence of some subjects' inability to participate must constitute a significant challenge to theories of the neutrality of difference in social justice discourse. It requires us to develop a moral or ethical position that allows for legitimate respectful action in nonreciprocal relationships of caring, and demands that we examine our requirement for perceived autonomy and agency as a ground for entitlement and subjectivity. Seen through the lens of the ethics of care, the empowerment paradigm breaks down where it does not recognize the value or the subjectivity of those of us who will, sometimes or always, need the community's assistance to live.

> A compassionate morality departs less from our responsibilities to others than responsiveness in our relationships with them. In assuming a self that seeks connection, and is changed through dialogue, it recasts the "problem" of dependency. (Froggett, 2002, p. 122)

Positioning Empowerment

Even when legitimately "speaking for" a truly dependent Other, however, there is potential pain for the person using the paradoxical expert power in many of these contexts. In the same way that the words of the marginalized can be co-opted in some kinds of representation, the intentions of the activist can be used against the individual or groups for which specific solutions have been designed. For the helper who thinks of her work as acting as a bridge—advocating for some socially disadvantaged group with the bureaucracies managing the resources that will improve their collective circumstances—can sometimes find herself contributing to or even believing in a decontextualizing and depoliticizing rhetoric that feeds the larger system:

> When expert needs discourses are institutionalized in state apparatuses, they tend to become normalizing, aimed at "reforming," or more often, stigmatizing "deviancy." This sometimes becomes explicit when services incorporate a

therapeutic dimension designed to close the gap between clients' recalcitrant self-interpretations and the interpretations imbedded in administrative policy. (Fraser, 1989, p. 174)

The impact of such institutional empowerment structures is further compromised when evidence-based evaluations of the success or failure of an individual empowerment process are determined by the imposition of measures of accomplishment of a "desirable end state" (Ellsworth, 1992, p. 56) in the client or group. In effect, these processes determine autonomy or agency by the adequacy of dominant language use (voice) of those who are deemed to have been empowered. Is empowerment, then, only manufacturing consent? Or, in the event that the subject has learned the dominant forms well enough to register her disagreement with policy, does it functionally contribute to structuring a manageable predetermined resistance, one that is futile by definition?

The language used to describe these efforts often illustrates some of the difficulties created by the epistemological double-binds experienced in the field of international relations, where "reciprocity of equal respect and acknowledgment of one another . . . entails an acknowledgment of the asymmetry between subjects" (Young, 1997, p. 50). By and large, in the value system embraced by development workers, projects are seen to be valid only if the outcome is not, in the end, colonizing. In these situations, unequal empowerment relations are often conceived of as partnerships, but the alliances that are built on are seldom entirely understood, and the exact nature and impact of the power imbalance on the community receiving help are confused or obfuscated:

> Empowerment is when the powerless gain the experience and the confidence needed to influence the decisions that affect their own daily lives, and is the foundation on which (development) partnerships must be built. Professionals cannot give power to those without power. Those who are powerless must take and exercise power for themselves. (Rifkin and Pridmore, 2001, p. 3)

Some of the critiques of international empowerment interventions, however well-meaning in their conception, arise from a gender analysis of the impact of such alliances. First, in many cases the focus on "a development agenda, understood as being responsive to local communities, involves perpetuating gendered biases in those communities, where . . . feminist goals are often ignored" (Richey, 2002, p. 212). However, many efforts to empower women in international settings within a Western feminist agenda have been critiqued by third-world women (Mohanty, 1991; Trinh, 1989) for "the politics of saving" (Spivak, 1987), where "Western women scholars present themselves as saviors, ignorant of the reality of non-Western women, but able and willing to facilitate the retrieval of their voices for the sake of global feminism" (Razack, 2000, p. 42).

Researching Power

The encouragement, facilitation, or translation of experience into "voice" is conceived as the primary goal for some kinds of qualitative inquiry (Deshler and Selener, 1991; Fine, 1994a), particularly in community action research, which is described as "an approach . . . that seeks to affect empowerment at all stages of the research process through critical analysis of power and responsible use of power" (Ristock and Pennell, 1996, p. 9). This is another area where concern is expressed about the nature of the empowerment relationship, and some critiques of this practice underline, once again, the paradoxical potential of empowerment to become a kind of "savage social therapy" (Chanfrault-Duchet, 1991, p. 89), where the intended outcomes are distorted and even research relationships can

> reproduce the very practices of domination that we seek to challenge. . . . To utilize the (research process) as an occasion for forcing on others our ideas of a proper political awareness, however we understand that, is to betray an implicit trust. (Anderson and Jack, 1991, p. 148)

One of the areas where empowerment ideology has been embraced in the name of voice is in the area of feminist therapy, particularly in community and individual responses to violence against women and children (Fallot and Harris, 2002; Herman, 1992). In safe houses, women's centers, and counseling offices, a woman telling her story to someone who listens is itself framed as empowerment, in that "it is precisely through the re appropriation of language (the 'master's tools') that we are able to transform our lives" (Lawless, 2001, p. 49). Against criticisms of psychology's potential to personalize and depoliticize the gendered oppression of women and the abuse of children, the concept of the use of feminist therapy as empowerment is understood to be

> the practice of a genuinely revolutionary act in which both lives and society are changed. . . . The first and most important "client" of feminist therapy is the culture in which it takes place; the first and foremost commitment of feminist therapists is to radical social transformation. (Brown, 1994, p. 17)

Examples of the theory of empowerment as it is understood in feminist therapy and community psychology are found in the various applications or intervention techniques that use narrative process to support a discourse of resistance to hegemonic normativity, by recognizing the overlapping and intertwined nature of the personal and the political:

> In feminist theory, resistance means the refusal to merge with the dominant cultural norms and to attend to one's own voice and integrity (Gilligan et al., 1991). A feminist theory of psychotherapy, rooted in the call for radical social change, seeks to bring a better understanding of such personal resistance, and

of how to identify and strengthen it, reframing it as a positive and healthy act within a feminist social context. (Brown, 1994, p. 25)

An important critique of this use of the combination of psychology and empowerment rhetoric is that it can be employed in the interest of domination and control—reducing public dissonance by personalizing and depoliticizing inequities, in effect empowering an individual by increasing her ability to cope with, or adjust to, her systematic oppression (Sandell, 1996). The construction of empowerment as a technology of the self, or simply personal development, has met its most fierce criticism from feminist theorists, particularly in the recognition of its appropriation for use by business and government:

> Neoconservatives have used the language of empowerment as frequently as socialists and feminists . . . as part of a new managerial ethos in the private sector and as a strategy of cost containment for governments facing budgetary restrictions. In these contexts, the language of empowerment can obscure exploitative relations and conceal class conflict. (Pease, 2002, p. 136)

Managing Power

In perhaps the most obvious case of this kind of language use within the paradigm of what are termed "Just In Time/Total Quality Management" models of production in big business and manufacturing, some of the concepts of empowerment have been bent into a shape that is said to improve the lives of workers and, at the same time, benefit the companies who employ them, by reducing waste. A complex system of surveillance and control instituted by the manipulation of peer pressure and group loyalty is justified under the rhetoric of *kaizen*—a Japanese term that translates as the "search for continuous improvement" (Delbridge et al., 1996) by workers. This language is represented as enlightened management's commitment to

> acknowledge the individual employee as an intelligent, accountable, creative being, and therefore a productive resource for the company. . . . The use of *kaizen* implies the inscription into the human body (i.e., the kaizening body, the employee expected to carry out the kaizen activities) of a set of qualities such as creativity, the will to change, and the ability to co-operate. Through making use of these qualities, in terms of "taking care of operations" (for the company), kaizen provides opportunities for developing ethical behavior, i.e., "taking care of the self." (Styhre, 2001, pp. 795/796)

This construction of empowerment seems to be a far cry from the original intentions of Marx, or, more particularly, of Freire and of the many people engaged in the original field in which emancipatory theories were put into practice—in the various sites of adult education. But perhaps it

exemplifies their/our worst fear, that we, by using rhetoric and methodology of empowerment, could be reproducing or even serving the power
structures that we are committed to opposing. Could "we" be "they"?
And are we the exploitative management (with power), or the exploited
kaizening bodies of those who have consented to our own powerlessness
(powerless, at least, over the uses of our power)? And if we are they, or
like them, can we call ourselves empowerment workers—can we still claim
membership in this community? Are we, even as a community, even as we
engage in the liberatory politics that construct our communal identities,
furthering the interests of the dominant by using our intelligence and creativity to eliminate waste, the waste of productive lives (even our own),
the lives of those unable to participate in power because of marginalization
and lack of education? Are we truly the product of our own empowerment,
the "docile bodies . . . become a self-disciplined work force" (Walkerdine,
1992, p. 17)?

Have I critiqued myself right out of my belief system, into despair and
helplessness? Or is this fear another example of the reasoning that holds us
captive in the grip of the hegemony of those organizational double-binds,
those rational paradoxes requiring constant struggle to resist or even survive?
What is clear to me, at least, is that I am still operating from a subject position within the values of emancipatory ideology, or I would not be so hor-
rified at the thought of using or being used by power in such an oppressive
way. So for survival's sake, I need to go back—back to the theorists of critical pedagogy, to the conceptions of feminism and empowerment education
that invite us "to look beyond old critical premises and toward continuing
revision" (Lather, 1992, p. 126). Back to the community where it is acceptable, or even expected, that a Subject will question or resist every premise of
authority, and where the stance of questioning is itself constructed as an act
of responsibility and resistance.

> Many times resistance tactics are simultaneously feeding into power structures
> and ideologies at the same time they provide a critical commentary, alternative
> understandings, coping strategies, and/or the means for slowly delegitimizing
> disempowering communications practices. The mere questioning of an
> organizational double bind and the paradoxical language that created it can be
> seen as simultaneously legitimizing and delegitimizing the authority, ideology
> and status quo from which it comes. (Wendt, 2001, p. 17)

Thinking Critically to Construct a Self

So is it critical pedagogy that creates the possibility of imagining this
community, this hope of a collective influence? Certainly it is within the
tradition of critical pedagogy that the terms of empowerment have been the
most intensively theorized. Particularly in the discipline of adult education,
there are explicit expectations that the actions of an empowerment agent,

assisting the development of both individuals and communities of self-directed learners, will contribute to social change.

> Education, including adult education, comes to serve as a compensatory or readjustment mechanism concerned to promote the collective well-being of an identified disadvantaged or disenfranchised group. . . . Education becomes a political act, and development and action are held to be interwoven and part of a broad movement to attain social justice. (Brookfield, 1983, p. 69)

In educational discourse there is an assumption of larger goals and intentions that are met through the interventions of empowerment processes, including, "empowerment through the development of individual competence, empowerment through preparation for active citizenship, empowerment through critical consciousness, and empowerment through the affirmation of difference" (Kieran, 2002, p. 65). But it is in feminist critiques of liberatory pedagogy that a different emphasis is discovered, and the privilege and the responsibility of membership in this community are fully articulated.

> The lessons learned from feminist struggles to make a difference through defiant speech offer both useful critiques of the assumptions of critical pedagogy and starting points for moving beyond its repressive myth . . . feminist voices are made possible by the interactions among women within and across race, class, and other differences that divide them. (Ellsworth, 1992, p. 103)

It is in feminist critiques that we see ourselves as still at a starting point in the project of emancipation. Still struggling to empower ourselves, not finished, not sure, working within the knowledge of the logical contraints of this endeavor, where "to recognize the self-contained opposite is to recognize that the personal is political, the micro is the macro, that resistance can be oppressive, that communication can be silencing and silence can be expressive" (Clair, 1998, p. 19). It is in feminist theory that I can hope to find a solution to the problem of agency in empowerment situations, where asymmetrical relations are

> structured to move toward equality of power, in which artificial and unnecessary barriers to equality of power are removed. In this relationship there is an equality of value and of the person's worth between the participants, but there continues to be some necessary asymmetry in certain aspects of the exchange, in part designed to empower the less powerful person but primarily required to define and delineate the responsibilities of the more powerful one. (Brown, 1994, p. 104)

It is in feminist critiques of emancipatory pedagogy that I find an analysis that attends to real political and material differences in the lives of women and marginalized others, acknowledges possible structural limitations to any empowerment process, and makes some reference to the nonrational basis of individual power:

> Empowerment consists of four dimensions, each equally important, but none sufficient by itself to enable women to act on their own behalf. These are cognitive (critical understanding of one's reality), the psychological (feelings of self-esteem), the political (awareness of power inequalities and the ability to organize and mobilize), and the economic (capacity to generate independent income). (Stromquist, 2002, p. 23)

It is in feminism, too, that I find recognition of the problem of membership and subjectivity that was the motivation for this examination of the ideology of empowerment. It with some relief that I find myself at the end of this process not a traitor at all—still reluctant, but without the loss of community or meaning that I was afraid of. In fact, I think I have accepted that the very act of questioning, of refusing to accept as given the limitations of the theories under which I work, is actually what qualifies me as a member of this community. I understand that my state of unease with the paradox of the power of my position here and my experiences of powerlessness in other arenas is central to the subjectivity/self that is constituted by identification as an empowerment practitioner who is also a feminist:

> The women who undertake the feminist position—as a part of the process aimed at empowering alternative forms of female subjectivity—are split subjects and not rational entities. Each woman is a multiplicity in herself: she is marked by a set of differences within the self, which turns her into a split, fractured, knotted entity, constructed over intersecting levels of experience. . . . There is no unmediated relation to gender, race, class, age, or sexual choice. Identity is the name given to this set of potentially contradictory variables: it is multiple and fractured; it is relational in that it requires a bond to the "others"; it is retrospective in that it functions through recollections and memories. Last but not least, identity is made of successive identifications that is to say, of unconscious internalized images which escape rational control. (Braidotti, 1998, p. 303)

In the end, having been converted by education, by the consciousness of the workings of power and domination, I find that I am still an empowerment worker—I choose, even knowing the flaws and limits of this ideology, to continue to act in relationships with others in ways consistent with its values. I (and many of the professionals who spoke with me about this) choose to continue to use empowerment practice as a solution to the problem of how to live *knowing,* responsible to the sense of having to do something about power and pain in the world, its beauty and terror. I choose hope instead of overdetermination, I choose meaning (even arbitrary and partial) over anomie, choose action over passive helplessness. I choose committed critique over cynicism, and community over isolation. With William James (James,

1978), I take an inherently pragmatic but essentially religious position: I choose to act as if my life has meaning, with no rational proof possible or required. For this project, and for my work in the foreseeable future, I will continue to use both the ideology and the critiques of empowerment in my commitment to learning from the practice of speaking out for social change.

Terminologies: Positionality and Theoretical Use of Language

Since so many of the terms used in any discussion of subjectivity have evolved out of several different discourses, (that is, anthropology, sociology, psychology, psychoanalysis, epistemology, as well as rhetoric), my specific usage of some terminologies in this text may need some clarification. Because I am using a critical heuristic frame for looking at the material, an additional layer of critique of the language also seems to be required. Perhaps this process will also put on record some indication of my location and my biases as well, in response to the feminist ethical demand for a declared positionality, while acknowledging the limits of whatever transparency is available in self-reflection. Within the choice of three feminist research frameworks defined by Michelle Fine as "ventriloquy," "voices," and "activism," I believe that my position for this project comes closest to that of the participatory activist:

> Here, the researcher's stance frames the texts produced and carves out the space in which intellectual surprises surface. These writers position themselves as political and interrogating, fully explicit about their original positions and where their research took them. (Fine, 1994b, p. 17)

My concern for understanding the terminologies used in this kind of practice has been sharpened by a remarkable privilege that I have been allowed by virtue of the commitment and work of several feminist activists in Japan. Since 1992, I have been invited to many different cities there to give public lectures, to run workshops and training for practitioners, and to participate, however peripherally, in the development of community organizations and strategies for culturally relevant responses to domestic violence and child abuse. For the last several years, at the request of these same activists, I have also hosted a summer training seminar for Japanese practitioners at UBC, where I have been able to enlist the help of many local experts to provide a broad curriculum for individuals and groups interested in learning more about our (eroded) systems of support for those affected by violence and marginalization.

Because I have not in any way mastered the complexities of the beautiful Japanese language, I work with interpreters, several of whom have had a profound effect on my use of English, and especially on my decision to use (or to avoid) certain words. As a person who speaks quickly and very idiomatically, I have had to learn to consider my use of certain words, and, through the collaborative effort involved in managing simultaneous interpretation by these thoughtful people, I have gained an appreciation of the need for clarification of many of the terms that I had previously used without thought. Although I am also someone who loves theoretical terminologies, and although I believe that much specialized academic language is absolutely specific and necessary, in the context of this work with translation I have been given the chance to think through some of the jargon, so common to my field of practice, that tends to obfuscate rather than clarify the ideas it is meant to convey.

To begin with, about eight years ago I heard myself say: "I can't talk about 'healing' any more, when we are talking about violence against women and children. I want to talk about learning." I was speaking to one of the first organizing meetings of an NGO that would become the Shien Kyoiku Centre (roughly translated as Women's Network for Education, Health, and Safety), a broad-based group of professionals and grassroots workers in support positions across disciplines: doctors, midwives, lawyers, policewomen, social workers, teachers, transition shelter workers, counselors, activists, and artists, all concerned with the issues arising from the kinds of personal violence that are as prevalent in Japan as anywhere else.

As often happens, my need to articulate something for that very focused talk provided me with an opportunity to find out what I have come to think and feel about a part of the work that I have been doing for over twenty-five years. I entered a graduate program trying to expand that opportunity for myself, by creating a space where I would be required to articulate and test ideas that have supported both my motivation and my guidelines for practice, for the most significant part of my working life. This book was written in the desire to somehow contribute to bridging the widening gap between the conflicting authorities of theory and experience that exists in the area of social activism, and it also represents an attempt to take responsibility for the fact that I am also teaching in this field, and I am committed to continue teaching, from a position of authority that in this context is particularly difficult to challenge. As an "out" incest survivor, as having grown up poor or working class, as the child of a mentally ill parent of marginalized ethnicity, as a lesbian, as a person with a physical disability, my complex marginal identities work in several ways to both support and undermine my authority, by virtue of the argument of experience.

So, I cannot call what is needed in this field "healing." Especially in the light of the recent research into the kinds of physiological and psychological responses that are predictable in situations of trauma (Herman, 1992; van der Kolk et al., 1996), we must acknowledge that the behaviors and emotional realities that we recognize as suffering are often logical responses to a kind of learning about the world, even if it is a world that normal society agrees to avoid. It is not sickness to be unwilling to trust after one's primary trust has been betrayed. It is not an illness to be despairing when one's most significant experiences are of powerlessness and pain. It is learning, and logic of a kind, to retreat from intimacy if intimacy has been violated. It is wisdom to avoid further damage after harm. I believe that if we can learn those things, then we can also learn new responses if we find ourselves in a place of relative safety, and this kind of *learning* may lead to what is meant by healing.

Having identified the intentional absence from this text of the normal medicalized language of healing, I must now discuss several other terms, since they will be used quite specifically in this context, although not without ongoing reflection and critique.

Marginalized

One of the issues that is central to my own work as advocate, educator, and direct service provider has been my interest in the ideas grounding the social justice agenda for the improvement of the lives of marginalized groups. I have been concerned for many years with the definitions of what constitutes *individual* marginalization, how it/they/we are represented— to the dominant center, and to one another—and how that affects both our ideas of self and our relationships. For the purposes of this study, however, I have chosen to focus in particular on some of those professionalized social connections that are constructed as helping relations: nursing, social work, counseling or community development, and some kinds of liberatory or engaged pedagogy, working in various contexts with those individuals who belong to what are known as underprivileged or marginalized categories and groups.

Even if I understand the idea of marginalization as a social category, however, I am wary of the potential for such a euphemistic and arbitrary geographical metaphor for membership (within or outside some bounded, owned, center or territory) to function in concert with other forms of social control that work against the goals of social justice action. Based on an essentializing and ultimately privileged hegemonic value of safe locatedness, this normative bias, as well as its representation or lack of it, is reflective of realities for the dominant group in any society, and the exclusion of those individuals and groups defined out of membership continues to support and maintain not the marginalized people themselves but the power positions enjoyed by the dominant. Even the act of helping can underline the power of the helper, at the expense of the perceived agency or independence of those in need of whatever is understood to be help.

So many of our strategies for addressing this problem in liberatory pedagogy or in other social justice arenas are grounded on, or firmly defended by, a careful analysis of power. But even the best-intentioned interventions based on this concept of the existence of less privileged Others/Outsiders have the potential to recreate the problem for which they have been designed. In fact, one of the ways that an individual finds out that she is unacceptable as a member of the center is to be the recipient of the kind of care or assistance that is created in order to minimize the effects of inherent power differences recognized in the social justice discourse.

I remember an incident in an adult education class, where I was co-presenting a section on poverty to people preparing for community practice. We were debriefing an exercise in which we had done a short version of "The Poverty Game" (Code, 1995, p. 111), and several people (including me) were upset by the experience. We were talking about the kinds of feel-good interventions that are represented to the general public as "how you can get involved" or "how you can make a difference (at little cost to you)" with such examples as Telethons, "Give a Kid a Coat" programs, and "Christmas Hampers for the Needy." One person talked about how ashamed he was when he realized that the other children in his class knew that his family had been on the list to receive a hamper—about $20 worth of food that his mother didn't know how to cook but that required his whole family to be seen as marginal. He had never before understood that he was different from the others, and was never again able to forget it.

This is not to say that I think we should not provide care—I have been an advocate for fair welfare for many years—or that the people who are engaged in the work of providing services to the marginalized are operating in bad faith. I am one of them. I use the term *marginalized* here, in spite of my critiques, because this expression has, within the word itself, the advantage of providing a sociological explanation for the plight of those designated. But I believe that in practice very often the use of this neutralizing language to describe the power difference inherent in helping relationships works to support two quite paradoxical feelings in the dominant group that allow them/us to continue to conceive of themselves/ourselves as either central to the problem, or at the center:

1. a kind of helpless and paralyzing pity—based on the sense that while they/we materially benefit by the underlying structures of inequity, they/we are not responsible for the creation of the conditions that support such structures and can't do very much to change the circumstances of those who suffer under them; or

2. a comforting self-justification, which suggests that, having changed the language in which we imagine or represent those outsiders, we have at least taken some individual responsibility for changing conditions for them.

Neither of these emotional possibilities poses a political problem in itself, but neither response guarantees any material change in the fundamental power relationship between dominant and marginalized. Rather, like so many images of far-off victims of famines, wars, and disease, the individual who is represented as an example of these impossible social problems is reduced to a nameless spectacle, at the same time that s/he is made multiple by her standing for the millions of pathetic or dangerous Others that wait, silently beseeching, for a response from those who observe but cannot imagine their experience. If we are morally challenged by our awareness of that multitude, we (the dominant) are constrained by the limits of our emotional response-ability. In our present environment of sensationalized "breaking news," so much information about atrocities and tragedy in the world overwhelms the rational faculties—and even our ability to empathize.

> Pity can entail a moral judgment if, as Aristotle maintains, pity is considered to be the emotion that we owe only to those enduring undeserved misfortune. But pity, far from being the natural twin of fear in the dramas of catastrophic misfortune, seems diluted—distracted—by fear, while fear (dread, terror) usually manages to swamp pity. (Sontag, 2003, p. 75)

But in the end it is only the victims of misfortune who are visible, even if they are rendered nameless by virtue of being atomized to a single example of numbers so large as to be incomprehensible. Even in language that recognizes oppression and valorizes justice, the facelessness of the systems of dominance and privilege that force so many outside is constructed as ubiquitous and institutional, leaving no mark of individual responsibility for those in the mainstream. Somehow the beneficiary of injustice is only the system, the structures on which we all depend but which can never be represented by any one individual. In contrast, only individuals suffer injustice, only those unfortunates that we see on the news who represent raced, classed, or other marked social identities. For example, "unemployed" and "homeless" are terms that apply to the individual, although very often the person's qualification for membership in these categories can be traced back to larger policies and systems that inevitably participate in various kinds of bland and impersonal injustice.

The use of the terminology of marginalization also plays an import-ant explanatory role in determining the proper response to this problem: if the problem is the outsideness of those on the margins, then if they would come in or could be brought in to the center, there would be no significant difference, they could benefit from the system, too, and there would be no injustice. Much of empowerment activism is undertaken with the intent of creating more inclusive systems, often without addressing how the shifting boundary of what can be included is either expanded or contracted by the changing needs of the dominant group. How much more uncomfortable is this location for those in the role of helper who, by virtue of training or association with some organization, find themselves identified with the dominant group even though they share significant markers of identity with the marginalized group: race, class, sexual identity/orientation, physical or mental disability, or a specific experience of victimization or trauma. My engagement with this issue is focused on the kinds of tensions and divisions that are often hidden *within* the caregiver if she sees herself as having the power to assist others by virtue of an alliance with the dominant or hegemonic centre, while at the same time experiencing or having previously experienced the very difficulties which put the marginalized in the position of needing help from her.

The ideology of social justice that entitles the subordinate individual to assistance operates as though the person who has the power to effect change is, in some significant and material way, different from the person who needs assistance. The importance of the maintenance of this difference is underlined in professional rules about appropriate boundaries. In most cases, this difference/distance is emphasized as a necessary part of the structure of helping and is supported by a rhetoric that states that the difference is in the interest of the client or student. In fact, although in all these contexts some forms of empathy or care for the student, client, or subject may be valued, the practitioner's credibility with her professional reference group is dependent on her avoidance of "over-identifying" with the recipient of her care. However, for both helper and the helped, this difference/distance is not neutral, no matter how euphemistically or modestly we describe our privilege, or how bravely or defiantly we deny our victimization/vulnerability.

In the process of establishing professional boundaries, a message is delivered to both parties about choice, autonomy, and agency. The helper's requirement to create and maintain appropriate boundaries decontextualizes and individualizes the difference between these two categories. First, it implies that the helper has the power to choose the agency (often conflated with voice) that affords her the valued membership in the more powerful group. She does that by identifying with her professional peers (the helpers) at the cost of the loss of membership with her personal peers (the helped), a cost that is seldom reckoned into the supposed benefits of membership. Perhaps she is understood to be fortunate to have been given the choice, or, more commonly in empowerment contexts, she is seen to be an exceptional individual among her marginalized group. Either way, the difference or the true boundary between her and others like her is her agency, her ability to choose, which comes from the very definition of the *inability* of the marginalized—they do not have the choice. The absolute necessity to choose the dominant as valuable, as a reference point, as a place of legitimization or voice in order to make any difference for the marginalized group, is rendered invisible. This choice is, I believe, central to one of the most important components of the ideology of helping in social justice situations—the problematic representation of any individual as inhabiting the social role of "victim."

Victimization and Agency

For this project I am choosing *not* to use the term *victim* in represent-ing any individual person. This decision has been determined by several considerations, not the least being that many years ago, and in company with countless others, I made what at the time was the political choice to describe myself as a survivor, rather than as a victim. In the late 1970s and early 1980s, at a time that I was helping to develop and manage two differ-ent nonprofit agencies providing support services to children in care, I par-ticipated in the feminist politicizing of the issues of domestic violence and sexual abuse of children, partly by the public disclosure of my own experi-ences of victimization. Although not unproblematic, even at the time,

> the use of survivor was meant to help draw attention to the abuse of women and girls as an institutionalized practice in our culture, something common, unquestioned, and almost expected. The accentuation of the worst—that women and girls were dying—was to show the public how far the "typical" could go, to show how horrible it could get for women along this continuum of hardship. (Lamb, 1999, p. 119)

In the setting of my professional practice during those years, the "accentuation of the worst" was not, in fact, any exaggeration. More than one of the girls who had been in my care during their years as adolescent street kids were later among the large number of Vancouver's "missing women"; one young woman's DNA was uncovered at the Pig Farm murder site, along with other physical evidence of the deaths of at least twenty-six sex workers from the Downtown East Side of Vancouver. Many others who had been in the care of the agencies that I was responsible for have died or disappeared in the interim.

But even at that time, my analysis was not limited to women and girls. My programs also provided supports for many of the boys and young men who were being exploited as street "hustlers" at a time when HIV was spreading unchecked in their already dangerous environment. A significant number were lost to AIDS long before the development of the miraculous medical cocktails that have reduced the fear, if not the danger, of those who are on the street today. My relationships with those young people, many of whom did not survive to find "voice," expanded rather than contradicted my feminist analysis of the individual and social costs of such monotonous and everyday violence. My experience of their beauty, their intelligence, and the brave defiance in their sometimes contradictory resistance and resilience has ever since grounded my practice and my political commitment to the ones who have survived. I have many times stated publicly that when I speak "as a survivor," I am aware of the need to recognize at least two others—one who did not survive and one who has not yet spoken (and may never speak) what s/he knows.

Besides my historic personal relationship to the political uses of the word "victim," at least one other reason for my decision to avoid the term results from an examination of some of the ideas behind the conception of who qualifies as a "victim" in the social justice discourse. It seems to me that a significant conflation of concepts from psychology and activist politics is in play in much of the marginalization (read victim) discourse, and I hope that a careful articulation of some of the individual terms will clarify my analysis of the necessity for recognizing agency (the Knower, conscious, self-conscious, and capable of choice) in our uses of rhetorical speaking out as activism. I contend that the idea of victim is at the core of a confusion in one of the founding conceptions of dependency and the helping relationship, where an apparent opposition between social structure and individual agency reflects a lack of distinction between first- and second-order abstractions. My arguments related to this tautology are expanded in the following chapters on voice and silence, but for this clarification of terms, I want to shift the focus to a more direct look at the experience of "being" a victim.

I have seen many situations in my practice where a person who seems to be living on the extreme edge of survival—living as a prostitute, addicted to street drugs (or over-the-counter medications), or risking HIV by sharing needles—has made the decision to change her/his circumstances. Many people have done this successfully, whether they get help or not, and many others have failed to make the change, whether they get help or not. Almost all of them have insisted at important times that they were *not* victims: that they *chose* the life, or the drug, or the risk. None of them would have been happy to give up some responsibility for their own situation, even if the need to say "It was my choice" made them guilty of creating the circumstances of their own destruction, implying, if not insisting, that "It was my own fault." This, in fact, is one of the well-known defining characteristics of victimized people: that many hold themselves, as individuals, responsible for their negative experiences, however systemic the violence that created them. And they don't do this alone. All the social representations of "victim," and many of the practices of helping, contribute to their need to describe themselves to those offering help either as helpless or as deserving self-blame for their tragic situation.

The relational components of this painful dialogue have implications for the worker as well. In the first construction, the people who need help can't help themselves (have no choice)—they are truly marginal, or victims—in which case the person who helps is doing a good thing (even if this is work for money), because she is fulfilling the obligations implied by the "rights" set out in a just society. In the other situation, if the persons who need help are actually able to act (or choose some other alternative) in some form or in some contexts, it means that they are not victims, in which case society is being exploited, and the person who is deciding to help is being manipulated, or acting in a codependent way, oppressing or patronizing the person by setting up a dependency. The apparent paradox of this problem of whether it is the responsibility of the privileged helper to discover (recognize) or to allow (empower) the agency of the marginal or subordinate person, along with the current individualizing contexts within which "care" is delivered to marginalized populations, creates the need for service providers to determine whether or not the person deserves whatever level of care is available. This circle creates the potential for what Tronto calls "unsympathetic disregard" (Tronto, 2006, p. 11), which requires "a reorientation towards the management of risk . . . [and] allows people to distance themselves from the emotional impact of their work, watch their backs, and mind their careers" (Froggett, 2002, p. 81).

An important element of this assignment of the authenticity of victimhood is the person's sense of entitlement, since demanding or asking/begging is conceived as having (or making) a choice about what they will or will not take (refusing the turkey in a Christmas food hamper, for instance, for a vegetarian family; or even refusing the hamper, for a person who is unwilling to expose the fact that she needs it or that her family has no place to cook the food, or who would rather just have the money and make her own decision about what to eat). If the subordinate person behaves in a way that shows that she understands that she has no entitlement, she will qualify as a victim and the helper will qualify as a good worker, but if the marginalized are seen as influencing, by some agency or choice, either the form or the quantity of response from the helper, then they are not "real victims" and the helper is perhaps being naive. Thus the representation of the helped as real victims is necessary for the helper to represent herself as doing good work. And further, for that helper who shares some determinants of marginalization with the helped, her choice to be a helper requires her to relinquish any entitlement she may have as a result of victimization by the same inequities that are the cause of suffering for her own constituency.

Other problems inherent in the representation of the margins follow from some obvious implications for the effects of social mirroring in the theory of the social construction of subjectivity. In the safety of membership in the "norm," members of a dominant culture can assume that how they represent themselves to others is neutral or automatically acceptable. But the marginalized—people with no representational power of their own—will be forced to accept the prevailing negative representations of their group as individually true of themselves. Learning who we are in the mirror of the dominant, those relegated to the position of Other will internalize not only the devalued image of themselves but also the justification for the original power difference that produced it. Individually and collectively, those on the margins must work very hard to resist definition by the norms of the dominant group, and much of social justice practice is defined as supporting that resistance. But even then, if the empowerment of these individuals is to be recognized, the forms and conventions of their resistance are very often co-opted, absorbed, and subsumed into the center, as they are assigned to predetermined "resistor" positions within the structures of hegemony.

An additional issue of representation arises when academic or professional narratives attempt to articulate explanations for the continued existence or even possible success of so-called oppressed people or peoples, even in inhumane or unjust circumstances. According to the Hegelian concept of power relations, both those relationships that could be described as power-over and those that may be better seen as power-with are similarly collusions between the dominant and the subordinate. In these conceptual models, the significance of power difference is first denied, then neutralized, and finally even justified by any survival or success (voice, or attainment of subjectivity, in philosophical terms) by the subordinate individual. Perhaps these ideas are even supported by the fact that so many people in the position of subordination refuse the definition of themselves as "victim." For some feminists, this refusal is in response to the medical and social pathologizing of those seen as irreparably damaged by trauma; a position based on the recognition of the way in which this operates to depoliticize the original reason for speaking out about victimization: "When a victim does 'move on,' she herself becomes wary of continuing to call herself a 'victim,' because the label has become associated with the multiproblem, dysfunctional image" (Lamb, 1999, p. 111).

But what if that refusal of the definition is exactly the form (representation) of resistance that is prescribed by the dominant? And what if refusing the claim of victim status reduces the person's entitlement to the services considered to be within the rights of ordinary citizens? An example of this conundrum exists in the deep division between the ideologies supporting and contesting the provision of harm reduction services to injection drug users, where for some, maintaining addicts who do not wish to be abstinent is seen as a waste of public health resources. Even more convoluted is the argument against the provision of condoms built into some of the aid programs offered in response to the HIV crisis in Africa and elsewhere.

The main reason that I will not use the term *victim* for an individual is that I believe that "victim" is a social role that absolutely negates not only the agency of the person but even her knowledge of her own situation. Speaking "I am a victim" is, in fact, not *being* a victim but *playing* a stereotyped universal "victim" for the dominant and can be said only in the silencing of the individual. But if being a victim is a requirement to be seen as deserving of help, how do we learn how to "play victim"? And can we play victim without representing ourselves as persons who want to learn how to "stop being a victim"—how to come in out of the margin? If we use educational language to describe a model of the useful dialogical relationship that can work to change power difference, such as the potentially patronizing conception of lifeskills training, or the creation of "legitimated peripheral participation" (Wenger, 1998) to assist in the development of "knowledgeable" subjects, we have to ask ourselves: what is it that the marginalized persons are learning? Are they really learning how to become the experts who will then be the helpers (how to join the center)? And if so, and if they are successful, what does that success cost them?

So many adolescents in the care of my organizations went through a period while they were moving away from the street when their definition of success would have been to attain the status of one of the professional people in their lives—a child care worker, a social worker, a teacher, or, in exceptional cases, a lawyer. Some did, indeed, go on to be border workers, and I knew one young woman who funded her whole undergraduate study and the first two years of law school by her work in the sex trade. Is this agency? Does this mean she was not a victim? Would her relatively powerful use of the limited benefits of a dangerously marginalized position disqualify her for consideration as a rape victim when a trick went bad? If I think that no individual can be reduced to the status of victim, does this mean that I agree with the pernicious new-age truism that "there are no victims"? Absolutely not.

I believe that in the "no victims" argument, we (the dominant nonvictims) originally begin the discursive exercise of defining ourselves as simultaneously powerful and immune from censure (good) in good faith, by trying to say that we are all valuable, no matter how much power we have or don't have. But somehow that gets turned around to mean that we have all experienced, or could all experience, subordination somewhere, so our power-over doesn't really count, or hurt anyone. I'm afraid that no matter how often we reassure ourselves that we all experience both subjection and privilege, the argument ultimately serves to remove responsibility from the dominant, to neutralize any complaints by the subordinate, and to continue to allow us to define the helpless into an abject position. Somehow, the victim is still represented as choosing to "play victim," to be outside or on the margins, simply by virtue of not being able to choose anything else.

I think of this position as "victim-blind." Although often taken with the desire to recognize the relative nature of power and privilege, constructed in an effort to honor the different kinds of agency experienced outside "white" or "centered" hegemony and seen as supporting resistance, this stance is analogous to the race-blind position articulated in some recent discourse on race. I want to use the victim-blind/race-blind analogy to expose the victimizing consequences of victim-blindness in the same way that race-blindness has been exposed as harmful.

If, for instance, we can see that "the rhetoric of equal treatment and color blindness operates to normalize whiteness" (Oliver, 2001, p. 117), then can we not recognize the way that victim blindness normalizes dominance? If we can refute the essential categories of race as a basis or justification for power difference, this does not change our need to acknowledge the power and dominance present in systems of racialization. Similarly, if we refute the essentialist (and it is always essentialist) category of the victim to define those who have experienced some harmful form of power-over, we should not be allowed to therefore pretend that there is no system or prevailing ideology that perpetuates victimization. If race has operated historically as an explanation/justification for the abuse of individuals, then even more circular is the victim explanation, which somehow equates the identity "victim" (invalidated by complaints, anger, or other inappropriate or unattractive social behavior) with the events or structures that constitute the victimization. Individuals do not represent the victim any more than an individual can represent race, but individuals are victimized, just as individuals are racialized, by classificatory systems and exclusions.

In fact, I think that they/we are not in fact excluded by the comforting and neutralized language of marginalization, we are shown only where we belong—outside and in constant danger of being seen as essentially responsible for our own situation. In many of our emancipatory projects, the conditions for entitlement to service or treatment are based on accepting a very particular role in the larger culture, as the Performer of Marginalization—the Abject, by definition helpless, voiceless, choiceless— so that the observer/helper has the role of someone with something to contribute. Voice or choice or agency implies responsibility for the conditions of subordination. Only innocence exempts us from the charge of collusion in our own pain. And, finally, only the innocence of the victim confers innocence on the helper.

The Border: Authenticity and Authority

The idea of the border is a continuation of the geological metaphor for social space and its inhabitants. If I use the concept of the center and the margin, it is not because I endorse a logic that depends on the border as a clear demarcation of the line between the two. Rather, I assume a kind of "fuzzy math" (Kosko, 1993), which allows for the multivalent logic of a continuum between two apparently oppositional states, where people inhabit the empty set: they are and are not members of the communities on either side. These are the people who have accomplished what is called *empowerment* but who disappear from the analytic screen as they move out of the margins to gain the power and the credibility of membership in the mainstream. Many significant shifts in policy and practice in pedagogical, psychological, and medical models for service to marginalized populations have reflected the "street theory" of practitioners in these positions, but very little effort has been made to examine the experience of the workers themselves. In many social justice environments, and particularly on the front lines of education in literacy (Horsman, 1999), health prevention strategies (Egan, 2001), and community-based social service, we rely heavily on the commitment and the advocacy of these individuals, but we often do not know who they are, how they made the shift in position that allows them to provide help, rather than to receive it, or what that shift may mean to them.

Empowerment or emancipatory discourses suggest that multiple relations of domination and subordination implicate us all, but many of the operations and structures involved in social responses to marginalization divide the field between those who have the authenticity of "real" knowledge of the margin and those who have the authority to do something about it.

The border worker is an anomaly in this environment, an open challenge to the lines drawn between helper and helped. If her authenticity can inform the authority of those dominant institutions in some way that improves the lives of others, and/or if an institution or organization gives her the authority to make a difference, then her experience of marginalization can be made into valuable cultural capital. Any decision to use academic or cultural capital to further the interests of those who are without representation sounds like an admirable action in support of social justice. But in practice it appears that sometimes, even in our best attempts to recognize diversity across these boundaries, an exercise of authenticity can become another function of outsiderness, where

> diversity is not ignored in the dominant cultural apparatus but promoted, in order to be narrowly and reductively defined through dominant stereotypes. Representation does not merely exclude, it also defines cultural difference by actively constructing the identity of the Other for dominant and subordinate groups. (Giroux, 1992, p. 58)

Paradoxically, privileged access to those designated as truly Other has also conferred an important kind of authenticity on the professional or the academic who captures the voices from the margin. Any professional meeting or conference will feature the sharing of some war stories—specifics of practice difficulties, descriptions of the work with particular individuals that position the speaker as participating in the "real thing," providing her with a status or street credibility borrowed from the vulnerable subjects who populate her stories. Any legitimate attempt at researching the margins must necessarily negotiate these difficult contradictions. It is significant that the position of the researcher has been the most highly theorized context within which the activist is called on to account for herself—her work, her constituency, and her authority—and where questions are raised about her right to speak (to represent or as a representative) for a voiceless minority. In many of these cases, the researcher or writer must establish her credentials as a "culture broker" (LeCompte, 1993, p. 11), in some explicit disclosure of the power of her personal location in relation to the subject.

Because authority and authenticity are dichotomized in a similar way in practical terms in many service or helping relationships, the brokering role described by LeCompte is often performed by bordered activists who live in a space created by a split somewhat analogous to the separations and connections under examination in the research relationship. For this study, I have used my own experience of this location—on the border of alienation and recognition—as the entry point for a social constructionist investigation of some of the contexts and consequences of self-disclosure, identity, and shifting membership within the paradoxical power relationships present in situations in which helping is informed by the political and ideological goals of empowerment.

For me, any attempt to delineate the relationship between the implications of social construction and the action-driven theories of empowerment is troubled by what appears to be a double bind of first- and second-order conceptions of marginalized identity. At the first level, an individual is not "marginal" except by membership in some group that is convention- or context-determined. Groups are marginalized in relation to other more powerful, dominant groups. But social construction theory and social justice ideology hold that membership in such groups creates problems for individuals that demand a social response, that require the work of a helper. The identity of helpers as nonmarginal depends on the roles they assume in their work with identified populations or groups, and the people who require help are determined to be members of a group marginalized in some way in common.

For the bordered worker, perhaps one of the most poignant paradoxes of empowerment ideology is the nature of the power relationship created by the action of one person or group seeing themselves as working to "empower" another group or individual. As one group assumes responsibility to carry some knowledge/power to the other, they are significantly positioning (Ellsworth, 1997) both parties to the transaction. It is my belief that the practice of self-disclosure of marginalized identity is a strategy often used by bordered workers in a very complex ethical response to this problem. For those of us who use this strategy it is sometimes important, both personally and politically, *not* to "pass" as dominant, even while we use the power and authority of the position assigned to those who do our work.

Living on the Border—Not Passing

The precarious space of speaking out as an advocate for others extends across a broad continuum: from the entirely face-to-face personal/therapeutic/medicalized to the activist/public/politicized. Some people have entered (and subsequently left) this territory as expert observers from the outside—as researchers or journalists. Academic accounts of bordered individuals are often concerned with the ethical issues faced by those who approach this border from a position of relative power, such as Haig-Brown's educational "border workers" (Giroux, 1992; Haig-Brown 1992/1993).

But like those researchers who have entered the ethnographic field as "insider/outsider" (Chaudhry, 1997, Narayan, 1993) or who have managed dual identities, as "halfies" (Abu-Lughod, 1993), some of the helpers working with marginalized populations have also entered the border from the less privileged side, and some have chosen to remain there —to live and work in the space between the authenticity of their membership in the marginalized group and the authority assigned to them with their professional roles.

Of those practitioners becoming bordered from positions of less privilege, a large proportion have chosen to literally pass through the border into the dominant population, never using the knowledge of their histories as a part of their public or professional identity/credibility. But this project has been undertaken in order to examine the motivations, the ethics, and the knowledge of people who have decided to live in this borderland and, for the purposes of their work in the space between, have chosen not to pass. As a result, my choice of informants has been limited to those who not only share this location but also have chosen, or have been chosen for, some public forum for the performance of a certain kind of identity/knowledge—a telling or disclosure of a story of a life marked by trauma, marginalization, or oppression that is offered as an action of uncovering: "speaking for others" (Alcoff, 1991), speaking out, or speaking truth to power.

The ideology of empowerment and much feminist textual practice is founded on the belief that such speaking out is not only valuable but politically necessary; nevertheless, the practitioners whose voices are first encouraged, occasionally broadcast, and eventually interrogated are generally observed by the researcher/theorist from the outside. In attempting to better respond to a social justice agenda, and sometimes in order to conform to the necessity for client-centered or evidence-based service, much social science is conducted in situations in which individuals are asked to explain/disclose their experience of marginalization. This process, while understood by all parties to be for the benefit of persons other than the informant, is ethically justified by the implied belief that the experience will prove to be, if not actually helpful (Nelson, 2001; Ristock and Pennell, 1996; Weis and Fine, 2000) at least not harmful to those who are given the opportunity to speak about their social condition (Alvesson and Skoldberg, 2000; Benmayor, 1991; Borland, 1991).

But once the speaking and the gathering of voices is over, the critique begins. Many academics see the individual case of the messy use of identity as rhetoric as providing at best a questionable social performance, perhaps because of the perennial professional risk of being exposed as inadequately critical and holding a politically naive belief in the innocence or transparency of the subaltern speaker. In almost any individual instance, a statement of witnessing is open to several truth examinations, and speakers are required to answer to charges of fabrication or, at the very least, exaggeration. The critical research stance sets up an essentialist conflation of identity and knowledge and supports a search for the romanticized ideal of the "heroic," authentic, subaltern (McLaren and Pinkney-Pastrana, 2000)—one who is, by definition, incomprehensible. This shift of the listener's focus to critique, as in the examination of "the impact of unreliable narrators on audiences" (Meiners, 2001, p. 110), functionally depoliticizes the acts of those speakers in particular whose representation of identity/knowledge has been constructed with a political intention. The end result is that those who, acquiring power and authority from passing as members in the dominant culture, choose to use the disclosure of private or previously marginalized experience as a rhetorical strategy are often interpreted as unreliable, simply by virtue of their evidently political (or politicized) motivation. Either they are seen as exceptional, and therefore not truly representative of the group, or as living evidence that other members of the population could (and should) overcome the limits imposed by their marginalized status in the same way that they have done.

The border worker, whose authority is based on her mainstream membership as a helper, but whose identity and professional credibility is bound up with the authenticity of her membership in a marginalized group, is presented with some particularly poignant choices if she chooses not to pass. She must make decisions about contexts for speaking, about what truths to tell, and which speaking voices to use. In health, social service, or counseling roles, the rules of confidentiality foreclose the possibility of speaking about the experience of the client to the public, in effect silencing any accounts of marginalization that may identify an individual other than the worker. But at the same time, the rules of professionalism (formal or informal) discourage a practitioner's self-disclosure to clients, and a public disclosure of the worker's personal experience of victimization or oppression can operate as a threat to her entitlement to her role. At the very least, such behavior signals a breach of professional distance. To try to represent her presence in this company, to give an accounting of how she got here from there, she faces the problem of holding open a space between pregiven roles defined by hegemonic discourse; she must operate somehow between the tropes recognizable as the Hero or the Victim.

In order to address the limits of these stereotypes for the comprehension of some of the political/rhetorical stances taken by such subjects, I have chosen to honor the use of voice in these situations as counterhegemonic action (Nelson, 2001), having political meaning and *not* simply the automated responses of cultural dupes, acting in accordance with Foucault's description of "confessional culture" (Foucault 1990, p. 60). I understand these professional performances of self-disclosure to be operating in the way that Hannah Arendt described the uses of narrative in the development of political responsibility:

The space of appearance of the polis is such that it calls upon everyone to show an "original courage" which is nothing else but a "consenting to act and speak," to leave one's safe shelter and expose one's self to others, and with them, "be ready to risk disclosure." (Kristeva, 2001, pp. 15/16)

The accounts that constitute the data for this work also lead me to argue, with Judith Butler, that the reflective struggle with the idea of a collectivity as "a political space made up of shareable particularities" (Kristeva, 2001, p. 18) is the site of the development of an ethical position and that the process of refining and delivering what she calls "an account of oneself" in a search for recognition constitutes the construction of the subjectivity of the speaker. Further, in the struggle to reconcile the strains implied in the acknowledgment of difference, speaking from outside the dominant norm also demonstrates the emergence of a recognizable political entity—the ethical subject.

The divergence is always between the universal and the particular, and it becomes the condition for moral questioning. The universal not only diverges from the particular, but this very divergence is what the individual comes to experience, what becomes for the individual the inaugural experience of morality. (Butler, 2005, pp. 8/9)

In this project, I have engaged people who are experts in a particular practice of speaking out, in an attempt to outline some of the conditions that may help to determine the political effectiveness (or ineffectiveness) of such an action—but also with a desire to identify those conditions or safeguards that could, to some extent, predict or limit the risk of private, personal, and emotional consequences of disclosure for the speaker. With the intention of creating such distinctions, and in the hope of providing a context for speaking to me that would not set up negative consequences for my subjects, I have articulated a framework where speaking out is conceived as a political act and where the bordered speaker's actions could fall into one or the other (or both) of the following categories:

- *The Performance of Dangerous Knowledge*: where the person uses his/her own experience in the context of the rhetorical authority of speaking for others as a member of a solidarity, probably in public—certainly with a public or political agenda and intention—supported by a careful assessment of risk and/or benefit; and/or
- *Performing the Abject*: where the person finds her account of her experience exposed in a context where her individuality is obscured by her apparent powerlessness and/or questionable veracity, and at the same time is highlighted by the belief that she is telling only her own story, and ". . . the dissident knowledge . . . focuses not on the intentional self but on the self made bereft of intention, not the legitimate person but the negated subject, whose negation makes her collective and minor" (Berlant, 2001, p. 49).

The Abject — Performing the Victim Who Is Not a Victim

Since I am not going to use the term *victim*, what do I mean here by the Abject? The most common uses of the term refer to Julia Kristeva's *Powers of Horror* (Kristeva, 1982). While I am at pains to sidestep many of the details and implications of what Spivak calls Kristeva's "Christianizing psychoanalysis" (Spivak, 1993, p. 17), I find the poetic potency of her visceral definitions of the Abject to be a powerful expression of the experience of having fallen, by self-disclosure, into the loss of individuality and of a valid self as the consequence of perceiving, through the lens of dominant subjectivity, a view of ourselves as stigmatized Other. The Abject, in this sense, is recognized only as a "type" of person: one who lives in the space of the unimaginable, reduced to less than a social object, the source and simultaneous embodiment of shame and pain—not only a victim but also an example of the dire consequences of life outside the norm. Living close enough to society to be visible, yet coming near enough to operate as a warning, the Abject serves to maintain the border, allowing or requiring the Subject to separate itself, even to set itself up, in opposition to the Other.

Most textual references to the Abject as the necessary Other that allows the assumption of a dominant speaking position describe it from the point of view of the dominant, for whom the idea of the Abject functions (in a way similar to Spivak's idea of the subaltern) as a challenge to entitlement: ". . . as a stand-in or trope for supplementarity and for the activity of deconstruction itself. . . . The alterity of the subaltern interrupts the claim of an elite position to be a, or the, subject of history" (Beverley, 1999, p. 102). This interruption sounds uncomfortable, a bit threatening to the security of the status quo, but not dangerous. Liberal or social justice ideology would perhaps assume that it could even be a good thing—a wake-up call—and that giving up or losing confidence in the privilege of the dominant might have a salutary effect on individuals confronted by their own participation in social structures of domination, or even that the Others who provided the interruption might be appreciated, if not respected. I believe that it is in the context of this assumption of a kind of dialogue between knowers, in a search for a better (morally and ethically neutral) understanding of foreign worlds, that the "voice of the victim" is sought. It is assumed to be good for us to know about this Other perspective.

Yet Kristeva insists that we (that is, the spoken we of dominant membership) have a different response to this challenge, when it comes from the Abject. She accuses us, in our response to abjection, of experiencing

> one of those violent, dark revolts of being, directed against a threat that seems to emanate from an exorbitant outside or inside, ejected beyond the scope of the possible, the tolerable, the thinkable. . . . Apprehensive, desire turns aside; sickened, it rejects. (Oliver, 2002, p. 229)

Iris Marion Young sees the social function of the Abject as that of providing the "ordinary citizen" with an opportunity to be a bystander at a spectacle of the impossible: a tourist visit to a repudiated location that, although avoided for our safety and in the service of membership in the dominant group, we don't actually ever completely give up. Operating as a reminder of what could happen to us if we lost our status as a valued Subject, a person in abjection is an embodied object lesson:

> The abject provokes fear and loathing, because it exposes the border between self and other as constituted and fragile and threatens to dissolve the subject by dissolving the border. (Young, 1990, p. 144)

This is nonetheless still a sketch of the view from the position of the one standing in a place of safety, marveling at the difference, at the distance or lack of it, between us and the rejected thing, even while justifying to ourselves our rather extreme emotional reaction to it. It does not describe the experiences of those who live and work on the kind of border between the acceptable and the unthinkable that this project is meant to map. For those multitudes who live outside the safety of the *Us* of normativity, the line that marks the border separating the self from abjection is inside, and the rejection of the stigmatized Other is a rejection of some important fragment of our history, our memory, ourselves. It is the repeated experience of this discrediting abjection, inspired in the bordered person by both external and internal prompts, that requires the work of risk assessment before speaking and constitutes the harm of saying the wrong thing, or of speaking about ourselves in the wrong contexts. Falling into the performance of the Abject is a profound loss of power: in the moment, it carries the feeling of a return to the original trauma or the devalued identity; in the long term, it consigns us to a state worse than irrelevancy. Compared to this, silence is comfortable, silence can be a refusal, an act of agency; the nonparticipation of silence is resistance.

The meaning of the word "Abject" and the experience of abjection are both entirely relational. In his examination of what he calls the Abject Hero in literature, Michael Bernstein states that for his purposes,

> abjection is a social and dialogic category, and its expression is always governed by the mapping of prior literary and cultural models. Abjection is only felt in conversation with another, and a voice, whether internal or external, whose oppressive confidence arises through its articulation of the normative values of society as a whole. (Bernstein, 1992, p. 29)

Expanding on Bakhtin's "carnivalesque," Bernstein refers to the servility of the "licensed fool" and speculates on the self-consciousness of the person who chooses (?) to perform in this way, suggesting that the fool finally becomes an Abject Hero in his/her "self-contempt . . . due to their haunted sense of only acting according to 'type,' of lacking authenticity, even in their suffering, where they most need to feel original" (p. 22). This comment may begin to approach a description of this experience from the inside, but this text also finds many of the individual examples of the trope, even in literature, "distinctly repellant" and "vile." It is also significant to me that it is this sense of self-consciousness, the knowledge of the self as contemptible, that elevates the Abject to the Heroic, at the same time that he is given credit for enough agency to choose such a position. It is exactly this conflation of agency and self-blame that leads me to reject, along with the Victim position, the tendency to romanticize the subaltern speaker as the Hero. I see this as simply a more seductive version of the Abject.

My use of the term *Abject* (and my desire to avoid creating abjection in anyone) comes from my conception of abjection as a kind of relational suffering arising as a logical consequence of the social construction of the self as marginal. In identifying the Abject as the negative pole on a continuum that I am calling Disclosure Consequences, I mean to talk about the risks of self-loathing—especially after we intentionally out ourselves as the despised Other. I use this dramatic language to explain stories like the first three excerpts in the introduction to this study and those of countless other people who have suffered from telling, from having and using what we call "voice." I want to describe the impact of seeing ourselves reflected in the gaze of someone who can understand us only as Abject—that we can fall into the hate for ourselves that we have been taught in the mirror of marginality. This collapse of the sense of ourselves as creditable, as believable persons with some authority, requires us to return to a rejected vision of ourselves that has been dictated by history or by some dominant One outside our control. Caught, seeing ourselves in the way we have been seen, revolted and repulsed by our own complicity in outing ourselves in the light of that disgust and disapproval, as Abject we are truly subordinate, Subaltern; we are selves silenced, knowledge annihilated.

If we have survived the event(s) or the social conditions that have created us as Other, the destruction of ourselves as Knower puts that survival under threat once again. This is the true confrontation with the Abject—it is IN us, it is part of us, and we cannot avoid it. The bitter humiliation of begging for acceptance and for recognition from someone (or some culture) that has already made any agency we may have impossible by definition, dismantles our rhetorical validity. This is not silence—voice is irrelevant—we feel like we are lying even while holding up the irrefutable evidence that supports our truth.

The political language of difference serves as a way of neutralizing both the reaction of the normal, social subject and the risks of exposure for the Abjected. What self do we create when we disclose some identification with those who are seen to be not just different but lesser in some way relative to the norm—speaking ourselves out, when outing means making ourselves

OUTsiders? We actually catapult ourselves out of membership by choosing to make our difference visible. By insisting on our difference, by engaging in what Spivak calls "clinging to marginality" (Spivak, 1994, p. 162), even if we remember the strategic reason for it as a claim to knowledge, we are risking a loss of credibility not only with our privileged peers but also with the marginalized group with whom we identify: those who do not have the privilege of passing. Those Others for whom confession is not necessary or possible, those who are visibly Outside, are not in a position to welcome those of us who have the choice to pass.

By operating from a position of privilege while retaining a political or personal need for claiming subaltern identity, we are also risking our own credibility with ourselves. For if what we are exposing was not visible, not even true, until we said it—if it is true only IF we say it—then what we are actually doing is marking ourselves, slipping back into a fold of the disallowed. And even if we do not continue to doubt the truth of the story we are telling, we still have learned to distrust our motivations for making it true, as though hiding, or not knowing, is our only innocence. Foucault's belief that confession is made with the expectation of redemption doesn't explain why we should suffer from speaking—if the sin is in keeping the secret, then the virtue endowed by the confession is construed as an entitlement to forgiveness. But for the Abject, which side of this mirror of rejection offers redemption?

Abjection is the feeling of knowing that we are hated, hateful, untrustworthy, unacceptable. It is an internal reality but entirely relational, dictated by our unshakeable expectation that anyone else has felt /will automatically feel the same revulsion that we feel for ourselves. It is the ultimate externalization of the hostile gaze of self-loathing: images from a camera in the hands of someone who is disgusted by us. Seeing the film expose our pathetic helplessness, our base desperation, our responsibility for our own pain, we inhabit "an empty castle, haunted by unappealing ghosts—'powerless' outside, 'impossible' inside" (Kristeva, 1982, p. 49).

We are all too familiar with the public uses of abject representation—as an apparently necessary component of fundraising strategies; as evidence of some social consciousness; as proof of the urgency for involvement in appeals for justice. The image of the victim is a commodity, essential for the construction of the social activist. So, even if the victim is reconstituted as a speaker, and even if she can be induced to express gratitude or endorsement for the social justice project being sold, her evident subalternity is consumed as a sign of the nonreciprocal obligation of the privileged: the social obligation to care about the group she represents.

When the pain of intimate others burns into the conscience of classically privileged national subjects, in such a fashion that they feel the pain of flawed or denied citizenship as their pain . . .[then] . . . those with power will do whatever is necessary to return the nation once more to legitimately utopian odor. Identification with pain, a universal true feeling, then leads to structural social change. (Berlant, 2001, p. 129)

Those of us who use the strategy of speaking out for social change need to know as much as we can about the risks we incur in the process, and those who wish to empower/facilitate/use our voices in this way need to know what it may cost us to participate. This study was undertaken to identify the connection between the ideology of empowerment and the possibility of these risks and painful outcomes, but also to make more comprehensible an important part of the practice of a particular group of people working within both the constraints of their location and the limits of discourse. Because the concepts and the constructions just described are often so much a part of any interrogation of life experience outside dominant culture, the construction of a methodology that can honor the intentions of those who choose to participate is crucial. This requires researchers to be aware of these potentials in their interactions with subaltern speakers.

Conversations in Which Silence Is Not Consent

Much academic writing on interview methodology is centered on such practical problems as how to go about asking the kinds of questions that will allow us to create a coherent text—whom to ask and how to represent the answers. But the need to ask is rarely questioned, and the hierarchical division of "Knowers," which allows one group to ask and requires the other to answer, is largely taken for granted. The many investigations that are undertaken with the express intention of improving material conditions for the marginalized respondent (or those presumed to be represented by, or included in, the respondent's position) imply that, in order to be useful, these knowledge-producing conversations must take place with individuals or groups who are less privileged than the researcher, or are somehow in need of the interventions suggested or enacted by the research process.

The social justice orientation of much of the ethics discourse on qualitative research encourages the researcher to see herself as legitimate only if she uses her authority on behalf of others, but the integral split between the researcher and the researched highlights the need for the continual re-evaluation and redefinition of what constitutes ethical behavior in these relations of power. In this, one of the most highly contested areas of research ethics, "feminist researchers have clearly gained the most ground in the rethinking of our relationships with 'subjects' and of the politics of power that loiter between us" (Fine, 1994b, p. 14). The decision of a choice of methodology for the conversations that formed the textual material for analysis and representation in this study required me to attend to some of the most difficult dilemmas present in contemporary theory on the question of voice, location, and the complexity present in research relationships, and it was made particularly cogent by my own membership in several different marginalized identity groups.

Understanding that even in the most idealist of feminist action projects, "the issue of power remains, regardless of our attempts at sisterhood, thoughtfulness, and sensitivity" (Ristock and Pennell, 1996, p. 68), and, aside from the possibility that my insider-outsider identity with this group might confuse the issues of power and/or severely limit my ability to hear new information, I felt the need to acknowledge the power structure in practical terms, terms that go beyond a simple (or even a complex and nuanced) statement of my own location. And that location was and is relevant here. Even if my identity/reputation as researcher might not be compromised by some evidence of insensitivity; my larger, longer-standing, and more personally invested identity as counselor and community activist required that I take particular care (responsibility) in power relations with this group. A feminist articulation of this concern is expressed in "an ethics of responsibility," whereby

> specific moral claims on us arise from our contact or relationship with particular others whose interests are vulnerable to or dependent on our actions and choices. We are obligated to respond to particular others when circumstances or ongoing relationships render them especially, conspicuously, or peculiarly dependent on us. (Walker, 1997, p. 64)

Without assuming any direct relationship of dependency because of my choice of relatively powerful subjects, in that I would not be dealing with some of the moral dilemmas faced by researchers in situations of extreme power difference, it was my sincere desire to conduct myself in this project from an ethical position that would go beyond the basic prescription to "do no harm." I am inclined, because of my long professional experience with vulnerable people, to disagree with those who would wish to lower the standards for the protection of research subjects. And I disagree that if we cannot gauge the potential consequences for those subjects, we should "just get on with it," in the name of knowledge production. I believe that there are, in fact, quite a few consequences that we can predict, and I think that we are obliged to inform ourselves about those possibilities and to take them into consideration before we begin such conversations, if we agree that "guidelines which ensure only that subjects are not harmed permanently or deceived without adequate institutional review are inadequate for seeking to engage the silenced in research on themselves" (Lincoln, 1993, p. 39).

If we take for granted that even, or perhaps especially, in a research conversation, "the presence of the Other is the occasion or prompt for the development of self-consciousness" (Alcoff, 2000, p. 328), then to be seen to be ethical, it seems to me that we are required to account somehow for the impact that we have on the Other, as well as to recognize her impact on us. From that point of view, when we are asking people to disclose deeply personal stories, we must find some way of holding ourselves responsible for the power we have over the other in the interaction. In his theory of Communicative Action, Habermas articulates a way to see this dialogic vulnerability of the other:

> The person forms an inner center only to the extent to which she simultaneously externalizes herself in communicatively produced interpersonal relationships. This explains the danger to, and the chronic susceptibility of, a vulnerable identity. (Habermas, 1989, p. 46)

Could this be the ground on which to build a criterion for the choice of methods in research? If, while we are talking, we are aware that we are implicated in the coproduction of a description of the "inner center" of a self, (as we are in various ways in counseling, teaching, and research relationships), could that help to guide our questions, our answers, our interventions, and the final public product of our work? What kind of a self are we helping to create? In a frame that he calls a "rhetorical-responsive version of social constructionism," Shotter describes this situation:

> The "things" supposedly in our "inner" lives are not to be found within us as individuals, but "in" the momentary relational spaces occurring between ourselves and an other or otherness in our surroundings. (Shotter, 1997, p. 3)

Could holding myself responsible for the co-creation of a part of another's inner life guide me in my conversation with such a person, as it guides me in my work as a counselor? Should it? Would such a strategy work to balance my resistance to engaging in any kind of patronizing protectionism with my desire to avoid an unintended construction of abjection? Or is it possible that simply recognizing silence in another way could enact (in our contact), and reflect (in the text), my deep respect for, and confidence in, those for whom a move to agency has involved such a complex self-rejection? The problems and negotiations of the daily work of people in this position are directly relevant to a central question for many feminist researchers:

> how do theorists respect the integrity of informants' consciousness and narratives, place them within social and historical context, and yet not collude in the social scientific gaze, fixation, moral specularizing of the poor and working classes? (Weseen and Wong, 2000, p. 54)

Positioning the Question

At first I therefore felt the need to ask myself: "What are we actually doing when we invite someone to tell us about her life?" In this project I asked powerful experts to tell me stories in order that this practice of telling and hearing could be better understood from the position of research. In response to me, in the researcher position, and (as in so many other contexts where this happens) in the name of knowledge production, these people have agreed, as individuals who have been subject to some painful life experience, to collude in recreating the experience in their own words. As a part of that engagement it is understood that, as the researcher, I will create an overview or analysis of the answers they provide me and offer some added framework or structure to the questions raised in the exchange.

Regardless of whether I am able to contribute any further meaning to the stories after the fact, one thing is clear. In the intimacy of an interpersonal conversation we have brought a painful experience into the room. We have brought the history of it, or the selective memory of the history of it, into the body of the person who is telling the story, and the same feelings, the same sickness, the same dread, some of the same shame or anger that are associated with the original event are brought into the person's mind by talking. In most contexts, even though we may operate within a theoretical framework that acknowledges the construction of a self in language, we don't really know how that works. So one of the most important considerations for methodology in this instance is one that perhaps needs to be broadened into a general question for those researchers looking into subaltern experience. If we recognize the potential for this kind of negative consequence to the speaker to arise from what could be read as an authentic response to questioning about her life, what safeguards do we need to put in place in order to proceed with research questioning? How can we find a way forward that will create conditions for safe disclosure and still allow us a reasonable chance of constructing relevant knowledge?

It is exactly this problem that I have asked the respondents in this study to address, because it is precisely their expertise in the practice of telling some difficult personal story that is needed to answer this question. I chose to pose this question as an expert in the practice to other experts in the practice, and much of my specific methodology followed logically as a result. For instance, in choosing to conceive of the border we are attempting to describe as a lived space and not as a line of demarcation, I needed a research process that could allow my interlocutors to articulate the conditions of life within that space with a minimum of translation. This required me to articulate a position on "position."

Particularly when research is framed as advocacy, or empowerment, we are often starting from a position that suggests, as a founding justification, that the voices that we are documenting need translation. So we are positioning ourselves as powerful enough to enable a public recognition of the subject. Even in the most idealized forms of research as political action or as pedagogy, we begin with the twin responsibilities of holding the power of first, interpellation, and second, address and explanation. In the context of researching the silenced, to be asked to be interviewed is constructed as a kind of privileged invitation, its inducement all the more powerful if the respondent is indeed un- or underrepresented. A journalistic assumption of the benefit of access to public acknowledgment is built into the request for research participants, where

> to be addressed is not merely to be recognized for what one already is, but to have the very term conferred by which the recognition of existence becomes possible. One comes to "exist" by virtue of this fundamental dependency on the address of the Other. One "exists" not only by virtue of being recognized but, in a prior sense, by virtue of being recognizable. The terms that facilitate recognition are themselves conventional, the effects and instruments of a social ritual that decide, often through exclusion and violence, the linguistic conditions of survivable subjects. (Butler, 1997a, p. 5)

The choice of how we address our participants is thus the first act of power in the research relationship. Taking into consideration the "linguistic vulnerability" of persons in relationships in which "the address constitutes a being within the possible circuit of recognition, and, accordingly, outside of it, in abjection," (Butler, 1997a, p. 5), my first and possibly most important criterion for a choice of methodology was based on the necessity to call on the subjects of my study in a manner that would recognize their identity as already having power of its own. I needed to find a way to address them that would honor their agency and their important knowledge; one that would acknowledge them as always already constructed as survivable subjects; one that would not require them to answer the call to existence by a performance of abjection. But the research relationship involves a dialogue, and it was also important to me to think about my own role as listener and how that might contribute to the kinds of stories I could hear.

I "called" others like me to tell stories about power and pain. Much of the literature on oral history or life story research emphasizes the developmental or transformative therapeutic potential that forms a part of the explanation of how the subjects can benefit by the process of telling the story of their lives. Yet I think that we must ask ourselves if we actually have the right, as researchers, to act as the co-producer of this kind of meaning for those who consent to be researched. One of the real concerns for me in undertaking an interview-based research project was the need to distinguish my role as researcher from my other roles as speaker /teacher /counselor. Since I bring to this process a long practice of the various uses of dialogue (rhetorical, pedagogical, and archeological), I had no doubt as to my ability to initiate and sustain relevant and meaningful conversations with people, even in situations in which there might appear to be little potential for reciprocity or continuity. This made me aware of a particular responsibility for my role, in light of my commitment to protect respondents from possible disclosure consequences in the interviews. I am fully cognizant that "the openness and intimacy of the interview may be seductive and lead subjects to disclose information they may later regret" (Kvale, 1996, p. 118).

So for me, an important criterion for my choice of methodology for this process was that I needed to create a context in which I could engage with research subjects only in the role of researcher, and not as a therapist or counselor. I believed that this commitment must go beyond the obvious necessity to avoid interviews with those who are, or have ever been, in a therapeutic relationship with me. But this left me with a further question: what about those roles that I play in other parts of my life? Could I leave out aspects of my own multiple marginalities in my role as a person in these relationships? How could I justify or account for the impact of my personal authority in the role of researcher with this particular group of people?

One of the ways this sense of the power of the researcher is often legitimized is by a vision of research as an opportunity to use the authority of the role in the formation of a "deliberate relationship," entered into "in the interests of teaching and social change" (Tom, 1997, p. 17). If, as a researcher, I am refusing the role of therapist, would it be any safer to think of myself as a teacher? Another meaning assigned to "address," which includes the teacher's position as holder of definitions, further expands the power of the researcher (if one could be even more powerful than to be able to decide if another person deserves recognition!). It is this sense of address that is used by Elizabeth Ellsworth, speaking of the relation between teachers and students:

> When teachers practice dialogue as an aspect of their pedagogy, they are employing a mode of address. The rules and moves and virtues of dialogue as pedagogy are not neutral—they offer very particular "places" to teachers and students. (Ellsworth, 1997, p. 49)

Even in recording life stories, the rules and moves and virtues of research relations also imply a continued power difference not erased by the contract implied in the consent form signed by the informant. If we listen to stories using the roles assigned within a pedagogical paradigm, it is very difficult to avoid the trap of positioning ourselves as the teacher, by definition the person who has a superior explanation:

> We constantly run the risk of pushing our stories against the stories of others and in a sense demanding that others rethink their stories in light of our stories . . . asking, if not insisting, that others interpret their stories in light of ours. (Cottle, 2002, p. 535)

However, I was concerned that if I would need to avoid creating the definitions (acting as a teacher) in my engagements with respondents, in order to produce a true textual representation of someone else's life story, then I would not be able to outline to them my interest in the study. While acknowledging that my description of the problem could potentially change some of the informants' thinking (change some of their definitions, at least), I decided that, in order to frame our conversations, I needed to explain the theoretical basis for my questions at the beginning of the interviews. Was I teaching while I did that? Was I engaging in consciousness raising with pedagogical intent? I did not consider that these conversations were entered into on my part with the desire to change anyone's mind about the topic. Rather, I was asking for comment on my ideas, engaging in dialogue with people who share a practice that is underrepresented in both professional and grassroots theoretical language. But perhaps one is not required to act as either therapist or teacher in the text-creation stage of the process, but the skills and frameworks of a therapeutic and/or pedagogical stance could still be of use in the interpretive process. As a response to this need to incorporate my intellectual orientations and to use my best skills in the process, I chose an arts-based methodology for this project.

Arts-Based Research

> Art can create two things most crucial for the witness—the address to and the creation of the other, and the emotional urgency resulting from the encounter with strangeness, with knowledge we do not know we know. (Davidson, 2003, pp. 164/165)

One way that interview-based research has been re-imagined in recent years, is "not as a method of gathering information but as a vehicle for producing performance texts and performance ethnographies about the self and society" (Denzin, 2001, p. 24). Though embedded in, and reflecting, many of the values of both the action and the educational forms of engagement in knowledge-production, this approach, it seems to me, offers a possibility for a meta-form: *NOT art as research but research as art.* I conceive of this as a positioning of the research process itself as a kind of ethics-based or moral philosophical conversation, a tool to use for communication, and a way to honor both speech and silence, both the action and the stillness of turn-taking in the exchange of subjectivities required for a shared construction of meaning. In "arts-based research the *expression* of meaning becomes central compared with science, where meaning is *stated*" (Butterwick, 2002, p. 243).

My decision to use this methodological framework for my study was based on several considerations, both academic and personal. If I can approach the research process as the medium to be manipulated, and if

I have decided that my goal for the process is expression as much as it is description, then some of the problems of the crisis of representation could be resolved by appeal to aesthetic criteria; then questions of validity could perhaps be based on the level of skill with which the material is used, rather than on the need to establish the subjects' credentials as oppressed-but-resistant, or the researcher's credentials as reluctant savior. It may even be possible to argue that in using "performative" or arts-based inquiry, I could see myself as responding to a very current demand in qualitative research,

> a call for a kind of validity after poststructuralism in which legitimation depends on a researcher's ability to explore the resources of different contemporary inquiry problematics . . . position[ing] validity as a space of constructed visibility of the practices of methodology. (Lather, 1994, p. 39)

The choice of this methodology met some of my original academic needs for the purposes of this study, primarily in the freedom it gave me to allow and account for some of the possible meanings of the silences between stories. Speaking of "the language of the unsayable" in an introduction to "the poetics of interpretation," Annie Rogers and her group identify the difficulties in recording and analyzing resistance and negation as a "crisis of knowledge for researchers":

> If we assume, as we do, that the unsaid can contribute something valuable to our understanding of how an individual understands the world, then what language can we use to present what is unsaid? Furthermore, how can we interpret its meaning in a systematic way while remaining sensitive to issues of authority and validity? (Rogers et al., 1999, p. 80)

The arts have always been a language used for the expression of the irrational, the unsaid. They have been used for centuries to create an opening to the unspeakable and are used in the present as illustrations of the postmodern belief that "there is no real world. There are no originals. There is no original reality which casts its shadow across the reproduction. There are only interpretations and their performances" (Denzin, 2001, p. 30).

An arts-based inquiry is also a personal fit for me as researcher. Outside my roles as counselor or teacher, it allows me to use one of the strongest parts of my experience in order to approach this most fragile knowledge in myself and others. As a visual artist, it is easy for me to understand silence or stillness as a negative space or a dark area in a complex chiaroscuro; as a singer, I can see those things as rest notes, punctuating and forming the basis for the rhythms of the whole piece. If an arts-based understanding of narrative can help me express, rather than expose, the local knowledge that I and others hold—the direct, "lived" knowledge of some of those spaces between victimization and power, helplessness and agency, silence and speech—then the product will be something I can share with others, even within the ethical constraints I have set myself. Rather than falling into the fixed choices of available representations of historically oppressed groups as victims or heroes, I hope that perhaps something produced within this frame can help to fulfill the need for

> writing that spirals around social injustice and resilience; that recognizes the endurance of structures of injustice and the powerful acts of agency; that appreciates the courage and the limits of individual acts of resistance, but refuses to perpetuate the fantasy that "victims" are simply powerless. (Weis and Fine, 2000, p. 61)

In this effort, I want to contribute to writing (and/or practice) that allows for a moving articulation or illustration of the paradox presently so difficult to reconcile in our contemporary division of identities into the categories of authenticity and authority: "that these women and men are strong *is not evidence that they have suffered no oppression*" (Weis and Fine, 2000, p. 61). My intention was and is to honor both the suffering and the strength of so many without collapsing any of us into an Abject victim position, and without enacting the defensive possibility of "a surrender to cynicism" (Adorno, 1985) that lives in a distancing critique, or even irony. For this purpose, I have chosen to engage in the research process by conceiving of it as a part of the innately human practice that has always supported endurance and survival by the transformation of pain into metaphor, allegory, music, and art.

> The abundance of real suffering tolerates no forgetting. . . . Yet this suffering, what Hegel called consciousness of adversity, also demands the continued existence of art while it prohibits it; . . . it is now virtually in art alone that suffering can still find its own voice, consolation, without immediately being betrayed by it. (Adorno, 1985, p. 312)

Representation—Portraiture

Sara Lawrence-Lightfoot and Jessica Hoffman Davis describe the "art and science" of social science portraiture in terms that convinced me that this is the most appropriate choice of representation for my project. Even beyond my initial satisfaction with a commitment to an artistic process, this framework offers me a familiar and comfortable position in relation to the subject: the interest, the engagement, and the curiosity of the "portraitist."

> Portraiture is a method of qualitative research that blurs the boundaries of aesthetics and empiricism in an effort to capture the complexity, dynamics, and subtlety of human experience and organizational life. Portraitists seek to record and interpret the perspectives and experience of the people they are studying, documenting their voices and their visions—their authority, knowledge, and wisdom. The drawing of the portrait is placed in social and cultural context

and shaped through dialogue between the portraitist and the subject, each one negotiating the discourse and shaping the evolving image. The relationship between the two is rich with meaning and resonance and becomes the arena for navigating the empirical, aesthetic, and ethical dimensions of authentic and compelling narrative. (Lawrence-Lightfoot and Davis, 1997, p. xv)

The position of portraitist also addresses what is likely to be the strongest argument against an arts-based approach: the awareness of the hermeneutic involvement of the researcher at all levels and stages of the process. "As all of portraiture can be understood as interpretive description, it is difficult if not impossible to isolate moments at which voice is not acting as interpretation" (Lawrence-Lightfoot and Davis, 1997, p. 110). But this calls up all the concerns about excessive self-reflectivity, as well as the problems of the crisis of representation. If I say that the research process is the medium, and the product of it is expression as well as description; if I agree that "our texts are built more in relation to fiction and storytelling, rather than in response to the norms of science and logical empiricism" (Tierney, 2002, p. 385), then how do I manage the need for validity or "truth"? What or who is actually represented in this portrait, and how can a text made up of pieces of thirteen people's conversations be a portrait? In particular, how can I produce a portrait of a practice? An analogy from art theory might be helpful here to describe my intentions in using the language of the portraiture genre.

I am operating from the position that Realism is a convention in Western art analogous to the norms of truth-claims in social science research; working within an aesthetic that values the representation of "how things really look," Realism can be described in visual terms:

technically, as the replication of an optical field by matching its color tones on a flat surface, whether or not the subject matter has, or could have been seen by the artist; iconographically, as the subject matter of everyday, contemporary life as seen or seeable by the artist, whether recorded photographically, or by other modes of visual report. . . . Realism disapproves of traditional and fictional subjects on the grounds that they are not real and visible and are not of the present world. Realism argues that only the things of ones own time, things one can see, are "real." (Gardner, 1986, p. 836)

The most apparently Realist genre in art, possible only through scientific and technical assistance, is, of course, photography. At least until the arrival of computer-based and digital photo manipulation, a photograph has been assumed to be a more or less reliable representation of what is really there in the visual field of the person holding the camera. Treating photography as an illustration of the real implies that there has been no mediation by the camera itself and does not recognize the impact of the social location, or the technological and artistic expertise of the artist behind it. Neither does it account for the rhetorical intentions of the artist in the darkroom or on the computer, manipulating the final representation. Portraiture, on the other hand, even if it conforms to the conventions of realism of its time, is understood to be entirely mediated—it represents the vision of an individual artist attempting to communicate something more about the subject than what is strictly visible from a single point of view. Contemporary portraiture is not trying to be photography; rather, it recognizes photographic realism as also being made up of conventions. Both in terms of art and of social science, these conceptions of the Real are deeply embedded Western ethnocentric historical conventions, which contribute to the construction *not* of what "can be seen" or, in the sense of text, what is "sayable," but of "what can be read" and "what can be believed" as it is represented. If ethnography or positivist social science research is analogous to photography, then a certain kind of research text and certain kinds of stories, disclosures, and performances are analogous to portraiture.

> The research portrait, a written narrative, is imprinted with the researcher's understanding of and relationship with the individual or site that is represented in the text. . . . Portraiture is based on a belief in narratives or stories as primary and valid structures through which personal and professional identities are framed, sustained, and shared. The narrative in portraiture is respected as an essential vehicle for meaning making in the life of the individual or group. (Davis, 2003, p. 199)

For this project I wanted to produce a portrait of what is "unsayable," "unseeable," something moving and changing, something that is changed as soon as it is seen. By talking about movement, I wanted to hold myself still for just a moment, just long enough to hold a focus on a view through a particular window, to learn the words and a rhythm with which to tell a story about a practice that requires this most fragile knowledge in me and others, this crossing of borders, this passing. I wrote this as a story of disclosure, because this whole project is a disclosure for me, a performance enacted with full consciousness of the kinds of consequences I may face, and with the same intention, the same fear, and the same hope of an outcome that I suspect also motivates the people whose stories I have worked to share.

> I wanted to be understood finally for who I believe myself to be, for the difficulty of and grief of using my own pain to be justified. I wanted my story to be unique and yet part of something greater than myself. I wanted to be seen for who I am and still appreciated—not denied, not simplified, not lied about or refused or minimized. . . . Writing is an act that claims courage and meaning and turns back denial, breaks open fear, and heals me as it makes possible some measure of healing for all those like me. (Allison, 1994, p. 180)

Methodological Intentions

One of the familiar cultural forms of interview-based research as art is the documentary film, wherein the conventions of documentary film-making usually work to represent social and structural relationships within a realist tradition, analogous to the more objectivist strands of "truth-finding" rather than "truth-making" in qualitative research. One of the theorists I have used "to think with" (Catherine Bateson) in the process of determining how to deal with representation for this project is Trinh T. Minh-Ha. In the context of creating documentary interviews that "take for granted that objective reality can never be captured" (Denzin, 2000, p. 32), she articulates her concept of the characteristics of the "responsible, reflexive, dialogical interview text" as including the following elements, many of which correspond to my criteria for choosing a methodology:

- It announces its own politics and evidences a political consciousness;
- It interrogates the realities it represents;
- It invokes the teller's story in the history that is told;
- It makes the audience responsible for interpretation;
- It resists the temptation to become an object of consumption;
- It resists all dichotomies (male, female, etc.);
- It foregrounds difference, not conflict;
- It uses multiple voices, emphasizing language as silence, the grain of voice, tone, inflection, pauses, silences, repetitions;
- Silence is presented as a form of resistance. (Trinh, 1991, p. 188)

Although I could not hope to adequately fulfill all those criteria in one project, this articulation of the ideals and possibilities of an arts-based interview practice has given me a fine, high target to shoot for and allowed me to imagine a strategy that could help me to find and hear "voice" (both my own and that of others like me) in a place of silence, but at the same time to honor what Levinas calls the "ethical resistance" of the Other:

> not the resistance of another power to mine, but the "resistance of what has no resistance," a mode of resistance constituted in the very exposure of the face of the other to my power . . . the sense in which the other comes to me in her/his "destitution" not as my servant or my equal but, paradoxically, as my master, the one who commands me to be concerned with his/her fate. (Levinas, 1969, p. 200)

I have tried to produce work where the content matches the process, where the art of research is applied in a larger conversation about relationship and respect. I have attempted to use the tools of qualitative research interviewing to produce an expression of love and compassion in the form of a portrait of a kind of empowerment practice—one that asks each person to hold herself in responsible relation to what Levinas calls "the face of the other": "the other as a unique, singular interlocutor . . . who is exposed to my powers, vulnerable to my strength, and yet resists my power in the way s/he calls it into question as interlocutor" (quoted in Hendley, 2000, p. 33). The next section describes my strategies for the interviews that facilitated the gathering of the unique and singular voices that I borrowed for the purpose of constructing this portrait.

Vignettes: Stories to Think With

Once I determined the overall framework of the study, I was left with the complex task of finding an interview methodology that could satisfy my pressing, but sometimes contradictory, concerns for both the process and the content of my study: my need to create and identify conditions for safe disclosure, my interest in the mechanics involved in constructing identity stories for rhetorical use in speaking out, and my commitment to present a portrait of concrete and specific examples of how this little-understood practice is developed and enacted. I decided to do the research in two stages, conducting the initial interviews with a larger number of subjects and returning to only half of the group for a longer second conversation. For the first interviews, I framed my conversations with the participants using a "vignette" approach to the questioning. This was a strategy that solved several of my problems. It offered the opportunity to outline practical problems in hypothetical terms in a way that could identify some of the very specific issues dealt with by bordered practitioners in our daily work; it addressed the discussion of the practice in the form of stories, and at the same time it reduced the potential for self-disclosure. I did not use vignettes for the second interviews.

For this first stage of the research, I wrote seven scenarios to use in structuring open-ended conversations with the helping professionals who volunteered to speak with me. I presented these stories as tools for talking, but in particular as a safe way for participants to respond in expert voice and without the necessity for self-disclosure of specific personal experience. The scenarios raise questions about probable motivations and ethical concerns for the practitioner in the story, and I asked them to discuss some of the potential outcomes, both personal and professional, that might arise from such self-disclosure in various social/political contexts. The vignettes were presented in recorded interviews of 1 to 1½ hours in length, and each story allowed for a discussion of one or more of the complex ethical and practical issues involved in helping relationships. Many of the stories were sketches of situations very familiar to all the participants. They were framed with the intention of encouraging indepth discussion, not only about the social structures that might affect the choice of whether or not to refer to personal experience in a given situation but also to the language and self-description that marginalized individuals might use or offer one another when operating from an ideology of speaking out.

Vignette methodology has been found to be particularly valuable applied with the goal of eliciting attitudes and assumptions about topics when more direct questioning might be considered to lead respondents to answer in socially programmed ways—providing answers that might reflect what they believe they should do or think, rather than what they would do or think in real life. Particularly in cases in which the interview or study is related to socially undesirable or stigmatized behavior, such as needle-sharing by injection drug users (Hughes, 1998), some findings suggest that vignettes produce more valid responses, by providing people with the chance to "flirt with risky behavior at no personal cost" (McKeganey et al., 1995, p. 1259). Although this project is working with an entirely different set of definitions for risk, it is true that for many professionals, acknowledging the use of self-disclosure in some of these settings is itself a confession of a possible breach of the ethics of professional distance—another kind of risky, undesirable behavior. Another argument for the use of vignettes in this case, however, is expressed in this observation by an early researcher:

> Vignettes move . . . away from a direct and abstracted approach and allow for features of the context to be specified, so that the respondent is being invited to make normative statements about a set of social circumstances, rather than to express his or her "beliefs" or "values" in a vacuum. It is a method which . . . acknowledges that meanings are social and that morality may well be situationally specific. (Finch, 1987, p. 105)

Setting aside for the moment any discussion of whether this description of situationally specific morality could represent the ethical commitments of the subjects in this study, the significance of specific material conditions for the process of decision making was amply indicated in their responses. The literature indicates that the main critique of vignette methodology is based on a concern for validity, related to what some researchers have called "satisficing": "a tendency for subjects to process vignette information less carefully or effectively than they would under real or ideal conditions" (Stolte, 1994, p. 727). This suggests that any material gained in response to such hypothetical questioning would not necessarily represent the subject's true practice. For my purposes, however, this was not a relevant concern, since I was encouraging individuals to discuss the thinking processes that they might go through in order to decide whether or not to use self-disclosure in a specific context, rather than seeking to determine what, in fact, they might do in daily practice. The whole engagement with these practitioners was undertaken with the shared assumption that the practice of self-disclosure, although already defined as questionable within the constraints of a common discourse of professional ethics, was something that they had done, intentionally, in various contexts.

A vignette . . . is selective, producing a "snapshot" of a given situation. This offers participants distance and space to provide a discursive interpretation within the context of a vignette. Where this "snapshot" does not offer enough information for an individual to make a decision or provide an explanation—characterized by an "it depends" response, the situated context of a vignette can be used to explore the main influencing factors. (Hughes, 1998, p. 383)

In the conversations based on these snapshots, we were able to think about elements of our practice, different from those that might have been elicited by direct questions about what we should do in the abstract. In contrast to the ways the technique was used in some other studies reported, the questions were not constructed in order to limit the answers to fixed-choice responses; each vignette contained some specific details that would make it difficult to predict a decision either way. However, in this study, "It depends" was the most common first response to all of the hypothetical scenarios. The discussions were focused for at least ten minutes on each scenario, ensuring a certain level of thoughtfulness about the content. In fact, it appears that, far from "satisficing," respondents were able to think more deeply about their practice as a result of trying to answer the questions posed in the vignettes—many of the participants expressed surprise at the conclusions they had reached after discussion about some of the potentials for each of the scenes.

JAMES: I realized that in some of the situations I had advocated a certain position in the beginning, and then after interrogating the subject for a while, my opinions shifted a little bit; so that was disconcerting—because I like to think of myself as someone who sticks to what he says—but at the same time, I guess that what the situations forced me to realize was the complexity of the moral choices that we are making in the discussion of these things.

Another area of criticism of the vignette strategy, common to any methodology employing open-ended questioning, is "that one sacrifices some comparability between respondents" (Finch, 1987, p. 106). Since I was more interested in discovering the shared epistemologies underlying decisions taken in such circumstances, I did not consider this possibility a problem. Rather, the vignette methodology served more than one very important function in this project. First, by focusing discussions on what were presented as specific situations, the scenarios allowed us to speculate about the motivations, external conditions, and possible power relations that could be operating as a background to the decision making of the protagonist. Placing these particular conditions beside the more or less universal ethical constraints imposed on helping professionals allowed for the articulation of some of the deeply held theoretical positions on which many of the decisions about self-disclosure are based. At the same time the participants identified some of the consequences arising from a decision either way. At the beginning of the second-stage conversations, I asked the participants about their experience of working with the vignettes in the first interviews. The answers to that line of questioning were an indication of the success of the strategy for this purpose.

> KATALINA: I do remember thinking that the questions were such good opportunities for me to really think about how I think, or how I deal with clients. I never get that opportunity now, because I'm faced with clients and their issues, and you just play it by ear—not really thinking how each one follows your thinking or your philosophy, or what your philosophy is. So, in that sense it was very—"interesting" is too mild of a word, I think—it was really a good experience. It was eye-opening to really think about it from that angle, an opportunity for me to learn what I think.
>
> ANISE: In terms of process, I thought it was interesting to look at those little cases that you gave and think about all the different permutations of—I guess what I would call "moral questions" that came up around disclosure. And as I do some research in ethics, I'm interested in looking at questions like that, from an ethical perspective. So that was interesting, just the process.

Perhaps most important for my particular ethical concerns, beginning our conversations using scenarios of some familiar but quite specific disclosure situations had the effect of ensuring the initial positioning of the participants as experts in the practice and allowing them to reflect on their experience without requiring them to tell their own stories in any recognizable way. To create the conditions for this, I decided that it was necessary, early in the first interviews with each individual, to tell them why I did not want them to talk about their personal pains. First I explained that my goal for the study was not to examine the specific harms of whatever marginalization each of us has lived with/through but rather to look closely at how we use the story of such pains with specific intent. But perhaps more important, I explained that I believe we are often put in the position of exposing ourselves as marginal—demonstrating our authenticity—in order to establish our right/ authority to speak about some of the difficult things that may be happening in the lives of others. I wanted to establish that authority without references, partly because the expertise I am seeking to theorize is not, in fact, the capacity to survive painful social or personal situations, or even the resilience that makes a life rich beyond mere survival, however hard-won. I take both of those things for granted in the lives of those people I was privileged to interview.

In various ways during the different conversations, I expressed my interest in discovering the epistemology of speaking out, as it is conveyed by the self-disclosures of people like them, whose practice is a performance of the capacity to operate as caring and ethical, responsible persons in full experiential knowledge of the damage and danger in the world. This departure from the more commonly used neutral questioning position was intentional, and I entered into the process with an awareness that, of course, my bias would influence the content. But I decided that to do anything else would not be consistent with my position on self-disclosure—that my choice to be present in the data required me to ante-up, even in the way we talked to each other, and that whatever impact this positioning may have on the product would, in fact, be central to the point I wish to make about the practice. Some of the respondents, familiar with the norms of research, also commented on this aspect of the interviews.

> ANISE: The other part of the process that I thought was interesting—it seemed to me that you had ideas that were seeping through into how you were talking, and I liked that. I think it's very new when we actually don't have, necessarily, a research where we're pretending to be in an unbiased position, but that your ideas were coming forward.

I was most particularly concerned, because of my methodological interest in "the price people pay to tell the truth about themselves," to open up the possibility for us to talk about the potential harms of disclosure. To do that, I felt that I needed to introduce the subject early in our conversations, and so I framed it as a theory central to my practice and to this study, introducing the idea of "Disclosure Consequences," as described in the introduction to this work. Working from within this critical framing of the risks of overdisclosure, I believed that it was of paramount importance, from the first conception of this project, that I find a strategy to reduce the possibility that any participants could experience themselves in this context, even for a moment, as Abject. My choices in direct conversation with participants, then, were based on my intention to match the practice to the theory, offering openings for the description of possibly painful personal experience framed as relevant knowledge, and not subjected to any interrogation or doubt.

> JAMES: . . . and so you set out a certain—a thought experiment. You provided me with a set of hypotheticals, and one of the rules of those hypotheticals is that I was not going to talk about the personal information that I could have brought to the table—as a very part of the structure in which we were talking . . .
>
> LZ: Absolutely—taking for granted the structure within which you *know*, the basis for your knowledge on the topic!
>
> JAMES: Yes.

Besides taking care of my concern for the possibility of painful disclosure consequences for the participants that could result from talking to me, the use of vignettes has also enabled me to further protect the anonymity of my subjects, blurring the line between the particular instance and the shared truth of the stories represented, at least in part by focusing the details of individual stories on specific kinds of hypothetical experience. The fact that several of the respondents had been in very similar situations gave each of the conversations a potential for a disclosure of the kind of knowledge that comes from personal experience, without making it necessary for anyone to be explicit about what those experiences might have been. This strategy has produced data that can encompass both generic and particular experience, allowing for the creation of a portrait without requiring the exposure of the exact truth of any one person's account. It also blurs the lines between their words and mine.

My own voice is directly represented in the recorded conversations in two ways. The first interview recorded for the data was the result of the support of an experienced researcher who used the vignettes to interview me as a participant. My first intention for this step was to test the scenarios as stories, to see if their content would, in fact, stimulate thought about the issues I was hoping to address, and to better understand the impact of the questions on the feelings of the person answering them. When reading the transcript of this first recording I was interested to find that, even though I wrote them myself, I was sometimes surprised by my own responses to the situations described in the vignettes. As I continued to work with the data, my gratitude for the skill and support of the person who conducted the initial interview with me only deepened.

Another reason for recording this process was that I wanted my own participation as a bordered practitioner to be represented in the data. Consistent with my intention to blur my responses with those of the other participants, I have chosen a pseudonym for this part of the data, in the same way and for the same reasons that I invited participants to name themselves for the purpose of the project. In some of the direct quotes from interviews with other participants, I have chosen to include my own prompts or reflections where they seem to be a necessary part of the dialogue, since during our interactions I gave certain indications of my own experience, as well as expressing my opinion on various topics of the conversation. In this way, my participation is recorded in three voices: the researcher, the interviewer, and the informant.

One of the significant characteristics of this practice captured by the use of vignettes in this study was the respectful compassion for others like them that each of these practitioners demonstrated in their responses to the hypothetical ethical dilemmas so familiar to bordered professionals. Because all the participants are very experienced practitioners, they would not necessarily consider themselves at risk in similar situations, but the framework of the vignettes put them in the position of thinking of others and acting as mentoring experts to the helpers in the scenarios. This strategy allowed them to express their concern for what each of them understood to be the dangers of disclosure, or overdisclosure—to the speaker, and, in some situations, to the listeners or witnesses as well. Another unforeseen benefit of this process was the recording of a wealth of positive examples of practice decisions—direct solutions to the problems confronted every day by bordered workers in the various fields represented in the subject group, shared with the wisdom of long experience and with the compassion for each other of those who truly understand both the pains and joys of working in this way. In almost every case provided at this stage, the respondents not only thought about the safety and protection of the worker, but they also offered practical suggestions for how the problem could be handled in a way that would serve the interests of both the worker and the client (or the public).

I used member checks after the first stage, providing the participants with the transcriptions of our interviews, both to guarantee that what I had captured in this way was acceptable to them and to help me to determine which of the original group would be willing and able to participate in the longer, indepth interviews. For the second series of conversations, I was able to talk with six people from the original group of thirteen about their own direct experience of disclosure, without necessarily referring to the content of their professional stories. For these deeper conversations I tried to select a varied representation of those who were interested in a more theoretical engagement with the discourses and the frameworks underpinning the value-laden practice of such speaking out. As a result, these longer interviews were conducted with two men and four women, each of whom identified themselves as having lived with at least one of the primary "differences" or social justice problems that are presently assumed to benefit from empowerment interventions: racism, ethnic or religious discrimination, disability, AIDS, mental illness, homophobia, domestic violence, the abuse of children. All these people currently work in various professional roles recognized as possible advocates for, and interpreters of, their clients' interest. In some cases, a single person inhabits more than one role at any given time: health practitioner, psychologist, social worker, professor, researcher, and/or community development activist.

By building on the original relationships developed by the use of vignettes, a return to the conversation the second time allowed us to move seamlessly into more personal conversations and/or disclosures, creating a spectrum of data where the lines between the hypothetical and the real, or the particular and the general, are not necessarily visible. Although undertaken for different reasons than those given by Hollway and Jefferson in their work with "defended subjects," the strategy of the second interview had similar effects on the process:

> The second interview is significant in that it feels like resuming an established relationship rather than starting out as strangers, as in the first. Interviewees' preparedness to open out intimate material also reflects the building up of an expectation that stories are what the researcher wants—that they are interesting, relevant, and valued. (Hollway and Jefferson, 2000, p. 44)

Essentially, I started with stories, because I wanted to understand something about the narrative construction, not only of the particular stories of these bordered selves but also of the kinds of subjectivities created by the telling of them. If in this project I manage to express something about the paradox presently so difficult to reconcile in our contemporary division of identities into the categories of authority and authenticity, helper and helped, it will take form in a story. Not, however, a story from a single position but one that reflects the common-ness—more factual, more common even than the solidarity—of those who have learned to speak, through the windows that language allows us, about a world outside speech.

The next chapter outlines the respondents' interactions with my vignettes and begins to sketch the outlines for a portrait of a practice in the daily decisions that must be made by ethical professionals living and working on the border.

CHAPTER 4

Vignettes: Professional Confessions

In the first series of interviews recorded for the study, participants responded to hypothetical scenarios outlining several possible helping situations in which a bordered professional would be in the position of deciding whether to "tell" about her own experience of a relevant issue. These scenarios were constructed with the desire to provide openings for discussion of ethical positions or practice suggestions without the need for personal disclosure by the speaker. Each of them was designed to attend to a superficially different social condition (the content of the disclosure) and also to address the need to think about some of the larger issues involved in any decision to self-disclose. Some of the issues that were built into the vignette questions were these:

- Safety: Who is "safe" enough to tell the story? Who is "safe" enough to hear it?
- Why not stay silent? Identification, risk, and rescue.
- Who is the story for? Politicizing/contextualizing experience.
- The ethics of speaking for others: Exploitation or empowerment?
- When is speaking out rhetorical? Moral authority of witnessing.

- When is it a knowledge claim? Professional identity/knowledge.
- What makes a speaking performance "good" or "successful"?

The scenarios were constructed using situations that are similar to some that are very familiar to me, either from my own experience as counselor, teacher, and public speaker or from reports from colleagues and clients. Each participant was given the scenarios by email or in hard copy at least ten days in advance of the interview, and a hard copy was provided at the meeting, along with copies of the previously signed consent forms. People engaged with the scenarios at different levels of complexity, some feeling that the answer was obvious at first reading. For most of the conversations, there was consequently considerable engagement with elements of the story that were not necessarily visible on first examination but were provided by the participants' first-hand knowledge of similar contexts. The various roles of the protagonists in the stories that matched the specific professional and/or personal life experiences of the individual participants increased, rather than limited, their engagement with the issues imbedded in the questions, although every person was willing to take some ethical position on every case presented. In very many cases, the conversation included suggestions on how the protagonist could solve the problems posed by the vignettes, supporting the (sometimes contradictory) demands of their personal and professional interests in creative ways. This chapter concentrates on the discussions about the individual vignettes, organized in the order that they were introduced.

Scenario One

Monique works in a community drop-in program for people with mental illness. She is asked to speak by the organizers of a public gathering in protest to service cuts to the population she works with. Should she "tell" about her own experience of mental illness? What are her concerns if she does?

This scenario offers a very familiar context, where the incentive to speak out is clearly in the service of others. The sense of urgency, and the necessity for some emotional appeal, is obvious—as is the idea that Monique is being honored, by being asked to share her special knowledge in a way that could make a difference politically. This would seem to be a situation in which Monique could demonstrate her empowerment (voice) and also see her action as fostering voice and empowerment for others like her, or like she used to be. This kind of empowerment ideology and other semitherapeutic discourses often support the many occasions when bordered helpers are put in a position to provide the public with a "victim voice" to legitimate a claim for service or to "show the human face of the problem"; with this in mind, it would appear to be an easy choice for Monique. Consistent with this assumption, some of the respondents felt that any risks that might be involved in such an action could be balanced by a larger positive impact than might be apparent in the moment.

> JAMES: . . . And I think when you start looking at the difference between short-term social goods and long-term social goods, the benefits—although they seem very small in the short term—can have quite a large effect in the long term. And I think it is through the concerted effort of people speaking about their experience and being able to . . . articulate—in a way that other people can understand what it is that is precisely happening in them when they are experiencing mental illness—that allows for broader social change. I think that process of transforming the very images and the very stereotypes that we use to describe mental illness is ultimately a very positive outcome.

But for all the expert participants who looked at this scenario, making any decision about speaking in a situation such as this would first require answers to several important preliminary questions: Who are the organizers of the public event? Would Monique be representing a government or non-government agency? Do the people in her workplace know about her history of mental illness? Is there philosophical support in her workplace for the concept of survivor-supporters, or even consumer-advocates? What is she risking in terms of her professional credibility—with her colleagues, with the peer work network that she participates in, with her clients? Who will be in the audience? What about others in her personal life who may not know, or who may contest, her description of herself and her life experience?

Then, even if all those conditions are met in a way that would encourage her to speak, there are still more questions: Was there coercion in the request? (This goes beyond the question of the power dynamic between her and the person requesting this action; beyond the issue of whether the person is her employer or above her in some hierarchy.) Besides her job, what else might it cost her to say no? If she refuses, will she be written off as weak, unempowered, possibly not "healed" enough to do the work? Not supportive of the program? Not a political ally?

All these issues come up even before the question of whether or not she believes that her exposure could, in fact, make a difference to funding. One of the most significant considerations that respondents had about entering this kind of public arena was whether the original goals would or could be met by the specific action of personal disclosure.

> ANISE: Her purpose here is about cuts—service cuts to the population—so, I would say that she needs to take into account what will best serve that purpose. And her purpose may be undermined by sharing her own experience of mental illness. It might open her up—first of all, to stigma, but also to dismissal of her concerns.

I think she would have to weigh her safety against her exposure to stigma—[personal, as well as] the broad stigma of "special interests"—as though those are real [that is,] that special interests, period, get dismissed. Which is, for me, just a way of reinforcing dominant perspectives and marginalizing already pretty marginalized perspectives.

BETH: In this situation—specifically, around mental health—it's such a closeted issue still, and it's stigmatized, and there aren't a lot of safe places for people to talk about that. And if she says something, if she comes out with her own personal story, the message about the funding cut is going to get lost. It's going to become a story about her. Not funding cuts.

Although taking seriously the political intent of those who may find themselves in such a situation, many of the respondents who described themselves as having had similar experiences expressed serious reservations as to the political benefit of speaking out in this way.

NED: I've done this stuff! I mean gathering in protest to service cuts. I mean, it's strictly throwing meat before lions, and it's a circus! It's usually a circus, and it's usually enormously cynical, and it's strictly not even 15 minutes of fame. It's more like 7 ½. And I don't think it's worth it, because whether or not they're going to cut service probably has absolutely nothing to do with what she says or doesn't say—nothing. It's all been decided. So this kind of performance is usually, unfortunately, smoke and mirrors.

One person had a further political critique of the practice, questioning its presentation as a knowledge claim that could be generalized for any purpose other than specularizing. This response is the first example in the research data of a specifically strategic argument against using the individuating tendency of a personal account in the service of a larger group. In offering a solution to the problem of what kind of content the speaker could or should use to establish authenticity, particularly in this public setting, she suggests that, as professionals working with social conditions that we have ourselves endured, we should incorporate a broader sense of what constitutes our personal experience. She indicates that it is important politically to reference this expanded source of knowledge in any representation of whatever is understood to be relevant about our having lived through the "experience."

ANISE: So, to me, this personal experience probably doesn't have finite boundaries around it where it's just about her own labeling experience or hospitalization experience—whatever she's had—but also how that interfaces with a variety of other people who experience mental illness and stigma and cuts and so on, you know, out in ripples. . . . She has experience of not just herself, but herself in relation to a whole bunch of other people who have had similar experiences. So I think that's a problem—reifying one individual personal experience and holding it up as some kind of meaningful evidence, in and of itself.

There were other questions about the way that the sense of personal exposure resulting from such an event could affect her emotionally. Right at the outset of the interviews, and from this first scenario onward, the participants began to talk about the need for the speaker to have control over the content of her story, in order to take care of herself. She is understood to be vulnerable partly because the external conditions of the public context do not provide her with the familiar feedback of a speaking situation with a one-to-one interlocutor. The fact that there would be no time of listening to the other's reaction to her would mean that she would have no opportunity to take a moment to change direction, to clarify, to consider how much she has said, or what to say next. Except in extreme circumstances, she would be operating with little or no indication of how the audience is receiving the information, which could lead to what one experienced participant described as a "runaway story." Every response to this question acknowledged the potential for a speaker in this context to say more than she wanted to say or to say something different from what she had intended, exposing more of herself and her experience of pain than she might be comfortable with after the fact.

> BETH: I've seen people do it often—where they go to speak as an expert in a professional manner, and they end up talking in a personal way, and hadn't intended to beforehand. You know, speaking publicly like that is—well, you talk and you talk and feel safe in the moment that you're talking. And people are paying attention and focused on you, and it sort of engages you to say more than you're thinking that you might say. And you keep talking, you keep talking, because nobody is interfering and asking you questions. And then, before you know it, you've said everything.

For a great number of people, just speaking in public about the most innocuous topic is a very stressful situation. How much more likely it is then, that the exposure of some marginalized aspect of the person's experience in a public situation will be overwhelming in its emotional effect. This vignette provoked many expressions of concern for how someone might feel in the moment and also led to descriptions of how it might feel for the listener to see someone in that position:

> ELLEN: I have watched people speak, in public, a story that I have heard them speak in semipublic—in a support group or even a classroom—then I've seen them speak in a rally, and the adrenaline of speaking in front of a large group of people has propelled them into storytelling and a particular form of expressing the story that is itself emotionally draining and exhausting. I've seen people who started out just making an observation remark at a public rally suddenly grabbing a bullhorn and threatening to punch somebody.

> BETH: If you know the individual really well and you know that they're not prepared to tell the story, it's heartbreaking to watch them. Painful—because you know they haven't considered the consequences.

Scenario Two

Anita began volunteering as a support worker at a rape counseling center after she was herself raped by an acquaintance. In a phone session with a rape victim, the caller describes a situation almost identical to her own experience. The caller feels that no one can understand the difficulty she is having in deciding whether or not to report her victimization to the police and that no one will believe her if she does file a complaint, because the man was someone she knew and trusted. Should Anita talk about her own rape experience? Why or why not?

This scenario offers another common dilemma. In a setting where very often the helper is a person with her own experience of the issue, the need for safety is expanded, in that the helper must consider the safety and comfort of the caller, but anyone observing the helper has concerns for her as well. For this vignette, several issues become obvious immediately. The fact that the caller is in crisis requires a level of careful professionalism that was immediately identified by every participant. The distance and lack of intimacy of a phone call was an important element to be considered in deciding how much to say about the helper's own experience of rape. The first concern in every interview was a focus on the needs of the caller.

ELLEN: [In a similar situation,] one of the things that we wanted to be sure we did not do was steal into the other person's story. And unless Anita is extremely skilled, I'm not sure how she could say, "This has happened to me," and not end up telling her story.

ANISE: There's more danger in usurping—in this case, the caller—and her being overwhelmed by somebody else's experience. There's nothing worse than saying, you know, "Here's my experience" and laying it out to somebody, and somebody else saying, "Well! You think that's bad! Wait till you hear mine!"

NED: I've had people come in and say, "I don't want to hear about thirteen women's rapes. I don't want to hear about thirteen, or twelve, even eight other women's experience. I want to talk about mine, and I want to talk about some solutions. And I don't want be in a room full of people, you know, going 'me too, me too, me too!'" Until then, I thought "me too" was a good thing.

Almost every respondent had suggestions for increasing the caller's confidence and connection with the helper, without increasing the risk of "usurping" the caller's story. Many of the suggestions clearly illustrated the participant's belief that, as much as Anita's professional expertise would be useful, some offering of connection and solidarity would be necessary to provide the kind of support needed by a caller in this context. What these responses did *not* provide was any kind of a formula or pat answer guaranteed to work in every situation. In fact, in several conversations, informants argued against many of the common conversational strategies that might otherwise seem logical or automatic, illustrating a depth of understanding of the caller's vulnerable position.

> ELLEN: I don't care what the scenario is, that's what victims feel: "Nobody's going to believe me." And one of the things that I know is that Anita can persuade her that these are real fears, these are real concerns, and yet there are success stories. What we try to do is to persuade her that, "Yes, indeed I do know. I do know what you're talking about." And if you get into "Has this ever happened to you?"—which I think is a common place that people will go sometimes: "You can't possibly know what I'm thinking—feeling, experiencing." The answer is "You're right. I can't. I don't know. So, tell me."

> JACQUES: When you call somebody over the phone, you are in crisis, you are confused, and both know it. You are asking someone to listen to you, rather than to tell you what to do. And . . . "No one understands me"—it means, at times, that I don't understand either. So, by saying that "I understand you!"—you could be interpreted as belittling [her].

> RENEE: I don't think there's a clear right or wrong in this one. But again, my inclination would be—there are ways for her to express understanding and empathy around this, and around this woman's indecision—you know, to support this woman in the difficulty and indecision she's having, without making a personal disclosure that may or may not be helpful to this woman. Most women in acquaintance rape situations face that kind of struggle. And you can talk about that, and express understanding of the indecision, without shifting the focus to your own story.

The implication that the caller needs to make a choice about reporting was understood to increase the helper's power in the relationship, and to amplify the helper's need to be aware of responsibility for the possible influence she may have on the decision if she over-identifies by comparing her situation to the caller's present experience. Some of the ethical ramifications of the subjective quality of "knowledge from experience" are illustrated clearly in the profoundly contradictory responses to this scenario. Some respondents assumed that, in her professional role, Anita would need to work toward convincing the caller to report, and they wondered if a disclosure by the helper would increase the caller's confidence; others believed that her responsibility would include warning the caller about how difficult it could be to go through the legal process.

> NED: I'm concerned about the client. I don't know what the client needs. I don't know if the client needs disclosure from Anita, or if the client needs just Anita going, "You're right! You know what? The truth of the social situation is, you're just going to get revictimized by the police." Like: "It's a really nasty experience. You're not going to get justice; you're not going to get famous; you're going to get to be the cog—the unpaid cog in the wheel—where everybody that deals with you is getting paid to be there, except you."

ANNE: I would share that with her. I would say, "I know what you mean. I went through something similar. And yes, it is—it is horrible, because you know no one will believe you. But I'll believe you." And that's where I would start from, and work with that.

. . . And, you know, if she doesn't want to report it, that's fine with me. I don't know what I would do in that same circumstance—because I was that same naive person, and I'm not naive anymore, so I'm not that person. But there was no way I would've reported it if I was that person today. I know I wouldn't be believed.

A recurring issue in the discussions about this scenario was the recognition of the risk for Anita if she decided to disclose over the phone. This was largely not read as potential loss of professional credibility, as in the case of Monique, especially since all participants acknowledged that the peer setting of a rape crisis center is likely to have at least some workers who are specifically bordered, in that they may have been previously subjected to sexual violence in their own lives. Instead, this scenario provided us with the opportunity to talk about the fear that she would have personal consequences as a result of the call, whether she disclosed or not. This led to conversations about self-care for such workers in front-line situations and provided suggestions that would support an assertion that helpers like them believe that "talking about it" is still the best remedy for this kind of pain. Participants offered suggestions for the provision of useful supports for workers in this situation, clearly expressing an awareness of the real vulnerability and resilience of those who work in this way.

RENEE: This is one where I would feel it has the potential—there's more potential there for it to go the wrong way and end up being about Anita, or triggering Anita into something that she may or may not be supported in dealing with in this moment.

ELLEN: It seems to me, Anita has to be able to integrate her stories into her work in a way that's meaningful for her and for other people. And to be aware that sometimes she's got to really take care of herself, like this situation. You know—all the alarm bells should be ringing that it's going to take more than a cup of tea to solve this one.

. . . And that's okay. It doesn't mean that she shouldn't be doing this work, or she's not able to—it just means that today was a bad day.

RENEE: She says it's very close, and it's reminding her of her own experience; as soon as you start going down that road, self-disclosure gets—whether it's for the benefit of the person that's calling or whether it's something where you're sort of doing your own storytelling work, becomes much muddier.

This muddiness, the alarm bells, and the "wrong way" are some of the euphemisms used for referring to the knowledge these participants have of some of the truly negative disclosure consequences that are discussed further in another section. In a therapeutic setting with a client, I might see examples of the use of that kind of language as cues, entrance opportunities where careful questioning could open up a deeper exploration of what the person has experienced. This scenario was presented, however, almost at the beginning of the conversations with each of these people, and I generally chose not to "dig" for what could have been more direct disclosures at that time, hoping to get back to those places, if it seemed appropriate, in the more in-depth second stage interviews. Although this choice may seem patronizing, in that these very robust participants could have very easily responded or chosen not to respond, it was consistent with my original ethical commitment to avoid taking a therapeutic position in the research relationship and supported by my intention to protect respondents from self-disclosure in this first meeting. The grounding for this intention was beautifully expressed by one participant:

> ELLEN: Mmm—I always resist making politics out of someone's personal trauma.

Scenario Three

> Ralph is a teacher who has had his experience of child sexual abuse by a priest made public, during the course of a long court case that resulted in the payment of damages to several victims. He has returned to work after a period of stress leave, only to find that there is a controversy in his school regarding the possibility of inappropriate sexual behavior by the school's basketball coach. Some of his colleagues are unwilling to believe the reports and are finding it difficult to support the boy who has come forward with this complaint. Should Ralph make a special effort to speak for the child? Should he let the boy know that he supports him? Should he use his own experience as an example when he talks to the boy?

This dense scenario provided the foundation for much very interesting conversation. Within the context of an imagined staff group in a school setting, people were presented with many of the problems faced by witnesses to disclosure or reports of violence or trauma. With the introduction of the court process into Ralph's story, participants were reminded of some of the legal consequences that could follow from some kinds of self-disclosure in our social context. In this story, the possible self-disclosure is once again in the service of the other (the abused child, or other children possibly being abused). Since Ralph has already been "outed" by the publicity surrounding his court case, it is not necessary for him to talk about it for himself. Or is it?

One conversation covered some of the most important motivations for speaking for others in a context such as this. It also introduces some of the potential risks of homophobia and the current assumptions associated with being a survivor of sexual violence, as well as referring to a belief that there could be physical or health consequences to a decision about how and when we self-disclose:

> NED: I wouldn't be able to be silent in a staff lunchroom or something; I would feel like I had to speak. Principally for that child but much more metaphorically for my own child inside of me—that I would speak for that child within that school. But I definitely think Ralph should make a special effort to speak for the child. It's on Ralph, because that silence becomes a kind of betrayal.
>
> LZ: You think that if he didn't speak to the staff group that he might not feel safe in the school, that the environment that he was in would be kind of polluted for him?
>
> NED: Yeah. It would be toxic for him. It may be toxic anyway. . . .
>
> LZ: It may be, in fact, impossible for him, but also, what about the assumption that a man who is an abuse survivor is more likely to be an abuser? Can Ralph afford to take that risk? Is Ralph gay? Is Ralph straight? Does Ralph have a wife and three kids?
>
> NED: I don't know those parameters; I mean, who he is then becomes a question of—those are very real dangers. . . . But is Ralph's silence—potential silence—going to put him in danger of a real emotional collapse, as profound betrayal? And that's got to be weighed against the potential social consequences.
>
> LZ: Um-hum.
>
> NED: I guess he could go back into silence. But the odds are, if he does that, he's not going to be seeing me: he's going to be seeing interns, in about two years—because his body's not going to take it. So I think it's a bad bet. I think the silence is a bad bet. But he doesn't have to disclose to not be silent!

This vignette, more than any other, brought up the issue of the truthfulness of a disclosure and the question of believing the speaker. How a disclosure is heard, and whether the content is taken at face value or translated into another set of meanings, was seen as an underlying tension in all of the scenarios. In this story, there are two people disclosing, and the respondents acknowledged that concerns for validity may be significant in both cases, though for different reasons.

> ALMA: I think that Ralph wouldn't be able *not* to speak for the child. I think that in talking to the other people in the staffroom or wherever he is, with his colleagues, I think that he actually would be ashamed of himself if he didn't speak up for the boy, because one of the things that happens there is the sense that if they don't believe the boy, then they don't believe that he was abused either. And so he is going to be in a position where just to be able to stand his colleagues, he's going to have to make a statement of belief in the kid. Now, it could be this kid isn't even telling the truth, but he's still going to have to take that position—that people need to believe the kid—because he needs to believe in himself.

In these responses, it is apparent that the professional's self-disclosure is sometimes used in the service of providing an authoritative support to a weaker claim. But why do we think that Ralph would be believed any more than the child would? If he is believed, is it because he is an adult? Does his successful court experience give him credibility? Or is it because the staff don't know the particular offender he has charged? It seems that the respondents expect him to be believed, partly because he is a professional. But he is a professional using an expanded knowledge claim. If he can maintain his professional stance when disclosing, he is then speaking with more information on the topic than is available to the child, and the only reason for referring to his own experience would be to establish that he holds more information on the topic than is available to the other professionals who have not been abused in this way. It is the extra knowledge carried in his disclosure that has the rhetorical effect.

Many of the respondents were concerned that the child be supported, whether or not he is telling the truth about the coach. This illustrates a complex and sophisticated set of political commitments to a professional response to the truth that such things can happen, without depending on the facts of this particular claim.

ANNE: It's also tough, too, because—the school's basketball coach is—you know—sports, it's that sports stuff, too. It's so macho. I mean, I understand why people don't want to believe it. But they have to. They have to try and get past that part and find out what really happened, in a way that's safe for the boy. That's what matters.

KATALINA: The school doesn't want any trouble, da-da-da-da. . . . That, of course, is there. But also this whole issue that maybe the boy has problems or comes from a broken home, da-da-da-da. So, to try to balance that issue, it doesn't hurt for somebody who's already spoken openly about this to say he's been there. Even if it turns out that the boy was lying. If the boy was lying, he's got other issues anyway!

LZ: That's right. Exactly. Maybe he was abused somewhere else.

KATALINA: . . . So it doesn't hurt for Ralph to say, "I've been there!" I think. It balances it, so that discussion can start. It doesn't necessarily mean the boy is right, or the boy is lying or that basketball coach is right, or that he's lying.

Besides the obvious expression of a commitment to professional support for children in this situation in general, this vignette elicited some responses that suggest that one of the motivations for speaking about our painful experiences, in contexts like these, could be the individual's sense of a moral obligation to share the extra knowledge gained in such a difficult way.

ELLEN: I can imagine it being most effective where he says, "Well, as you all know, I had this experience—and one of the worst things that happened for me was . . . ", and to just use himself as a credible authority. And I feel quite strongly that there's actually an ethical imperative to do that . . . and we all have an imperative to protect young people—anybody, for that matter—but in this case, a young person. So we also—everyone has the need—it's a righteous thing to speak up. He's coming from a place of special privilege, although it didn't feel like it!

KATE: . . . Like he may feel that he owes him, or he may not want him to go through the ringer. I sort of think—some people really would feel the sense that they really wanted to, but might not think it's appropriate, and then they back off. And what I said initially is that sometimes, feeling that you owe people something has gotten me into trouble, [*laughs*] because I don't take care of myself when I do that. And I think it's really natural, especially in the context where there's all these things going on. I think that Ralph would either, maybe, feel he really owed him something, or just run like hell.

For many people, the first concern was for Ralph to protect himself. But there was also a recognition that there would be many different components to the decisions facing him: some external constraints, created by the specific discourses referring to the sexual abuse of boys, by homophobia and the description of male survivors not only as unstable but also as potential offenders—but also some consciousness of internal limits on how much Ralph can tolerate. Once again, the responses provided in the interviews reflected the idea that there could be a process that Ralph may need to have gone through, before this act of speaking out would be safe for him, or indeed for the person or persons he is speaking for.

BETH: The first thing that I was thinking about is where Ralph was with this—in terms of support, and process, too. You know, did he process any of it, or was it just this horrific experience that he's gone through and he's raw and doesn't realize it, because he has no insight or awareness, because he's had no process, or whether he's done some analysis or he's done some work around it, and he's strong, and can present it in that way.

See, that's interesting, because the theme that's coming out is: where a person's at, and the awareness they have about what they're talking about. It could be that he's thought a lot about it, and he's talked to a lot of people about it. He could make an effort to speak to the boy, and might become emotional, but it could be contained. And there's nothing wrong with that. But what if he falls apart? And then what happens to his professional credibility, and his reputation?

This scenario also provided the context for suggestions and conversations about the idea of allies, of social supports beyond the formal structures of supervision or therapy. The suggestions for how Ralph could proceed included many references to the need for allies in the staff group, not just as supports for Ralph but also to provide a measure of safety for the child if Ralph were to speak with him, or on his behalf. Much of the ethical discussion indicated sensitivity to the power dynamics likely to be present in such a situation and offered solutions that could be interpreted as informed recommendations for changes in policy, arising from a knowledge of some of the systemic components of the problems posed by the specific setting.

> ELLEN: I would hope that Ralph could—assuming that he had these supports as he went through his own process—call in his allies. To the school, to also support the child. This child should not have to stand alone. I think it shouldn't just be Ralph; there should be someone else there who—there ought to be other people there who will share the responsibility for that.

Scenario Four

> Joanne, who has struggled at various times in her life with severe suicidal depression, is a nurse in the emergency ward of a hospital in a small community. Someone she knows only slightly from the community is brought in to the ward after what appears to be an intentional overdose of prescription medication. There is no one else around when the woman regains consciousness and wants to talk. Is it appropriate for Joanne to talk about her own experience? How much should she say about it?

For the story of Joanne, once again the context is read as very significant to the decision of whether or not she should disclose any part of an experience that she shares with her patient. In this case, the awareness of the protagonist's professional role is highlighted by (what we could speculate might be) possible implications for dual relationships in the life of a nurse in a small community. On the one hand, she needs to be seen as completely reliable as a professional, as she may be the only constant health provider available to the people using the hospital on a regular basis; but, on the other, she is a visible member of a community, where everybody knows everybody's business. The main concern for Joanne was expressed in the form of worry that she would not be able to perform her role adequately if she were to self-disclose. Including attempted suicide as the content of a self-disclosure was understood to have the potential to be very risky for her, and while most informants indicated that, in any case, disclosure would not be appropriate in this context, some of the responses included suggestions for how she could use the specifics of her experiential knowledge in a very controlled way.

> JAMES: If she is talking to this woman about suicide, I think the woman's going to look to her as an authority, as a support network for her while she's in the hospital. I could even see it undercutting her ability to deal with suicide in a proactive way if she does actually disclose.
>
> LZ: And I think "authority," that word that you used, is a good one. So it somehow undermines her authority as a professional?
>
> JAMES: Yeah—which is weird, because in a lot of the other situations, I didn't feel that that undermining of authority was there. But in this situation, I really feel like it's definitely a possibility. . . . I've always thought that personal

disclosure actually gives you a kind of authenticity, and adds to your authority, because you've been there and you've seen it and you've done it.

LZ: Is this about suicide, do you think? Is it because suicide trumps everything else?

JAMES: Yeah. I mean, suicide is just such a—I guess it's a profound reaction to life. Or it's a profound denial of life.

ALMA: I think that the problem is that it identifies her in the community, right? That it means that the next time somebody comes to the hospital, they ask for the suicidal nurse. And that's why I think that she'd have to be really, really careful about what she said. She could say that anybody could be depressed, or that some people have more difficulty with depression than others, but that people can survive and live and have a good life with it.

Is this an act of solidarity? Is she speaking with the intention of advocacy, or even operating as an example of a person who has depression who could be a successful person? Maybe even then it's not appropriate, except to talk about something that she knows, some way that she knows something about this—that she understands that people can, in fact, feel so bad one day that they take too many pills, and the next day they want to live.

But the first concern for everyone who was interviewed was not, in fact, for Joanne. In an immediate response to the questions, everyone determined that the primary consideration for the nurse had to be the immediate safety and comfort of the patient. For some, this took the form of acknowledging how significant the first impressions of care could be for the woman's sense of her own value to others. The idea of a potentially positive personal connection was understood to rest not on the identity or experience of the nurse, but on how she treated the patient as a person.

MARY: Hmm. Well, from victims in this situation, I've had people tell me that what the person who was at their bedside said to them, immediately after they woke up, absolutely colored their use of suicidal language after that. The cases I can remember: One woman was told by the doctor, "I just can't keep cleaning you out like this." . . . And then another one said that the nurse on hand just yelled at her, "Don't ever come back here like this!" and it was her concern, sincere in the moment—it really affected the person who had woken up—that gave them the oomph not to do an attempt for some time.

One of the issues that emerged in the discussion of this scenario was directly reflective of some of the possible ways that the privileged or extra knowledge gained by experience could be used in a professional relationship. One powerful example was a reaction to the suggestion that, in a situation such as this, one of the motivations a nurse might have for speaking out about her own experience of suicide could be to assert that the patient's overdose incident was intentional rather than accidental, to move her out of denial.

NED: I think that's doing therapy without a license. I think that's intrusive. I think it's a complete violation of somebody in a really vulnerable, passive state. "I'm going to decide that you're in denial, which is—by definition (my definition)—it's not a good thing that for some reason you lied. At this time, it's not appropriate for you to be in denial." I mean, there's a reason—it's a defense mechanism. It defends.

LZ: Right.

NED: . . ."Given that wisdom, I'm going to insist that you confront my version of your experience." . . . ? Nah! Uhuh. . . . and "This is also for your own good." . . .

LZ: . . . and "Because I know—" . . .

NED: . . . not "Because I'm tired and burned out, but because I know—" . . . Uh-uh—I'm not going there. I think it's intrusive. I think it's rude.

LZ: Just as rude as self-disclosure in this situation?

NED: Um-hum. And disclosure supposedly augments/backs up/ supports the appropriateness of this intervention, because "I've had an experience, and now that I've had the experience, I know the appropriate reaction to that experience." Of course! [*sarcastic*]

LZ: So, what we're talking about in every one of these is: is our experience authority? And, in this case, you've just framed it really well—she would be using that experience not only as authority, but as an excuse for behavior we wouldn't otherwise condone.

NED: Well, you can stretch the word. From authority to authoritarian.

For every respondent to this vignette, there was a single imperative. The judgment of these experienced helpers was that the best illustration of knowing that any professional could demonstrate in this circumstance would be to provide the person with an opportunity to talk. The skill of listening to another's disclosure was not overtly approached in any way as a component of this first stage of the research, but the professional commitment and expertise of the participants were clearly expressed in their responses to this hypothetical problem.

ANISE: So, your first job is to listen. The woman wants to talk.

ANNE: No, I don't think it's appropriate for her to talk about her own experience, on a couple of levels. The first one is: the woman is coming out of a real drug state—not knowing what she's taken, but I know she's not going to be feeling good; and she wants to talk; and she wants it to be about her, at that point. If I was the woman lying in that bed, I'd think, "This isn't about you!"

ELLEN: Given my own experience with people who have woken up from attempted suicide: they want to talk; they don't want to listen.

NED: Your job isn't to talk to some poor human being that just woke up from an overdose. No. And there's no one else around when this woman regains consciousness and wants to talk. So let her talk!

SALLY: I've been around a lot of suicide in professional and personal experiences, and when they want to talk, they want to talk. And you don't disclose any personal stuff, because then you're taking away their power, because they want to talk.

LZ: And so you're actually connecting by listening . . .

SALLY: . . . by listening—not by pushing your own story.

LZ: So she should say nothing?

SALLY: She should LISTEN.

Scenario Five

Regina, a lesbian, is a sessional teacher in a conservative Community College and is leading a mixed class for people in a Certificate Program that will qualify them to work with children in care. In a class dealing with adolescent sexuality, several students exhibit homophobic and discriminatory attitudes about GLBT people. Although in class time the students appear to comply with the need for sensitivity around this issue, during a coffee break she overhears an inappropriate joke and sees a student, who she believes is gay, retreat from the group. How should she address this problem with the class? What will happen if she "comes out" to them?

This scenario, too, seemed simple on first reading. The changes in culture that have, to some extent, legitimized sexual difference would presumably call for Regina to take on this issue directly. Her relative power in relation to the students would seem to reduce the risk for her and increase her need to take a political stand on homophobia. For some respondents, the idea that a teacher should be a role-model was an important consideration, but there was also the recognition that changing social attitudes and individual differences in the teacher's age, training, and experience, might be at least as important for decision making as the conservative setting.

BETH: So, in a situation like this, what I would hope for a person who's teaching, is that they would come out. And they would address this just in a straightforward, confident way, and still say, "That's not appropriate."

LZ: But do you have to be a lesbian to say that's not appropriate?

BETH: Well, no, of course you don't, but she is. So, I mean, any teacher should do that but we don't necessarily have to—[*laughs*]—and not all teachers are that progressive. But I think all teachers should do that.

It's interesting, I think, that the age is an issue too, because I think it's easier for people who are younger to just be out there; they've had the advantage of a couple of generations of ground breakers. And if it's somebody who's older that still could have a lot of internalized homophobia, and it's an unsettled issue, then that'd be difficult. But if she's twenty, she has to come out.

In further discussion of this scenario, there were two important areas of practice that required some thought. Beyond this sense of the necessity that a professional may feel to honor their identity in a situation such as this, there is the concern for the student who may or may not identify him/herself as gay. Much of the conversation resulting from that part of the vignette centered on how to protect the student from such a stigmatizing experience and also to preserve the student's right to her own choice to come out or not. Some of the responses to this vignette were, in effect, arguments for the creation of a larger sense of inclusion and safety for anyone on the margins.

> ALMA: It's interesting to think about what kind of systemic or policy differences would change the nature of the decision that the person would have to make. Like, for instance: if, in the school, one of the very first parts of the curriculum was a discussion of homophobia as a problem, then when she got to this it would not have to come down to "her proof" and "his proof," or any of those things. Or maybe she would've come out in the first class, and it wouldn't be a big surprise to anybody. But, you know, there is a systemic response to almost all of these, which is to actually take into account the possibility that among "us," there might be a few of "them," whoever the "thems" are!, and that a useful systemic response is one that actually recognizes that that line is not so harsh.

Much of the discussion about this scenario had to do with the problem of imposing a set of values on others. No matter how important this kind of anti-oppression work was seen to be, the participants reported their concern for the difficulty of carrying a kind of moral authority on the basis of personal experience alone. Some of the subtleties of this complex sense of competing reference systems were expressed in the sometimes emotionally charged responses offered to this problem, since, for almost all of the interviewees, the powerful formal authority of the teaching position was seen to be necessary to confront this breach of an abstract ethical stance.

> ELLEN: And the issue here is, you are dealing with people who were going to be working with children in care, and children in care come from a wide diversity—and we are on record as honoring that diversity. So, you know what? You don't get to have that opinion. Oh well. So suck it up!
>
> I can't make it impossible for someone who's homophobic to get a job in this situation. But I can be very sure that they understand what the rules of practice are: you're not allowed to slap children, and you're not allowed to make jokes that are homophobic.

Regina's need to act in response to this situation is seen to be all the more urgent because of the pedagogical goal of preparing the students for a helping role with vulnerable people. The sense that her task is protecting others led many people to suggest a very direct use of her professional authority, but for some it also provided a perceived need for the use of the special knowledge of personal experience and for some, a recognition of the possibility that the breach of the ideal of impartiality may have other consequences.

ALMA: It depends on what her politics are, and how many semesters she's taught, and how many times she's had to hear these jokes—how tired she is of the whole thing. Because she could come back and just lay down the law: "I heard that. That's not funny!"

So, what's the difference between saying, "Cut it out" and saying, "I heard that. I'm a lesbian. Do you know why that's not funny?" I think the difference is authority. Either you're "PC" and you're just a righteous person and so you're upholding some imaginary rule set, which is the way this is being treated in this group, or you're the person who's an authority on this specific issue. Homophobia hurts.

MARY: If she comes out to the class, she will lose some of them in terms of being able to learn from her. This will mean that their work will be poorer, and she might get to fail them! [*laughs*] So, for this one, I'm kind of vindictive!

ALMA: Sometimes, it's like, "Whoa—how did you get in here?" But in supervising this kind of work, we have to lay out our expectations so that attitudes—not just expressions like this, but attitudes—are relevant! And that's not human rights. I mean, people have the right to be assholes if they want, but, excuse me! [*laughs*] I don't have to pay them.

Scenario Six

Marlene's father has been incarcerated for sexual offences against children. She has moved to another city and begun her practice as a psychologist, specializing in the treatment of child sexual abuse. A new patient, who has also moved from her hometown, has recognized her name and made the connection with her father's charges. The client wants to deal with her own sexual victimization by a family member and asks directly whether Marlene will be able to support her in her process. What should Marlene tell her client?

This vignette addresses some of the formal aspects of professional ethics more directly than any other. For almost every respondent, the ethical requirements of the role of psychologist were seen as more important than the question of Marlene's individual entitlement to personal privacy. The lack of details in the presentation of this scenario allowed for conversations that expressed people's attitudes about central questions for the bordered worker: whether or not a person who had been victimized could ever be a good professional. Further, what makes them "good"—experience/ knowledge? empathy? professional training? having done their own work? Many cogent responses were in reference to the implied question raised by the client: "Why would someone who has had the experience of abuse become a specialist in the field?" Some comments provide a moving assertion of support for the motivations of bordered professionals who enter these arenas, but almost all responses also recognized that experience was not necessarily a guarantee of good practice, or even of empathy for the vulnerable.

ANISE: Well, it's not. It's not simple at all, to my point of view. You know, so many of us that are in this kind of "helping" kind of role, are doing it because—*because* of our personal experiences. And that's not bad thing. It's a good thing, as long as you are using it in a really healthy, ethical kind of way. So, one would hope that Marlene had already gotten there. I was making that assumption. I'm making that assumption about all these people: that they've done some of their own work.

BETH: I find that, sometimes, people who come from a background of abuse aren't necessarily prepared to be helpful, or don't have the skills to be helpful, or can be misguided. I also know that there are a lot of people who come from those backgrounds who are amazingly effective. And that's one of the huge issues in this example . . . and how do you decipher that?

ANNE: I think [she would be useful] because she's been through it. She's recognizing that people are going to know her, at some point or other. It's like anybody with the last name "Homolka" or "Bernardo." Would I think that somebody who's named Homolka, say—if her sister was a psychologist, dealing with victims, would I think she could help me? Actually, I think she could.

Her extra knowledge of abuse has already been exposed to the client, but the fact that the text was not clear about whether Marlene was directly victimized by her father required participants to speculate on the possibility that Marlene could be someone who subscribes to the theories of the False Memory Foundation (Cohen, 2001; Daly, 2004, p. 141), or that she might feel that her father was unfairly convicted, justifying the client's concern for her ability to believe a story of abuse. Knowledge of this major debate in her area of practice was assumed by many of the participants to be a part of Marlene's expertise, and, in that light, several felt that her responsibility to declare her position on the topic would be based on a therapeutic need for safety for the client. This was framed in terms of transparency and presence and indicated the need for some level of self-disclosure presented as a component of her professional knowledge, in order to allay the client's fears.

ALMA: She needs to indicate, to the client who asked that direct question, where she stands on it. And once she's said that, after that it's not her business. And that's to protect the client, so it doesn't get muddied up. But I think that's a question: what are we disclosing? And in service of what, are we disclosing?

In the service of my authority as a practitioner, there are some places where, actually, the disclosure is relevant, and it increases my authority as a practitioner because I am willing to be honest. There are other places where such a disclosure decreases my authority as a practitioner. There are some places where it endangers my credibility as a human being.

BETH: You know, if there was a measurement of which person should definitely *not* talk about it, it would be this one. But I think that she only brings that she's honest about who she is, where she comes from, and assures the person, to whatever professional extent that they need, that she's aware of who she is, and can help her. And then, after that, that person's individual experience isn't a part of the process.

One part of the response to this scenario involved acknowledgment of the professional's fears that her disclosure may put her at risk. Being new to the field, being in a new city, and feeling exposed by the potential client's knowledge of her father's criminal status led several of the informants to feel that she might respond to her guilt by association with an unmanageable fear of the client. Some felt that the fear might be justified, and others felt that the situation could become so complex that she would not, in the end, be able to fulfill her role in a way that would be useful to the client.

> MARY: There is her own fear about how to belong in the new town. But if she doesn't face forward on it, if she doesn't just tell it in the moment—in the sense of presenting herself as responsible ethically in that working relationship and being prepared to support the person—like minimal disclosure, but lots of support—then it's going to become background. It's going to become gossip, and she'll be standing back, and she'll never know quite what happened.

> LZ: Well, that's the thing that we have to pay attention to, is that the people that we disclose to have access to others—that the story gets passed on, and you have no control over it.

> MARY: And the story gets passed on in ways that you just never would imagine—and you don't know what it was that was finally said that kind of tipped the balance. You never do actually find out, as far as I can tell, who-said-what-to-whom that was the final, you know, termite in the support system, or whatever.

> NED: Does the therapist have a right to privacy? Yeah. And also, you know, it depends how paranoid you get, like: did this client, as a child, experience this psychologist's father? You know, it could get really weird. The client knows far too much about the therapist already. And what should Marlene tell the client? Goodbye! Goodbye. . . . Just too messy.

Marlene's hypothetical situation also addresses more specifically the professional roles in which the practitioner is expected to provide care in a nonreciprocal relationship. Especially in the context of a therapeutic relationship, it is generally understood that *any* action by the practitioner must be taken for the exclusive benefit of the client. The respondents' adherence to this ethical position was illustrated in every one of the responses to the vignette. Developing a sense of professional responsibility for some public exposure as well as learning how to manage the boundaries required by her relatively powerful role in such a relationship were seen as necessary preparations for practice. In this context, self-protection for the counselor is framed as protection for the client as well, in that the client should not be put in a position where she is expected to keep secret some information that could damage the professional.

SALLY: But Marlene is a health care professional; because she's a psychologist, it's really most important to protect yourself. As a psychologist specializing in the treatment of childhood sexual abuse, she has to have bullet-proof walls around her, to protect herself. And so she has to make those boundaries known. So, she's only going to disclose what she feels comfortable to put out, on the billboard, on top of big buildings. And who cares what anybody else thinks if this patient wants to break her own confidentiality—because, as a helper, Marlene shouldn't worry what that patient says outside of her doors.

LZ: And the patient has the right to say whatever she wants.

SALLY: And if the patient wants to talk about her own experiences, that's her choice. So, it shouldn't matter.

LZ: So, is what you're saying that "Marlene has to be ready for this, before she opens her door, if she's also carrying the experience of abuse herself. She has to come out there knowing . . ."?

SALLY: Even if she's not carrying the experience of abuse herself. Her father's been charged, so she has to be ready. It's a small world. News travels.

Scenario Seven

Jennifer is a worker in a transition house operated by the same organization that supported her through a period when she was herself victimized by a partner and needed shelter. The organization is now doing a fund-raising drive to maintain a level of service after funding cutbacks, and they want to "use" her story as an example of the success of the program. She is asked to be a part of an educational video, speaking about the way the program helped her "get her life together." It is expected that she will also speak about her recovery from substance abuse, as they are now planning to extend their service to include drug and alcohol programming. What should Jennifer take into account as she decides whether or not to participate?

This vignette addresses directly the difference between testimony and the testimonial. The original questions posed by the first scenario are here re-introduced. Once again, the offering of the opportunity to use her voice is presented as a compliment. She is the poster girl who proves the value of the program. Isn't she proud of her achievement? Why wouldn't she be flattered, be happy to help? Questions about the level of coercion were, first, who asked her? Was it her colleague, her supervisor, a hired fund-raiser, or the director of the program? Second, how long is it since she was herself a recipient of the "care" or the organization? Might she need their help again sometime in the future? For some informants, the idea of a permanent record of Jennifer's story is much more questionable for her than even the situation where Monique is asked to speak in public. For some, even asking her to do this would be an indication of some power problems or lack of responsibility to clients within the program.

ANISE: It seems to me that there is automatically some kind of conflict of interest: she's working—she's a worker in a transition house, so now they're wanting to in a very permanent way cast her in the role of client. And it's not that I draw hard and fast lines between those, but it would take an extraordinary amount of effort to live that all the time, that dual identity. And it seems to me that, a lot of times, people belong to the worker persona, when they've made some milestones in their own process. And to sort of take herself back to that, and print it in a permanent way on a video. I think she'd be very, very cautious about taking such a public and permanent role.

It's different than Monique talking at one gathering; to put yourself on a video is different. She's being asked by her organization to do that, so she's being put in a somewhat coerced position. To be asked already suggests at least ignorance, if not abuse of power.

NED: Within a context where it's possibly good for the organization that she disclose, but has little or nothing to do with whether or not it's good for her—in this case, there appears to be some kind of threat of guilt, as well as some kind of emotional extortion, going on. . . . Because she's supposed to feel gratitude toward this organization that supported her through her period of victimization. And now she's working for them, so she should feel some kind of maternal/paternal "family" kind of feelings for this organization— and therefore should be happy to go forth and give her story to them, to be used outside the organization, for the support of the "family" organization. . . . I see!

And what should Jennifer take into account as she decides whether or not to participate? That she's being emotionally blackmailed and that she should see how much money they're paying her. How much money she actually needs for the next couple of months until she gets another job.

ANNE: The organization has a responsibility, an enormous responsibility, to protect both workers and clients, *and* former clients. We have an obligation to the clients to do—to meet our objectives, in whatever way. We have other obligations—we have our funders, we have an obligation to society, but we don't put people in danger. And that's something that could happen, later. You don't make people participate in something that might not be good for them later on.

LZ: So part of the danger is that it would affect her ability to have work, later.

ANNE: It might. It might affect her substance abuse. It might affect childcare. It might affect a court case later on about whether or not she's a fit mother, or it may affect her health status like in public health tracking for HIV.

A primary concern for most informants was the recognition of the fact that in most cases, Jennifer would have no real control over either the content of the video or the context within which it would be used. From the point of view of the social construction of identity, the process of permanently recording a partial identity as subaltern is understood to have potential danger for the person, perhaps especially for the development of more powerful or agentic social roles, not only in reference to credibility for future job opportunities but also in the sense of the person's ongoing positive self-esteem.

> ELLEN: No matter what she does, once she gives her story to somebody else particularly on a video, then she has absolutely no way of controlling the context in which her story is encountered—and she has no way to counter or mediate people's responses. And I think until that's happened to somebody, they don't really appreciate what happens when the twenty minutes of context turns into a ten-second clip, with some music behind it.
>
> She's also employed there now, so she's in a double power dimension. . . . And then there she is, the cameras are rolling—and odd things happen when that happens. And, particularly if she doesn't have the right to say, "Well, I don't want—I teared up, and I know that those are the money shots, but I don't want you to use it (because I don't want the world to see that)," and if she doesn't have the control over that, she could end up being really unhappy about the consequences, and . . . you know—she becomes the poster child— and then what happens?

With the introduction of the testimonial use of self-disclosure, some of the informants described the presentation of the story of the protagonist in terms of a rhetorical performance. This, for some, is articulated in terms of self-control in revisiting the experience, rather than in the terms used in earlier scenarios, where "having done her work" was seen as necessary for a safe disclosure. The conversations about the sense of performance began to examine the idea of a good, or effective, telling of the story, the awareness of rhetoric as a skill.

> JAMES: So then, it is a weird kind of instrumentalization of her story—you know, she becomes a tool, to be used for certain productive ends, for the transition house. And I could see that situation being very powerful. I think what they're looking for, in her account of her story of getting her life together, is a certain emotional tone. I bet they feel that if they hired an actor, that that tone would not be there that sense of authentically being through it. The voice of the victim is a very powerful voice.
>
> LZ: Why is that? . . . . What if it's a performance of the victim? What if it's a person who's already walked a long way from that, and in order to talk about their story, they go back into that voice? If that's a performance—does that take away from the authenticity of it?
>
> JAMES: No. I think it's possible to revisit that voice, and do it—embody it, in a way that makes it as real as if it was the first time you were talking about it.
>
> ALMA: I think that people really do want to give whatever they can to make it possible for programs to exist. People want to be productive. And at some level what we actually have to do, and we all believe this, in private, is to convince the people who have the power that the position of the helpers, or the position of those who need the support, is valuable.
>
> We use rhetoric that is a moral appeal. It's an emotional appeal. It's an appeal to people's better humanity. . . . And so when we do that, we actually

have to present it—like it's a performance. We have to present a kind of emotional subjection, to some extent, in order to justify the intervention—and some people are better at that, and some people get lost in it. And so when we're being chosen to do that kind of work—and it is work!—I don't think anybody outside ourselves can actually say whether it's something that we can safely do.

Faced with the loss of control of much of the content and most of the context in the production of a video that would be out there for a long time, individuals also had to consider why anyone would even take the risk. Some of the common motivations for speaking out are obvious here, but some interviews provided a deeper analysis. It was in the context of this scenario that some of the important practices utilized in the development of some kind of a tellable story were also articulated. Especially when the story is elicited for rhetorical purposes, the presentation of an intentional performance of knowledge is seen to provide the possibility of a distinctly personal achievement.

LZ: So, in all of these, the person risks falling back into feelings and emotions, because that's in fact what's being asked for in every one of these—except that, somehow, we're asked to hold that in some way that still carries authority, that doesn't just fall into helplessness and victimization.

JAMES: Yeah—where it becomes a source of strength.

LZ: So we're asked, in all of these situations, to be inspiring to others, carrying this by embodying the strength of being able to talk about it.

JAMES: Yeah. And I think there's another thing that ends up happening, too, when people revisit their stories over and over again. The story can lose some of its vividness—you know? And that can be a good thing—that you're letting it go—but, at the same time, sometimes that revisiting of it allows you to edit it and make it into a more compelling and succinct version than you were first able to tell, when you started dealing with that story.

LZ: So there's actually a benefit that's internal. It's a completely private benefit.

JAMES: Yeah—but I think it happens in, you know, a public discourse.

LZ: And it sounds as though, for you, it matters that it impacts the public. I mean, it isn't just that we're talking to a blank screen. It's that we're talking to somebody that moves, because of your speech. So, are we talking about agency?

JAMES: I think so. Yeah.

LZ: So: a relationship between voice and agency. If we could speak in a way that actually moves something, then we feel more powerful?

JAMES: Yeah, I think so. Because this hasn't happened often in my life, but I have been in situations where, for various reasons, I felt silenced. And you can definitely feel a lack of agency when that happens.

You know, I am aware of the powerful transformation when that story is told, but at the same time, it's often that I'm most acutely aware of it when the possibility is silenced—so I guess I've come to that conclusion through knowledge of its opposite.

For these informants, the speaker's control over the content of her disclosure is the most important factor in assessing the potential for negative consequences. But in the context of a testimonial, as in the structure of a research interview, the speaker understands that the material provided will be edited for selective use, based on criteria external to the immediate interlocutory relationship. For one experienced presenter, the desire to have her relevant truth acknowledged is framed as a motivation that can be manipulated by the threat of withdrawal of the time—the opportunity to speak—if she is not prepared to provide the rhetorical substance required for the aesthetic or journalistic intentions of the project. Her observation of the power of the translation required to fit her story to the agenda of the institution offering the space for such a voice, provides an eloquent description of the paradoxical potential for the "fall" associated with testimony—a kind of colonized disclosure. These are the times when, even while we are given a voice, the opportunity to speak can move us, unwillingly, from the authenticity and authority of the position of Knower, into the awareness of colluding with something that is not our own truth: Abjection.

> MARY: What happens in these situations is that if she doesn't agree to do it, and if she doesn't agree to disclose completely, they will say, "You're useless, then. We won't use you." . . . "Unless you're speaking the line we need, we won't allow you the time." Right? In which case, you're not speaking your truth, you're speaking a company line. And that really bugs me, whenever it happens—and it has happened to me.
>
> She has to consider her whole identity: her own recovery, her own hopes for the future, particularly the substance-use piece, because there's so much there that people assume is your own fault. So, I know you put "use" in quotes because you were trying to get that kind of response, but it is true that I have presented on other topics that was not of my choosing. And if you push a button, I can speak, probably!—but it's not healthy for me. It's been very hurtful, emotionally, for me to speak a truth that I wasn't prepared to speak.
>
> . . . Even when I've tried to debrief it—"Are you bitter?" That was one response I got.
>
> LZ: Bitter? Yeah.
>
> MARY: "Only on the really bad days," is what I said.

Voicing and Silence: Speaking for Others by Speaking about Ourselves

> Any discussion of a feminist "I" must take into account the register "we," a contested zone that resists definition but asserts its own existence. . . . Audre Lorde declares, "If we don't name ourselves, we are nothing" (Lorde, 1980). . . . those who are named by others have no way to exist in and for themselves. Yet the "we" is somehow in existence, known to itself, available for the naming. Audre Lorde frames a "we" that situates her clearly among those who are vulnerable to being named from the outside and thus, paradoxically, created for other's purposes while being eliminated for their own. (Perrault, 1998, p. 192)

An enduring paradox in the concrete operations that follow from the ideologies of empowerment theory and liberatory pedagogy seems to be a double bind of first and second-order conceptions of marginalized identity. To begin with, an individual is not "marginal" except by membership in some group that is convention- or context-determined. Groups are marginalized in relation to other more powerful, dominant groups. But much of social justice and social service policy and practice is based on the first-level supposition that it is membership in such groups that creates the problems for individuals that demand a social response in the form of some intervention that requires the work of a helper. The individuals who need help are determined to be members of a group marginalized in some way in common, so by definition, they are in need, but the solutions can be offered only according to specific needs, identified in individual terms in relation to helpers who are read as nonmarginal in the roles they assume as working in relation to particular populations or groups.

At the second level, the translation function of helpers requires that advocacy or assistance must be offered in concrete form as a response to an individual case, framed in the context of the more abstract explanation of the "damaged identity" (Nelson, 2001), which is the result of membership in a marginalized group. This requires a continual reinforcement of the master narrative of the plight of the marginalized—in the form of proofs of individual examples of need or helplessness—in order to justify the delivery of helping services to the group. Speaking with authority about the needs of people like me places the bordered helper in the middle of this paradox, and in a particular ethical and epistemological bind.

In health, social service, and counseling roles, the rules of confidentiality foreclose the possibility of directly speaking about the experience of a specific client to the public, disallowing any account of marginalization that may identify an individual other than the worker herself. So "I," for many bordered professionals, can be the *only* valid expression of a lived "we." But at the same time, the expectations of professionalism, such as those articulated for therapeutic relationships (Peterson, 2002; Simi and Mahalik, 1997), social work (Goldstein, 1997), and nursing (Fredriksson and Eriksson, 2003), question or discourage the practitioner's self-disclosure to clients, and a public disclosure of the worker's personal experience of oppression can operate as a threat to her entitlement to her role—at the very least it signals a breach of professional distance. By the ethics of many of our roles, even in face-to-face encounters, we are expected to manage a complex compartmentalization of personal experience:

> ALMA: Then we have to stand around and act as though all the pain is over there, and there's nothing over here—and it's a breach of professionalism if you don't. In order to be a professional, you have to look like, "That never happened to me!" And if you look like that happened to you, within the stereotypes of what a victim looks like, then you can't possibly be perceived as a professional.

So we are discouraged from speaking what we know about other people's stories, or about our common difficulties, except in the particular instance of our own experience. But speaking "I," as a helper, where I am invited to describe my painful experience as unique and outside of political context, opens up a complex contradiction of validity.

> MARY: Either we're "selfish" and "advocating for ourselves"—including ourselves as some kind of charismatic leader or something, or we are "not

able to be discreet," we are "not sensible," we are "not appropriate, in context."

Identified as a bordered helper, I am caught in a dilemma of speaking as a questionable exmember of a group that is perceived as either having no voice or having multiple voices that no one voice can represent. As a result, my relatively powerful role leaves me in a particularly confusing position:

1. Any explanation that allows me to speak about my marginalized experience *as a Knower* requires me to have a basis for knowing beyond my personal experience and to maintain some kind of analysis that suggests "I am not alone"—I have a reference group, a knowledge shared with others like me, or like I used to be . . .

2. But as soon as I can speak, I am no longer operating from the same location as those with whom I am claiming membership (often we are speaking about the experience of being or feeling alone—outside dominant culture/social membership—being silenced).

3. If I speak only of my particular, individual experience, I am considered authentic, even if possibly unreliable or unreadable (incoherent or even incorrigible).

4. But if I speak of "our" experience, I am vulnerable to the criticisms of validity that are common to the genre of testimonio—the idea that a political agenda discredits rhetoric.

So either what I say is true about my own experience, and therefore irrelevant to others, or relevant, because it applies to others, but not quite true.

> The metaphor of "finding one's voice" is one of finding one's self and freeing the self from the oppression of self-blame and self-loathing. The "authentic" voices that are freed from self-blame, however, are individual voices and no longer serve a transgressive purpose. That is, they no longer challenge the status quo; they do not lead to social change. (Lamb, 1999, p. 129)

The Heroic possibility for the "I" in this situation is only a thinly gilded variation of the Abject role and, in the end, unsatisfactory as a livable rhetorical position. As "I," my story, if read as a Heroic triumph, is depoliticized, drained of context and meaning, and I become a token of the different, the exception; once again, the exotic Other. This is not recognition, and this is not the kind of difference that is idealized in social justice language. But, although conscious of the possibility for our voices to be reduced to a spectacle of Otherness, many of us persist in speaking out. It is with the full awareness of the risks inherent in the performances of self that we call disclosure, that we, the "we" represented in this study, still choose to speak, that we continue to make the ethical choice to use our identities and our stories to connect with others.

Speaking into Relation

Rather than seeing such actions as speaking out, I have come to believe that we must understand any professional self-disclosure as speaking ourselves *into* relation, in that it is significant not only that we are engaging the other when we speak but also that we are, in the most important way, inventing ourselves in the process. In naming ourselves out when our marginalization is not visible, we declare our re-membering of a group experience in a context both personal and historical.

> On a phenomenological level, my experience of myself comes through the narratives that I construct to tell myself and my life to another, especially on a mundane and everyday basis. I construct and reconstruct my experiences for another, even if I don't actually ever tell them the narrative that I have prepared for them. It is the bearing witness to the other itself, spoken or not, that gives birth to the I. (Oliver, 2001, p. 207)
>
> BETH: As I gained the presence to just sit in my own body and witness that again, it's—learning those stories again. And it's analyzing them, and integrating them, into who we become, and how we are who we are.

Is there any "I" that is not embedded in some larger "we"? For this examination of voice in narratives of bordered identity, it is not only the construction of voice as power that concerns me. I am taking the position that it is the contested use of the voice of the *first-person plural* that makes any of these disclosures meaningful, that allows individual marginal experience to be understood as knowledge at all, and that reflects the intersubjective nature of the co-creation of our stories and our subjectivities, of our selves, public and private.

> JACQUES: At times, in different contexts, around different issues, when I have actually talked about my own experiences—when I have known that the audience out there are actually the caring ones, the ones who are there to change the system, and who may have different views, but in certain ways they are like-minded—it has helped me to better understand myself. And it has also kind of created me, given me the tools to be able to link between my own personal experiences, and use that as a bridge to understand other people's experiences.

The rhetorical identity that we speak from, as well as the language that we use to describe our singular position in the world, is co-constructed in the dialogue with/about the group that we are choosing to represent ourselves as belonging to by self-disclosure. Although we may not choose the cultural context with which the rhetorical act engages, it is part of the ideology attached to speaking out that we influence it by entering into dialogue with it. To do that, we are obliged to operate as identities in translation, speaking across the boundary. The use of "we" as a rhetorical position addresses the dialogic nature of the way our stories are constructed, honors the terms by which we recognize one another, and serves as a shorthand acknowledgment of those other speakers with whom we have been engaged in the testing and development of the terminologies and narrative trajectories that can be used rhetorically without harm to ourselves, to those people who hear it, and to those who we represent by identification.

> NED: I think when you've done the work, there's a spiritual commonality, and there's a tribe—or a brotherhood or sisterhood—and we recognize each other. And we know when we're bullshitting, and we know when we're fearing something. And there's a level of intimacy that also appears that's pretty rare outside of that.

The idea of this particular *we*—a group of individuals who live in the space that defines a boundary—is grounded in a membership of shared knowledge and mutual accountability and is precariously balanced with a painful recognition of our unique and specific differences from one another. The representation of this ephemeral collectivity operates as a fragile bridge over the contradiction of our awareness of the social invisibility that marginalization engenders and expresses our experience of the wish for the comforts of an impossible group identity. Rather than imagining a kind of "strategic essentialism" (Young, 1990), or any utopian concept of a community transparent to each other, this "we" is employed in the service of what Benhabib calls "a vision of a community of needs and solidarity, in contrast to the community of rights and entitlements" (Young, 1990, p. 230). The "we" of these stories lives in the concept "what we know" and not "who we are." Whatever details may be included in the stories function to provide a partial definition of "who we are not": we, who know ourselves as Others. This knowing holds within it, as self-consciousness and as an analysis, both a position and a challenge to dominance.

> The "I" has no story of its own that is not also a story of a relation—a set of relations—to a set of norms. . . . If the "I" is not at one with moral norms, this means only that the subject must deliberate upon these norms, and that part of deliberation will entail a critical understanding of their social genesis and meaning. In this sense, ethical deliberation is bound up with the operation of critique. (Butler, 2005, p. 8)

The Dialogic "We"

Taking into account Bakhtin's conception of the dialogical "storied self," the use of first-person plural in such narratives may also be understood as an expression of the internal dialogue ongoing in the self-representation of a complex, narratively structured subjectivity. In this construction, voice is conceived as

> the manifestation of a particular ideology or perception of reality . . . mediated by language . . . [where] the individual interacts with the world via a repertoire of such voices . . . a dialogue manifested interpersonally across the boundary of self and world but also intrapersonally as the play of internalized voices as inner speech. (Raggat, 2006, p. 18)

The inner speech in this conception, however, is not only a conversation between two (or many) individual voices, and certainly does not refer to the popular psychology construction of the possibility of multiple personalities, but also involves a dialogue with some internalized idea of membership, as "when Bakhtin refers to 'multivoicedness,' he has in mind not only the simultaneous existence of different individual voices but also the simultaneous existence of an individual voice and the voice of a group" (Hermans, 2001, p. 262). I believe that access to, and the integration of, such a repertoire of voices are important components of the development of ethical subjectivity, as well as a significant reflection of agency and accountability, or what Friere calls intentionality: "being *conscious of*, not only as intent on objects, but as turned in upon itself in a Jasperian 'split'—consciousness as consciousness of consciousness" (Freire, 1999, p. 60).

But it is only with the development of such consciousness that, for the purpose of "narrative repair," we can begin to talk back against the domination that has marginalized us, with the creation of a "counterstory: a narrative that takes up a shared but oppressive understanding of who someone is, and tries to shift it" (Nelson, 2001, p. 69). From this vantage point, also described as "double consciousness" by W. E. B. DuBois (Du Bois, 1903) and Fanon (Fanon, 1967), the idea of self-disclosure as a counterstory emerges as a logical response to domination, but the existence (and the content) of the story itself stands as evidence of the continuance of the reality it rejects. Even given the benefits of such a clear analysis, this revolutionary positioning has practical limitations for those on the border who wish to use a helping role supported by the dominant culture to improve conditions for a marginalized group. If the recuperation of the individual self as agent is indeed the intention behind the practice, then any marker of identity for the marginalized person that coincides with the negative stereotype must be categorically denied, essentially valorized, or claimed as intentional defiance.

> A counterstance locks one into a duel of oppressor and oppressed; locked in mortal combat, like the cop and the criminal, both reduced to a common denominator of violence. The counterstance refutes the dominant culture's views and beliefs, and for this, it is proudly defiant. All reaction is limited by, and dependant on, what it is reacting against. (Anzaldúa, 1987, p. 78)

If every story in the context of intentional professional self-disclosure is a counterstory, offered by a knowing subject in response to a prevailing or normative version of events, then in order to recognize the use of the collective voice in these situations as a counterhegemonic action, we must attend not only to the ways in which these stories construct meaning but also to the master narratives whose meanings they contest and within which they are defined. Any admission of doubt or uncertainty will not be reported as part of these stories, unless they are read as knowledge about subjection's power to impose false consciousness on those who are its object. Some stories of these parts of our knowing will have to be read into our silences.

> ANISE: Of course, the very notion of disclosure implies something that's hidden, and so it implies that you're walking across a dichotomy. So you pass as a "not abused" person, but what's in that category of a "not abused" person? Well, stereotypical thinking puts "not abused" persons into the "healthy" category, in the "mentally stable" category. And us, you know, poor "traumatized" folks, are in some other category.
>
> And this is highly problematic, because the people that typically are unable to hide their experiences are the people who are—just thinking about, say, sexual abuse as a child—they're typically the most damaged people that can't hide it. Those of us who have the choice, that have gotten to some reasonably safe place, we don't even make it into the research or into the clinical studies, or into the clinical populations or even known, because we can [choose to hide it].

In the end, it is this very double consciousness that produces the authority of the voice of translation—and part of this knowledge includes the awareness that there are some things that remain outside of translation.

> There is always something else or Other that exceeds our abilities to remember—that escapes our conscious grasp even when the repressed returns. . . . When we try to remember or reflect on our own experiences, what 'comes back' to us, is not what "actually" happened to us. Rather, what returns to mind and body are ghostly traces of what we manage to ignore and to forget yet again because of the very way we have structured the questions we ask about our experiences (Ellsworth, 1997, p 65)

Sometimes silence is the only expression of these experiences. But if we can see what is not said as living in the negative spaces between what can be communicated, we can learn something from silence. In these spaces, we can observe both the vulnerability of the speaker and the impact of the unspoken experience, in the same way that we get information about the shape and the strength of a hand in the imprint left in fresh clay after the artist has gone.

> Whether silence is institutionalized through the state or hidden in plain sight and explained away as forms of everyday random acts of violence, it

does contribute to the organization of our social realities. Silence, as a form of defiance through grassroots movements or the seemingly spontaneous expressions of resistance, demonstrates organization . . . takes on varied forms, and fulfills a variety of functions. Silence participates in the creation of our lives. (Clair, 1998, p. 187)

Silences, Not Secrets

ALMA: So, I'm trying to separate the disclosure, which is a story about what happened — it happened, it's over, so it's a story; but because it's my disclosure it's a story about me *and* about what happened. But the story is separate from the person, because we could choose to tell it or not . . . it's like the story is a map of the space of living between the secret and telling.

Pictures created by master narratives are so strongly resistant to evidence because what they say about certain groups of people is only common sense, what everybody knows, what you don't have to think about, what's necessarily the case. Single instances to the contrary—even many of them—haven't much power to alter what everybody knows. (Nelson, 2001, p. 148)

Even powerful counterstories, polished and refined, can be turned and broken in the face of some kinds of normative listening. Particularly if the authority for the story is a singular "I," the story of some apparently unique experience that contradicts what "everybody knows" is immediately translated by the listener into meanings that fit the speaker within a conventional social category, rounding off the specifics of the individual until she fits back into the anonymity of an othered group identity, familiar and predictable.

JAMES: Well, I think he stopped seeing me as a person, and he started seeing me as a diagnosis.

LZ: Right. Isn't that what happens with profound marginalization or stigmatization? . . . that we become a category, we are no longer an individual. And that's actually the loss to the person of that kind of disclosure.

JAMES: And I think there's something very—and I don't think this is the wrong word—I think that there's a violence in labeling in categories, categorizing people in that way.

LZ: Mmmhmm . . . .

JAMES: I understand the importance of having labels and understanding categories, but if you aren't able to see what slips behind the category, and what slips beyond the label, and the holistic picture of the person that exists outside of these things, then you are really operating in this sort of deficit model of understanding, one that really does do a grave injustice to the humanity of the person.

LZ: Their individuality—

JAMES: Individuality . . . and the difference of that person, from any other person.

Counterstories told as "we" represent the parts of the story of resistance that we can agree to—with one another, with ourselves. Some of the silences between these stories are placeholders for the worst of the "I" experiences—unmanageable, unexplained, not clearly understood or integrated, and still reflecting the power of the external definitions of normativity. These are the places where the attempts to "regain or retain a more positive sense of identity is an intense struggle—not only against external images and representations of [ourselves] objectified as Other, but also against all [we] have internalized from those images and representations, absorbed into [our] own two-ness, [our] own torn sel[ves]" (Pickering, 2001, p. 77). The problem of voicing any resistance to both the external pressures and the internalized master narratives that hold the marginalized in place lies precisely in the absolutely taken for granted nature of long-held personal or cultural stereotypes:

> Counterstories are up against a formidable foe. The master narratives they set out to resist are capable of hiding what ought to be opposed, of absorbing such opposition as might be offered, of penetrating so deeply into a belief system as to be uprooted only at great cost, of spreading their nets so widely across the culture that localized resistance can make no headway against them. (Nelson, 2001, p. 164)

In some cases, silence marks exactly what is NOT secret at all. It delineates the places where the strength and visibility of ubiquitous common knowledge makes resistance futile. If the only thing that counts as speaking in these contexts is telling a counter-story, then it is perhaps in the silences surrounding these stories that the truly oppressive master narratives can be seen to operate. These are the spaces where the incontestable stereotypes work so powerfully that there is no recourse in ordinary language to subvert them. For many, the repeated experience of confrontation with the powerful forms of normativity that persist in negative stereotyping has had the effect of re-inscribing us, over and over, as Abject, finally making some experiences untellable.

> In the face of this Other who is not-you, but taken-as-you by others . . . The representation seems to be one and the same as its referent, as if this objectification were the truth, the only truth, that there is to tell about you. . . . You are both silenced and spoken for. You are seen but not recognized. You are identified but denied an identity that you can call your own. Your identity is split, broken, dispersed into its abjected images, its alienated representations. (Pickering, 2001, pp. 77/78)

> NED: One articulate woman simply said, "I don't want to tell you what I do, because anytime I tell anybody what I do, it changes how they see me." I mean, it really only left two things that she could probably be doing at this juncture.

Falling into the apparent Truth of the stereotype, however, reframes our silence as secret; it constructs our retreat as a withholding that supports the norm as transparent and obvious, and it proves the rightness of outsider status for the Abject. What is then made secret is, once again, the dominance inherent in the unchallenged truth-value of the master narrative. In the end, the voice itself is so compromised that it is the structure and the processes of this re-inscription itself that are impossible to articulate.

> Voice becomes something of a dress that has been chosen from the cultural wardrobe according to the rules of fashion and decorum, which is then rewashed, pressed, and rehung on the victim by researchers, therapists, and authors according to similar but slightly different rules of fashion and decorum. What lies underneath the voice is not the naked truth but a body that also has been shaped by cultural rules and discourses. There is no concealed naked or unadorned truth. (Lamb, 1999, p. 130)

If silence can only be hiding, can only be read as secrets or lies, then the act of exposing what lies beneath the voice, what is hidden by silence, has the effect of creating something more true, more authentic, than what is voiced. But unless we have the choice of when to speak, and what to say about our own experience (unless we can claim the position of Knower) the exposure of this truth confirms us in the role of the Abject.

> ALMA: Part of the reason that I tell the stories is because I want people to know that someone who looks as powerful as I do could, in fact, have had these other experiences. I want that stereotype broken—but it creates a dissonance. There's a kind of terrible dissonance there for the listener; it's like a paradigm shift or something. If it doesn't shift, I'm crazy, right? If it doesn't shift for them, I'm lying.

However much it may be valued as authentic, the naked performance of the Abject is a profound loss of power for the person. In the moment, it carries the feeling of a return to the original trauma or the devalued identity; in the long term, it consigns us to a state worse than irrelevancy. Compared to this, choosing silence is an act of agency, silence can be a refusal; the nonparticipation of silence is sometimes the only resistance that escapes the dichotomy of the common denominator of violence. And, if silence is a chosen secrecy, then secrecy itself can be understood as a valued component of agency.

> Secrecy is a safeguard to freedom, Emmanuel Levinas argues (Levinas, 1985) . . . it is the inviolable core of human subjectivity that makes interaction a matter of choice rather than rational necessity—"Only starting from this secrecy is the pluralism of society possible." (Sommer, 1998, p. 198)

If, as listeners, we don't assume that silence is a choice, then either we are forced to see the subaltern as Abject, even in our best intentions, or we have to ascribe her silence to her need for a secrecy that is based on the shame of not knowing something important *that we know*: that she is valuable. Hilde Lindemann Nelson offers one explanation for silence or the lack of a coherent (convincing) counterstory that identifies some of the internal contradictions in someone who is struggling for voice but whose identity and self-evaluations have been constructed by the epistemic violence of marginalization.

> The difficulty for someone who identifies herself as unworthy of answering for her own conduct is that she can't re-identify herself as morally accountable simply by coming to the rational conclusion that her feelings of worthlessness aren't warranted, or by having others point this out to her. Because she doesn't trust her own judgment, it will be hard for her to hear, much less create, a counterstory that re-identifies her as a worthy person. (Nelson, 2001, p. 33)

This hidden conflict in the individual may, in fact, form a part of the reasoning that leads to a choice of silence. However, that a person has made the choice to be silent does not imply that she is without an intellectual understanding of the need for a counterstory, or even of her claim to one. Because I am taking the position that some kinds of silence can be seen as acts of agency, rather than as the absence of subjectivity, I am theorizing that the use of "we" in the dialogical sense also recognizes some of these silences as choice. In recognizing ourselves as accountable to one another, we must acknowledge the possibility that any one of us could make the choice *not* to speak until we are ready. The "we," in that case, is inclusive: I believe that we can know without speaking and that silence can be the expression of a choice, based on a clear assessment of the circumstances of speaking. In our individual and joint efforts to create the tellable stories that will allow us to step out of the limiting stereotypes imposed by marginalization, we must consider it a responsible option for a speaker to choose to reserve a part of her story as not ready for airing—and we must believe in her ability to assess her own vulnerability to the interrogation of her claims of truth.

> The idea of agency comes from the principle of accountable reason, that one acts with responsibility, that one has to assume the possibility of intention, one has to assume even the freedom of subjectivity in order to be responsible. That's where agency is located. (Spivak, 1996, p. 294)

Silence to Preserve Relationship

Even in the presence of a worked out counterstory, however, silence is sometimes also an offering in the name of connection, in an effort to create or preserve relationship. One participant described the use of silence as a way of respectfully recognizing the difficulty of those who are what he calls "citizens": people who do not have the experience of the margin, or of the stigma of stereotyping, particularly when they are involved in important relationships with people who have lived the kinds of stories that are hard to tell. "We," as in Ned's story, describes those who know, as opposed to the citizens who can't really be expected to understand.

> NED: I think there are stories that are impossible . . . I don't think I'm a citizen anymore. And I think being in certain businesses—like being a therapist long enough, and being a cop and being a prostitute, maybe truly being a minister or a rabbi or one of those guys, would take you out of the realm of the everyday citizen. And I think there are stories that occur within that lifetime—within that frame—that are outside of the realm of citizens.
>
> And what I was thinking about was . . . with the young prostitutes that I work with, and when they would ask whether or not to tell their boyfriends or girlfriends about their previous lives. And I would tell them not to—because the people that they're getting together with were citizens, were people who had certain conventions outside of which they had no experience. And because they didn't have any experience, they just had—like, movies, or projections, or opinions that weren't based on any real, visceral gut knowledge of what they were talking about. So I would usually advise, especially the young women, "If you get old and grey, you're sitting on the park bench or your porch, you can consider it. But until then, unless they did it in a past life too—don't! Because they can't always handle that information, and that information is just destructive, and provocative of fantasies. But they can't meet you there, and so don't tell them—at least certainly not for a long, long time until you've really got a real commonality between the two of you." So that's what I mean by stories that are outside of sharing.

Assuming the speaker's consciousness of consciousness, the decision to leave out some part of a story in an understanding of the overwhelming odds of it being heard as a complete counterstory with no recognition or reading of the silences, is an act of accountability and good judgment. It is a judgment formed in a process of inner dialogue, a selection made on the basis of the potential harms of a loss of credibility: in the moment, Abjection; in the long run, loss of connection or of the opportunity to help. It is a choice, based both on knowledge of the rhetorical environment that the story enters, and a deep responsibility to others, to the "we" who may hear it in a politicized pedagogical environment where "knowledge of the other is valuable only when it contains 'positive' representations" (Srivastava and Francis, 2006, p. 281).

> MARY: So yeah, how many stereotypes do you put in one pot? And when you do that, it's a matter of self-protection, to be aware of the stereotypes others are assuming about you, and make sure that you're being appropriate in those images in order to not lose credibility—depending on who is there.
>
> It's credibility with the victim you don't want to lose. The credibility with society—it may not, in the moment, be a benefit to have that. In some instances you'll be sought after for comment and stuff, if you disclose marginalization.

On the other hand, [if you lose credibility] you might have lost an opportunity to teach us all something.

It was many times illustrated in the interviews that one of the most obvious motivations for speaking from experience is to make use of the opportunity to teach us something. Many of the contexts for speaking out are explicitly created in the interest of popular education and have varied potentials for the authentic pedagogue. One of the most familiar contexts for this is the use of native speakers to provide content for anti-oppression training, whereby

> the production of knowledge is seen as an important goal—knowledge of the experiences of people of color, knowledge of the others' perspective, or self-knowledge. Combating our supposed "ignorance" of inequity, these workshops draw knowledge from its most "authentic" Knowers—nonwhite and queer participants. However, one of the implicit goals of this approach is to sidestep or erase, rather than to explore, the existing knowledge of racism and heterosexism that already pervades all our social institutions. (Srivastava and Francis, 2006, pp. 291–292)

The secrecy of some kinds of silence between individuals, (whether one of them is or is not a citizen), does not persist because these kinds of marginalization, victimization, or stigmatization are invisible in the culture in which the relationship between two interlocutors is embedded. In fact, information about such ongoing realities as racism, homophobia, intimate violence, even mass murder is prevalent in all our social environments as common knowledge, but in the abstract. What remains a secret, albeit one continually broken, is the fact that individuals who have been subject or witness to these experiences are real and present everywhere. It is ironic that these privileged Knowers are required to speak, to describe their experience and their identities in recognizable language, and within some conventional coherence—because it seems that it is only in the particular, in the specifics of an individual story, that the existence of these abstract realities is proved. As described in Shoshana Felman's work on Holocaust testimony, even the silence in such witnessing is a knowledge claim.

> Knowledge in the testimony is . . . not simply a factual given that is reproduced and replicated by the testifier, but an advent, an event in its own right. . . . [the woman] was testifying not simply to empirical historical facts, but to the very secret of survival and of resistance to extermination. . . . her silence was itself part of the testimony, an essential part of the historical truth she was precisely bearing witness to . . . this was her way of being, of surviving, of resisting. It is not merely her speech, but the very boundaries of silence which surround it, which attest, today as well as in the past, to this assertion of resistance. (Felman and Laub, 1992, p. 62)

The following three chapters demonstrate the study participants' sophisticated understanding of professional self-disclosure as a knowledge claim, as performance, and as political action, grounded by descriptions of individual motivations and strategies for deciding when, how, and how much to tell—to perform, in both voice and silence, our knowing.

CHAPTER 6

Preparation for Speaking Out: Polishing the Story

BETH: Well, you know, being able to tell the stories, being able to tell a story, is a skill. It's like writing. If you do it over and over, and you practice it, then you become better. And often people are thrown into situations and aren't even aware, necessarily, that they're going to tell a story, and then that can be painful—in a lot of ways, actually. Painful for the person who's doing it; painful for the people who are witnessing her do it.

But what it's making me think about is: when do you know? What is the difference between people who are able to do these things, and people who aren't? What makes that difference?

A significant portion of every interview in the study was focused on identifying some of the complex ethical assessments that are made by these practitioners as they make the choice to speak out, to intentionally use some appropriate, or safe, reference to their personal experience, rather than to operate from a rule-based assumption that self-disclosure is always required or would never be the right thing to do. Each person at some point articulated the need for the story to reflect that the speaker had done her work on the topic she would be addressing in speaking out or disclosure. When the conversation was expanded, it became obvious that what many people thought was the important evidence that this work had been done was an analysis: the reflection of a critique or of a resolution that could offer something useful to the listener. Every one of these experienced practitioners clearly articulated the belief that a speaker should have prepared for telling—should have dealt with the issue, worked out, practiced, or "polished" a story in order to be able to use it safely and effectively in a rhetorical/political way. This polishing appears to serve more than one purpose, and it involves more than one process.

> NED: If the story still has a lot of rawness, or unresolvedness or nakedness, or vulnerability in the telling, I'd tell her she should not do it. I would essentially be opposed to her telling that, unless I was confident that she was really in that place where it was "story," and—and not vibrant.

A Small Telling—Control of the Details

> KATE: I think the other thing is, always: how much do you tell and in service of what? You know, that's almost the worst thing to think through if, in that sense, telling implies telling the whole story.
> But, of course there's a way of just telling sometimes, that could be very powerful, and [you don't] have to start revealing a lot about what the experience was—it could be just a small telling.

In the transcription data from the interviews, there are many references to a process of integration of the narrative into a larger personal meaning, which is felt to be a necessary step in the preparations that increase the potential for a safe telling of the story of a self. Each person at some point offered suggestions as to how much detail should be included in a professional self-disclosure, as a safeguard for both speaker and listeners. It is evident in these responses that the agency of the person who has "made it a story" is exercised not only in the decision to speak but also in the moment-to-moment choice of detail, based on our reading of the audience.

> NED: I think the graphic details of a particular event are the beginning stages of the story. I think they're the crucible of the story. And when you're through the specific details—whatever "through" means—then you're left with the humanness of the feelings of that story. And then you can connect with everybody in the audience for whatever your purpose is.
> I mean, if we've come through those details, then we're able to make it a story—the loneliness of it, or whatever—we're sharing with everybody else, for whatever reason we've chosen to do that.
> RENEE: . . . [Detail?] Very little, very minimal—again, to connect with, to universalize it a little bit, to connect them with the ideas. "There are resources; there are ways to get help around this. There are possibilities for surviving this."
> ALMA: What have we disclosed? Do we go around and tell everybody, "This happened, and then this happened and then this happened, and then this happened, twice"?

No, I don't think that's it. We talk about what we understand from what happened.

ELLEN: I believe it's possible to not use your story but to use what the story meant, to be effective. To say, not "Believe me, I know!—nudge-nudge, wink-wink" but, rather, to use what a person has learned from her own experience to get across her sense of conviction.

I have been in situations where I have been working with someone, and have done that, and had the person look at me and say, "I believe that you really do." And it's not "nudge-nudge, wink-wink"—it's "I have used the conviction of what I've learned, from the story, to talk from that place just a little bit better."

For Katalina, disclosure of any personal material should be limited to a single sentence, and for some, the disclosure is limited to the use of "we" instead of "you" or "they" when speaking about people in the context of the issues being addressed. For Ned, the disclosure is actually present in the way questions are framed to the client, with some knowledge implied even if not specified.

KATALINA: I think it's okay for her to disclose if she's comfortable with the disclosure and if she believes that that will help the other person feel a little bit better about what happened to her, but that she shouldn't go into detail. Maybe it could be like a one-sentence thing.

NED: More and more, I'm very careful about disclosure. About the fit of the story, but also about the story no longer being necessary. I do enough disclosing in the question. The intimacy of the assumed knowledge, and the intimacy of the question, seems to be sufficient. I don't have to go to the story to establish a credential.

Many people stated that in most professional situations the details should be left out of the story completely. For rhetorical purposes, then, the point of the narrative is not to expose the specific content of the individual's particular experience but rather to articulate some conceptualization or resolution of the experience as grounded in a larger context.

JACQUES: In different contexts, I have actually disclosed a lot. And you kind of feel stronger, especially if you have dealt with the issue in your own mind. . . . I would, actually, talk about my own experience. However, I would be reserved. I would assess my audience. I wouldn't get into too much detail, but I would use myself to explore the consequences of a lack of services.

Protecting My Story/Myself

Several of the informants indicated that the details should not be required to establish either authenticity or sincerity but, even more importantly, that the story itself in all its complexity needs protection, because of its significance to the life of the speaker. Although none of these participants ever spoke directly to one another, some of their answers, even on complex topics, were remarkably similar.

> LZ: Rhetorical power is manipulative, it's persuasive, it's intentional. And so, when you say, "I will bring in these details, and I'll leave out those details, as an intentional choice," does that make it less authentic?
>
> JAMES: No, I don't think so. I think that makes us judicious. I think it makes us smart.
>
> LZ: [*laughs*] Absolutely. It certainly keeps us safe—that, too.
>
> JAMES: Yeah. Because if the authenticity was based on telling all the details all the time, then we'd get stuck in the situation where we would have to relive the story all the time—and I think this could happen, if we got caught up in a circle like that—the story would cease to have any meaning for us.
>
> I think when I disclose, no matter what kind of disclosure it is, I use an authentic voice. But, at the same time, I am selective about what I disclose.
>
> And, I mean, this is going to sound kind of weird, but my story is very special for me—it goes to the very heart of who I am and how I understand the world and it radically transformed my understanding of the world—so, as that kind of story, I feel very protective of it.
>
> NED: I think the story's probably always precious. And when we get to that place of the story as commodity, it's quite possible we're going to be doing ourselves a massive disservice, at a level we don't even begin to understand, if we've commodified the story.

The preciousness of the story that is offered as our truth makes the actions or attitudes of the interlocutor/witness to the telling very significant to the construction of the self of the speaker, at the very least within the immediate relationship with the listener. But if we understand the polishing or practice of "making it a story" as an incremental process, then it makes sense that at certain stages of the development of the story, the constructed self of the teller is more vulnerable to negative, critical, or stereotyped feedback. Under these conditions the person is more likely to suffer the generalized effects of disclosure consequences and/or a collapse into Abjection. One of the ways that the idea of the story and the self are connected is expressed in an interaction with Ned. He provides a description of how the way our stories are *heard* creates a space for us, how the response of a witness limits or extends the selfhood available to us in relationship:

> NED: If the telling of a story is a reaching out to be touched as an individual, as an intimate other, then getting rounded off and boxed is just being made into an "Other," period. The very intimacy of the moment is lost. The very reason that we would be telling that story is lost. And you've just become one amongst many, when, in fact, the offer of the story is to be one who is special

in that moment. And it's gone, it's just—a door slams! A door slams shut and probably is not going to get reopened.

. . . And now there's this whole part of us that we have to hide, because it will not be understood. And so it can't come out.

LZ: And there's also a breach in the relationship.

NED: Oh, yeah—there's a big breach in the relationship at that point. If we can't trust them with the story, yeah, then we've got to hide. And—

LZ: . . . or deny ourselves . . .

NED: . . . or deny ourselves, or have this little tiny bit of crazy operating. It's crazymaking. Because we have to be less than we are, we have to conform to some—in the moment—some newly created notion of ourselves in the relationship.

Sometimes the interlocutor's inability to hear the meaning of an individual's story diminishes the teller ("makes us less than we are"), but there is also a potential for the same inability or lack of comprehension to make us more than we are. There are times when the powerful presentation of a dramatic story is taken up by others and shifted into the creation of the "heroic survivor" or the "poster child" of a particular group. Ned told a story about another kind of construction of self that is a common experience for some who have chosen to tell stories of Dangerous Knowledge. He tells of a time when the story, for him, became something that was taken so seriously by listeners, that he became what he calls a "guru." As he became identified as someone with specialized knowledge, this experience of having his identity defined by others, even in an apparently positive or flattering way, once again had decidedly negative effects on his life.

LZ: In that sense, your knowledge was based entirely in your own experience, right? Your knowledge is not knowledge of some esoteric thing. It's a leadership by identity. And so, when that started, you could see your experience as something useful to others. And a story about yourself as something useful to others.

NED: Right.

LZ: And then, what you're saying is that it got very distorted, eventually.

NED: Right.

LZ: Do you think that it got distorted because you changed, or because you were bigger than the story, or . . . ?

NED: No, I don't. I think it's a group phenomenon, and I don't think I was bigger than the story. I think a story is something contextualized with other people's needs. Then when I'm in that position—when practically anybody's in that position—we're a lens. And we're a lens for all their projections, and all their needs, and all their love and everything else in the mix. And it's pretty hard not to get distorted.

It would take really being clean and really being clear about who you are in the world to not get wrecked by that. And basically I just got wrecked by it.

Using the Story—Risk Assessment

One of the most important themes recurring in these accounts of self-disclosure is an articulation of a continual process of risk assessment that each person described as being a necessary step in her decision making on entering any context in which self-disclosure might be expected.

> LZ: How can you tell when you've gotten your story to a place where it's actually safe, no matter where you go?
>
> ALMA: In every case there are some real risks. I think that there's a kind of a split in our belief about what we should be doing in speaking out, that people who don't speak out are "cowards," or that people who don't carry their survivorhood somehow more publicly are "letting us all down" or something, and that we should all be brave revolutionaries.
>
> And I think that we don't actually think about some of the really direct consequences that could happen. So that there's a sort of "get out there and speak about it!" when, sometimes, it's the wrong thing to do. And that each of us has to make these kinds of judgments before we decide to do that.

Once we have chosen to contribute to breaking the silence as a commitment in principle, there are still risks and responsibilities that must be taken into account before speaking from experience in the specific instance, whether in the direct one-to-one interaction or for political purposes. Many of the conversations provided deeply personal descriptions of the effects that a story of marginalization can have on the narrative construction of identity in relationship.

> JAMES: It's always such a risk . . . but you don't know if they are comfortable, even if you think it's OK—and there is always the off chance that we are totally wrong, and they just don't have the experience—and then you have just put your foot in your mouth.

"There are penalties for choosing the wrong voice at the wrong time, for telling an inappropriate tale. Far better, one might conclude . . . to keep silent" (Razack, 1993, p. 65). The ideology of empowerment and much feminist textual practice is based on the assumption that such speaking out is not only valuable but also politically necessary, but only rarely are the penalties or the potential costs to the speaker factored into the equation. Perhaps because I asked explicitly about these costs in the context of talking about my conception of Disclosure Consequences, a significant part of every conversation in this study addressed the possibility of very real harms resulting from this kind of self-disclosure. This came in the form of concerns for others in the situations presented in the vignettes, and then very often in descriptions of directly personal experiences of the kinds of pain I have described as "falling into the Abject." I believe that, even without using my language of Disclosure Consequences, the commonly expressed need for risk assessment as a part of this practice is evidence for the phenomenon. It is based on our experienced knowledge of the possibility of painful consequences arising from speaking out, both for the speaker and for those listening to the stories.

> LZ: And there's a kind of reality when we put something into words, when we say something—that we make it real in a way that wasn't real, before we said it. That it becomes concrete, and then the misery is so much bigger. It's like we created it by saying it.
>
> ANISE: And you know, we see this over and over again. [She tells a story of a specific situation where a research subject responded to the interviewer, in feedback, with] "I was pissed off for three days after you did that interview with me!"
>
> LZ: Exactly.
>
> ANISE: And she was just ranting and raving. She wasn't mad about the interview—she was mad about the impact it had on her. And we see that over and over again. It's not only anger; sometimes it's depression or—
>
> LZ: . . . or suicide or self-harm . . .
>
> ANISE: . . . or suicide or whatever! You've brought it all up and made it real, and yeah, absolutely.

Obvious risks, such as concern for professional credibility, fear of loss of authority, or even the possibility of losing one's job, were all taken into account automatically. Other, perhaps less obvious risks were described as arising from the likelihood of losing control of the story under the pressure of public scrutiny. The first of these was seen as the potential for both the personal and the political purposes for speaking being defeated by the action. One of the possible negative outcomes is framed in terms of the construction of an ongoing limited subject position or public identity for the speaker:

> ANISE: I think that it can disenfranchise you. I think that it can under-mine your intention—you know, your political intention. And it can solidify your identity in one place. Like, your lone identity is not lesbian. That's not the only thing you are, and yet in some ways self-disclosure can, in some contexts, keep you in that particular place and people can't see you as academic, as woman, as mother, as whatever (!), whatever your other pieces of you are, that all fit together.
>
> So it can be quite risky, I think, and quite dangerous, and not really accomplish anything.

Another risk for this kind of public practice was identified as arising from the limits of available language for experience and the norms created and supported in discourse. Some of the informants described situations in which an inadequately professional performance of the story has had the eventual outcome of playing into some oppressive stereotype, endangering or discrediting the group asking for voice and inadvertently making audience members who share the story even more vulnerable. It is perhaps the case that a significant part of the risk assessment of the intentional professional speaker is a response to a practical knowledge of the fact that in every disclosure we are speaking into socially structured relationships and offering our particular perceptions of experience from within the limits of an existing language. This language supports powerful regimes of meaning and maintains the structures of dominance that can redefine our actions and our intentions, since

> the very terms by which we give an account, by which we make ourselves intelligible to ourselves and to others, are not of our own making. They are social in character, and they establish social norms, a domain of unfreedom and substitutability within which our "singular" stories are told. (Butler, 2005, p. 21)

> ALMA: A public protest, a public gathering, in protest—really, what it is, is a rabblerousing performance, and it's intentional. And what happens if the person slips and falls into a kind of victim performance, is that it panics a bunch of people in the audience. And even some of the people who might be allies or helpers could turn away—not only from the person telling the story but from the other people in the audience that are identified with what she says. Then it just becomes kind of messy.

> ELLEN: I mean, it's okay to ride naked through the town if you actually get the tax cut. [*laughing*] But if you ride naked through the town and you don't get the tax cut—goosebumps, on top of everything else.

Many of the comments of the participants suggest that some of the goals for rhetorical self-disclosure are met by playing the limits of a stereotype against itself, as well as by reaching to identify with those who are without voice. In a situation in which those are the intentions, a failed performance of the power of voice has very real repercussions for the speaker's self-image in that relationship. It is in the exact nature of identification with the listeners to whom an appeal for membership is addressed, that the speaker is vulnerable to a particularly ironic loss of credibility. It is perhaps especially in the view of those with whom we identify that we are most subject to the possibility of finding ourselves redrawn into the pre-existing mural of marginalization. We can find ourselves substituted, in the perception of the audience, by the negativity of the internalized images of stigmatized identity that our disclosures are intended to oppose.

> ALMA: I think that we'd like to think that if the marginalized people in the audience can see that the speaker has made a pretty good life for herself, even though she has the same difficulties that they have, then one of the things that she offers, by speaking out, is a kind of role model of somebody who can overcome the problem. And I think that's the goal.
> But I actually think that in practice that is very often not the outcome. In practice, what sometimes happens is that the clients, who are coming in

with their own self-doubt and self-hate, and worrying about whether they're trusted, can feel that if the worker has the same issues, then they can't be trusted either. And so it sometimes works against us.

Disclosure Consequences

Each person also referred to a more personal risk. For each, there was a response that spoke to their own experience of disclosures that have gone wrong, where they have fallen into victim or been left with the kind of private emotional suffering that is re-activated by the exposure of the story in a context where our identification with the experience has operated to challenge our credibility, not just with others but with ourselves.

> ANNE: When I started working with sexual assault, I had some concerns about going and working with that group, because I thought, "You think you've healed, you think you've moved on—and now you're going to put yourself right back into that."
>
> JAMES: I think, like in a lot of these situations, it's going to force her to look back on very difficult periods of her life and reconsider what she did, why she did it, and I think it's going to throw her emotionally and psychologically backwards in her life, just even to be around this woman.
>
> And I think if she does disclose, that it's going to be even more of a powerful experience. I don't mean that necessarily in a positive way—mean powerful in the way that storms can be powerful.

One of the ways these storms were described, by James and others, was as the possibility of falling back into feelings associated with the bordered speaker's earlier painful experience. In their descriptions of personal pain and professional self-doubt, many subjects reported far-reaching consequences for disclosures in particular situations.

> KATE: And sometimes that's very subtle, and it's nonverbal, and there's a kind of jarring feeling. So, that's learning more about that—about the consequences. We're just [vulnerable], there's no control over how things are received.
>
> LZ: So, is it that if someone doesn't actually have some experience that allows them to identify with you, when you're telling that kind of a story, then they're basing a judgment of you on some stereotype that is externally defined? That the cookie-cutter stereotype of a person does not describe the story, even if the story lands in that space? The story dies, somehow, in that space. Is that right? Or is it the person who's telling the story that suffers somehow?
>
> NED: I think the person that's told the story suffers. I mean, the story's not heard, because it can't be heard.
>
> LZ: Right. So it's silent?
>
> NED: Well, it's worse than silent.
>
> If you're reaching out with that level of story, and if it's not just gossip—if you're vulnerable in that story, then there's a heart opening—a heart reaching

in that moment. . . . And if the person you're sharing that with can't hear it, then not only the story dies, but something very vulnerable and very young, and very tender, has been rebuked. Even if the person loves you. And you're going to get hurt in that process. And you're going to draw back, and so—both people get hurt in that.

The story, the vulnerability, the aliveness of that story certainly gets bruised and becomes probably a little more forbidden—it gets a little more smutch on it of social taboo. It's like, "Oh—we can't be in this story."

Does the story itself die? I think the story doesn't die; I think the story goes into retreat.

LZ: . . . Or gets translated?

NED: Yeah, I mean, my hesitation is that it would get translated. And the meaning of it gets translated—even with the best intentions—into what people understand (which is not coming from themselves or from the person telling the story). It's coming from some sort of external media definition of what they experienced.

ELLEN: I've just seen too many times where the story literally falls on ears that won't hear and won't change. So, I would be concerned that she might be setting herself up for a really profound sense of failure: "Not only do I have this stigmatized history in my life, but now I can't even use the story where it might do some good." When, in fact, rarely do stories achieve the purpose—that particular kind of purpose.

Some of the responses clearly articulated the position that the process of preparation to tell operates in stages or levels of competence, largely determined by the relative safety of the telling. At an early stage in the development of an explanation about what happened, or an understanding of what happened, both the story and the teller are particularly dependent on the response of the listener for meaning, and at that stage the supportive (empowering) response of the other is critical. For many of the participants in the study, this has important practical implications for an expanded sense of our responsibility as interlocutors in the process of facilitating voice in others. We have the responsibility to recognize that someone who is still at the point where what she needs from her audience is reassurance or validation is more likely to be harmed by an experience with a hostile or indifferent listener than someone who has a more practiced story. Katalina, who uses some self-disclosure in her educational work, had a very powerful reaction to some of the ways in which marginalized voice is promoted or encouraged in groups.

KATALINA: Like psychodrama. I don't like that. I really don't like it.

LZ: I don't like it either, but we risk something like psychodrama whenever we do self-disclosure as pedagogy. And it's really interesting to me that we don't name it that way, because everybody would understand what that is, then—but we don't actually name it in terms of responsibility for the kinds of personal relationships that we build in those groups.

So you don't want to stop or close her down, but you also don't want to add to the fire so that she has this big catharsis thing, right?

KATALINA: It's a very careful balance that you have to kind of strike. Or be, at least, aware of that balance that needs to be struck. You can't maybe always avoid it, but . . .

LZ: So do you have a theory about why doing that [avoiding it, shutting her down] is better than setting fire to her hair and having her do some kind of big dramatic thing?

KATALINA: . . . Because if the fire thing happens then she would require more care afterwards, more intensive care. And I'm not willing to do that. So, if I'm not willing to do that, then I shouldn't light a fire, because what happens to the people that are all lit and have nowhere to go?

I know how it happens. I really think that's very dangerous—to open everything up and then let it be. What are these people supposed to do with those opened-up emotions?

LZ: Exactly. But also that they opened it in a group—that they disclosed, in front of a group, more than they've ever said in their lives, and now what?

KATALINA: That can be so dangerous.

Steps to Safe Telling

ALMA: People find voice and they find power. And we move on, and we get on with some other part of our lives, and maybe we want to figure out how to turn some of "that" back, but by the time we're here, we're no longer talking about what "that" was like. . . . We've made a story of it, you know. And I'm glad. I'm glad for you, I'm glad for myself, that we've made it into the story, that it's not in our blood anymore. And so whatever we know about it is distanced, thank god!—and there's a certain amount of expertise that goes with that.

So, we're inviting people—and this is what it feels like, to me—we're inviting people, when we ask them to tell about themselves. We're inviting them to come on over here. Join the place where people can talk! Join the place where people can feel okay.

An important part of almost every interview for this study was the effort to identify the participants' expert strategies for preparations for speaking. The individuals in this group, knowing that disclosure holds the potential for some kinds of negative consequences, have many times decided to take that risk, to get the story polished into a form that we can use for knowledge production, for connection, or for purposes that may be political, journalistic, or juridical—to "give an account of ourselves." For some, this process was framed as having developed a story in stages. Some conversations described the polishing process as being a kind of coconstruction, a development of what can be said, and what can be heard, in dialogue. In this view the story results from learning, and testing with others, the categories of language and generic forms that are available for talking about such things, first in relationship, then in public, taking it on the road.

> ALMA: The beginning story is a very fragile thing. It is a story that didn't have any words at the beginning—it was invisible, a secret. Then, as we move it towards the light, as we move it towards the usage that we're putting it to when we talk about it, we're actually forming it . . . and we're forming it with other people—because we try it out over here, and then somebody jumps back with something, and then we kind of mould it and change it, and there's a discourse that it enters. And then we learn the language of that discourse, and we fit it somewhere—and we make meaning, finally.
>
> LZ: But if we think about that in terms of a joint construction of meaning, is what you're saying that: If you haven't told it before, then the listener has too much say about what it is?
>
> ELLEN: That's exactly what I mean. A good listener will not get in on it as much as a bad listener. I may not know whether the story is going to survive a bad listener, but it may also not survive the good listener. And I need to understand the story myself, first; and then I need to put it out there to someone who's skillful; and then I need to put it out there, if I'm skillful myself; and then I need to just let it go, because then whatever happens to it isn't going to really have too much of an impact on me.
> So, I see those as levels.
>
> LZ: Right—so the first level involves more interaction with the listener, and more kind of testing, to see if it's understood. By the listener . . .
>
> ELLEN: But also to get the listener's contribution.

Even in the conception of language as a necessary tool for meaning-making or identity formation, there is an acknowledgment that the language that we use to describe and understand our experience is developed in important relationships. It is perhaps with the hope of constructing exactly this kind of helping relationship that so many bordered workers position ourselves as not only facilitators but privileged listeners to stories that we ourselves could tell/have told/will tell, with the intention of empowering one another. It is with this understanding of the importance of language that these practitioners have emphasized the necessity for the preparation or polishing of the story itself. However, for one person with long experience in this role, the idea of the development of the story itself was secondary to the sense that for some, meaning-making emerges out of the simple good fortune of arriving in a situation in which they are offered a significant relational recognition—one of those "witnessing relations, [where] we can speak . . . because we are spoken to and only because someone listens" (Oliver, 2001, p. 183). This understanding represents, for Anise, an ongoing personal responsibility for her impact on others, a position that has specific ethical implications for daily practice.

ANISE: I think that people may be, ultimately, frustrated [in the struggle] to make meaning of their experience, if the entire world blanks out their experience . . . when the entire world reflects back to you that you're wrong. And if you never could find somebody to say, "Yeah! You're right!" what would that feel like?

So, I think there are those fortunate few in the world that, when they have an experience that's outside of the dominant perspective, they sooner, rather than later, run into somebody who says, "This is totally fine! It's totally normal!", and the coherence is there for them, and they can go down that path very quickly. . . . But I think it's a matter of that. It's not a matter of time or stages or points in your life. It's about: "How are *you* seeing me?" Which, for me, has a lot of implications for how we are with each other, right?

This particular conversation also touches on another theme in the discourses that work beneath the surface of the practice of professional self-disclosure, one that goes more deeply into the question of what we think we are doing when we tell our stories as professionals. If we extend the meaning of voice to the language of subjectivity, then perhaps in this view, in order to empower others, we may not only have the obligation to provide language, or even to share our stories, but also to witness, with care and recognition, to offer to another the "possibility of an interlocutor [that] makes subjectivity possible" (Oliver, 2001, p. 183). Anise also argued very clearly against identifying the practice of "using the master's tools" of hegemonic discourse as the only enabling condition for the individual's ability to speak. Her perception perhaps recognizes a significant separation of the story from the person: that the person carries the story, not that the story creates her subjectivity. In this and other conversations, the idea of the current positionality of the speaker was also seen as a significant determining factor for the use of the story.

ANISE: Yes, but you see I don't think that's just a function of the story. That's what I'm saying. I think it's a function of your positionality elsewhere, your security, elsewhere. It's not—it doesn't stand on its own.

LZ. Interesting.

ANISE: Well, because—certainly, I can say my story, whichever story I choose, has evolved and developed over time. And as I think I've got more sophisticated theoretical explanations for it, it's gotten clearer or whatever, but it's not just a function of the story—it's who I am, and my position in the world.

Now, if I had a serious alcohol problem right now, that would change the story, my willingness to disclose it to you or whatever, right? But I'm in a very secure position. You can't separate that out.

My willingness, and ability to tell whatever parts of my story, in whatever way, is not just what discourse I've got available to me, or how I've shaped the story, or how I've evolved it. It's my security, and my world, and my life.

JACQUES: At times I've noticed that it is how you actually disclose information—the tone, the content, the amount of information that you actually provide to individuals—these all make very much difference!

LZ: So, you're confident in your ability to manage that, to decide how much, and to engage the crowd, and make your own decision about all that. . . . But when we're looking at someone else, are we always confident about their ability to do that? Can we make a decision, in principle, which says everybody should? And do we make a decision in principle that says nobody should?

JACQUES: No—I honestly believe that it's always context oriented. And it depends on your position.

It's very interesting. I'm kind of finding out that the way I'm answering these questions is all—it's all new. I make it personal. Like, for the other story, I don't see Joanne or Jacques. I see the position, the status that Jacques has . . .

LZ: . . . the professionalism.

JACQUES: Yeah—and that status is more important.

LZ: Right. Because you identify both sides of it. And sometimes we choose the professional side and sometimes we choose the personal side. But can we actually ever say that we're always going to do one or the other?

JACQUES: No. No, because situation-to-situation it is different.

Taking Ownership of the Story

LZ: So, there's something about those early disclosures that are searching for truth, or something?

JAMES: Yeah.

LZ: So, can you think of a time where it became obvious that it wasn't actually up to somebody else to decide whether or not it was true? Is there a kind of ownership that we can take, of the story?

JAMES: I would say definitely, yes. My ownership of the story—it wasn't really until I was in charge of what people knew that I took ownership of it. . . . And really, I would say that it was after the last time where I felt I was compelled to do this thing, and after that I felt like, "OK, I did that. Now I can be selective; now I can control it." And definitely, I've learned how to—manipulate is the wrong word—but how to exercise control.

For some of the speakers in my study, the story and its development were seen as identical to the development of the self, while for others, this development or use of the story came about in some way that reflects a separation between the story and themselves. In either case, in the reports of how the stories are used intentionally, there is a sense in which each has experienced some kind of a shift that has allowed them to claim or own the story in such a way that they were no longer vulnerable to whatever outside response the story may find. Though many would agree that they are still vulnerable to the attitudes and responses of others in a personal disclosure, most declared that their professional disclosures no longer posed a risk to them in the same way.

> ELLEN: I'm speaking to you from a point in my life where I'm not relying on the people that I'm telling stories to, in those contexts, to acknowledge and recognize and accept this new woman that I've shown them. I don't need to do that.
>
> LZ: No. You're not looking for acknowledgment of that identity.
>
> ELLEN: Yeah. And when someone says, "I'm glad you told me that story. I understand you better. I'm grateful," then I'm happy that we have some more bridges to cross to each other, but I don't rely on being recognized by the persons that I'm talking to. And I think it's because we're talking, here, about my professional life.
>
> I still find it devastating when I tell a story in my personal life, and the person who I'm talking to doesn't believe me, or doesn't care, or is impatient, or isn't moved, or just starts to analyze or—you know . . . because I am sharing some part of myself. And that's frustrating and that's sad.
>
> ALMA: I could say my story in front of anybody now, and it wouldn't make any difference to me whether they puked. You know, I don't care what they do with it. But at certain stages of our lives, we are way more liable to have our stories twisted or made incoherent by the response of others.

Being "Believed"

In the context of protecting both the story and the self from this discrediting, this incoherence, this Abjection, the practitioners who spoke to me explained the necessity for the preparations for speaking out as a process, understood to be the way the speaker practices/learns the uses of the narrative form. Once she has done her own work, incorporated the information that the story is intended to impart, and prepared herself with practice, she will know the story well enough so that she/it has the authority to be able to withstand the power of the prevailing stereotypes or master narratives that she is defying: she will be able to sustain herself and her story, even if it is not believed. But the problem of being believed brings us back to the difficulty with maintaining any separation between our stories and ourselves.

> LZ: Now, can we go back to identity on this? Because part of what we're doing here is using a sense of who you are, when you tell those stories, right?
>
> ELLEN: Yes. Yes.
>
> LZ: You're coming out from behind the veil of a role to a particular experience. Yet, when we talk about authenticity of stories, if someone doesn't believe you, do they feel like they don't believe your identity? They don't believe that you're really who you say you are?
>
> ELLEN: Well, I think that that would be part of not believing me.

LZ: So, that's part of what the risk is, when you tell a story that you haven't really got a grip on?

ELLEN: Yeah, I've had people say, "I just can't believe that that would ever happen—you just don't seem like the sort of person that would ever have had that experience." And sometimes they say it in a sense of, "I'm really glad you told that story, because until you started talking, I always thought you were blah, blah, blah . . ." And so, it's a sense that they've acknowledged that I'm showing them some part of myself that they haven't seen before, and they believe that person.

. . . But I've also had people, although it's less frequent, who have said, "I just think you made that up, and I don't believe that that is you." And my response now is, "What can I say?"

Until we have accomplished some level of ownership of the story or some conviction that our perception or explanation of the events is true, the effect of not being believed can be devastating. The feeling of disconnection or silencing that follows from this may be what we mean by Abjection, or at least disempowerment. To the extent that being believed by another is dependent on a shared epistemology or paradigm for knowledge production, we will always be accountable to others in dialogue, but the way this is usually expressed is in terms of our credibility: if the story seems unbelievable, or the audience does not seem to believe her, then the teller has a need to prove something, not necessarily to corroborate the details of the story but to prove herself a credible witness. Ellen described this sensation, common to many bordered speakers, when talking about an incident where this happened to her, at a time when she was telling a "true" story about someone else's experience.

ELLEN: I felt absolutely awful. . . . I could see that there were some people in the room who were sceptical, who thought that I'd made it up.

LZ: Didn't believe it.

ELLEN: Didn't believe *me*. And there were some who really, so totally believed me, they had tears dangling in their eyes, and a transformative experience. And that's fine. People have different reactions. But I realized that if I was going to tell the story, it's really important that everybody there believed me. And I felt like I had to, in a sense, prove that it was true.

Our knowledge of the painful feelings connected to not being believed makes our responsibility for witnessing other's stories very complex. Once again, in situations in which believing can't be taken for granted, our intentions in the practice of self-disclosure are sometimes in conflict with the profound sensitivity to connection and disconnection that we use in helping relationships. The vulnerability of our identification with others who may share similar stories makes it confusing or particularly painful for us, if they refuse to disclose in a reciprocal way, or if, when they do, we cannot believe their accounts.

LZ: Well, you say that one of the reasons for doing self-disclosure in the first place is to reach across or to make a connection that allows the other person to understand that they're not alone. What happens if the other person then, in order to not be alone, tells you a story that sounds like what you want to hear? How does it feel?

KATALINA: "That sounds like" meaning that she may not be telling the truth?

LZ: Well . . . that she thinks this is what she needs to do, because you've done that.

KATALINA: Then, I've stopped disclosing.

LZ: Alright—but how does that feel?

KATALINA: Like I've been betrayed . . . I don't know. There was something similar to that when I was taking a class, where the instructor asked for a lot of disclosure for the process to happen—which is understandable. But I was annoyed, by the end, that she didn't tell anything about herself. Granted, she's the instructor. Granted, she does this every semester, every year, whatever that she does. So, in my comments at the end, I said, "I'm disturbed by the fact that there's so much disclosure in the room, but we seem to get none from you. And that made me uncomfortable."

Knowledge Claims

ELLEN: It is a knowledge claim. I'm telling the story, because it contains an aspect of my epistemology. And that's the part that I think gets missed, when people are talking about storying.

And that, I think, is the part where I can balance the risks of disclosure against the worthiness of the story-ing, because: I'm—if I cease to risk disclosing, then I cease to build knowledge. And those are all building my epistemology, but also exposing my built epistemology.

For all of the people who spoke with me, the disclosure, in whatever form was seen to be appropriate, was presented as knowledge. Each of these people saw themselves as reaching for what I am calling the Performance of Dangerous Knowledge. With full recognition of a complex process of polishing the story, a task undertaken to prevent the loss of subjectivity implied by the necessity for risk assessment, these speakers choose to present their knowledge, even their epistemology, in the form of personal narratives. These stories are, in themselves, performances of power—demonstrations of courage and the ability to confront dominance and difference, claiming the right to name ourselves, to value our named identities, and to honor our connections to others.

All forms of identity . . . are formed through telling or writing a particular life story that injects life circumstances with meaning in a personally coherent narrative. The coherence for which we strive, and which is portrayed as an identity, is realized in and through what we write, say and do. Identity is made in and through performance, whether this performance is a story told to oneself or another, written for others to read, or enacted in an activity involving shared expectations. . . . Identities reflect the meanings that we make of self in relation to others. (Cohler and Hammack, 2006, p. 167)

CHAPTER 7

Pedagogical Confessions: Narrating Empowerment for Knowledge Production

> KATALINA: I don't hesitate to disclose. But I personally believe it's the amount of disclosure that's the issue. It's not whether you disclose or not.

The use of self-disclosure as voice is so ubiquitous that it has become an almost invisible genre in what Foucault called our "confessional culture." Every day, justified by the ideology of empowerment, we can expect people to demonstrate in narrative form their first-hand knowledge of trauma, oppression, or injustice as a way to make a contribution to knowledge production and social change. On the news, on talk shows, in classrooms and workshops and treatment settings, in public or in one-on-one conversations, people are encouraged to tell about their painful experiences with the confidence that, even if the process is difficult for the speaker, it will be good for them in the long run. It is understood that "we"—the general public— need to know about these things and that "we"—the marginalized—need to talk about them. Some of the conventions of this confessional self-disclosure have always operated as a kind of shorthand, so that certain references to experience allow listeners to make assumptions about some predictable conflation of identity/knowledge, some recognizable category of selfhood comprising a whole set of assumed skills and knowledges that can be inferred from the speaker's narrative. For many people, this storied identification has become a passport, a way of representing themselves to the world.

> NED: I think these days a lot of people aren't assuming much of anything about the listener, when they bring you that story. I think these days they bring you that story as a credential, and they go, "I do this and I've done that, and that's my credential." And I don't think they're assuming much of anything about me, except that maybe they've been told I'm the kind of person who can bring those credentials, too.
>
> It's not until we get to a place where we're really talking about whatever that stuff is for them that they begin to check me out, as to whether I know what they're talking about. Because I see a lot of those stories in this culture like little badges. You know: "I'm an addict," "I'm a prostitute." And it doesn't matter what the other person knows—it's like a calling card.

However, the use of the conventions of representation that support a stereotyped identity/knowledge in this form holds very different potentials for the bordered worker than for the marginalized individual who does not also live/work in a helper role. Not only do bordered workers possibly have more to lose by the exposure of their marginalized status, but if we take into account the operations of a consciousness of consciousness as a significant component of the preparation of the story for this kind of political use, there are further implications. The fact that we are operating from the position of someone with agency, with the ability to make the choice to speak (or not), changes the meanings of both the content and the practice of such intentional storytelling. Whether in response to a forensic or journalistic call or to some internal political commitment to knowledge production, actions of this kind require the bordered speaker to consider several questions, personal and ethical—some of which were identified in the respondents' comments about the vignettes used in the first series of interviews for this project. In the longer second interviews, the informants were encouraged to explain more about their use of this kind of storytelling, particularly where ideological or value-based considerations could be identified as contributing to decision making around disclosure.

> ALMA: When we're carrying those stories, as part of ourselves, or if we think of them as an . . . I don't know . . . an identification badge, or a placard or something. Well, you don't have to have your cape open to the placard all the time [*laughing*], but you know you can flip it back any time you want. But how we carry it that way, when we're talking to people, depends on which one of those people we are talking to.

Perhaps the first ethical issue, and one that was touched on in almost every interview, was the question: "Am I disclosing this for my own benefit, or for the benefit of others?" The answer to this question came in many forms, often without my introducing it as a problem, and perhaps indicates that, for many who make the choice to self-disclose in this way, we must have prepared some convincing defense against the charge of "doing it for ourselves," long before we can make the decision to speak in a specific situation. While this may be partly a response to the common proscriptions against the practice in general, many of the comments indicate a complex interpersonal sensitivity that grounds an ethical deliberation based on relational considerations more familiar in the Ethics of Care framework, whereby choices made in the professional setting can be understood to be in response to the particular relationships involved, rather on the basis of some abstract principle. These responses provide a pragmatic description of a practice-based relational epistemology that necessitates and supports an ongoing ethical engagement with others:

> Attention to particular persons as a, if not the, morally crucial epistemic mode requires distinctive sorts of understanding, usefully described by Gilligan as "contextual and narrative" rather than "formal and abstract." The latter "abstracts the moral problem from the interpersonal situation," and the former "invokes a narrative of relationships that extends over time." (Walker, 1992, p. 167)

> ANISE: I probably am more comfortable in my own self when I am disclosing things in a more public forum, because then it's clear as to why I'm doing it. It's clear that I'm not doing this so you'll feel sorry for me. I'm doing it for public and political reasons.

> ELLEN: When someone says, "I guess you're just wanting to deal with your stuff," my own response inside is, "Phht! You thought that was me dealing with my stuff? You couldn't pay me to deal with my stuff!" But I need to have that response, and I need to know the difference.
>
> And I also need to be aware that often my initial response is anger. It is, "You think I don't worry about that? You think I don't take care about that? You don't think . . ."—you know. And the shoulders come up, and there's trouble. I'm aware of that, because it is a challenge to my foundational values.

From the many responses to this thread in the interviews, it appears that a critical component of the ethical stance that supports the bordered worker in deciding when, how, or how much to disclose is the recognition that we are, of course, in it for ourselves. But being in it, in this sense, is being in the position of working in a field that touches us, reflects our experience, or puts us in the position where we are reminded of our own pains. Some of the articulations of this awareness in the interviews clearly demonstrate the importance of the personal motivations that have brought so many dedicated bordered workers to their complex and difficult roles of activism and advocacy, and in many cases have kept them/us engaged beyond the limits of a normal career, in a life's work of helping with vulnerable populations.

> LZ: So then, what would you say is the meaning, for yourself—the meaning of doing this kind of work, in relation to your life?

KATALINA: It's turning what happened that was very negative into positive. That's what it is about, and that I have recognized from the beginning.

LZ: And it's an active response to a negative experience . . . because you don't have to do this. You could do something else.

KATALINA: Right. But if I did something else, the negative would most likely stay negative in me. So I almost have to do something about it, to make sense of it.

Our professional interactions with others can contribute greatly to our own lives if the work itself provides us with a sense of meaning, as well as whatever financial benefits a job may bring. And if by "turning the negative to positive" the specifics of the work allow us some meaningful response rather than just passively knowing about their difficulties, then we are active in helping to alleviate some of the pains and harms of those like us or like we used to be. But for each of the people interviewed, there was a clear expression of the imperative to remember, as a first rule of professionalism, that we cannot use the helping relationship with vulnerable others simply to get our own needs met.

LZ: So, in your helping relationships . . .

SALLY: You default to the professional. Your job right then, that you're getting paid for, is to help that person, not to get your own . . . whatever, benefit. And through that relationship, you do get benefit from that, and you do get some healing from that. And that's a bonus . . . but you can do that without revealing yourself, because that puts you in a position where you are in the job to get your own counseling. . . . Which we all do! I think that's a normal thing; we work in helping relationship areas, because . . . okay, that's a generalization! . . . but a lot of those people work in these areas because it's close to them, in some way.

MARY: Yes, a theory about how it [self-disclosure] gets done is different from who does it. Because actually, yes, we all do it; and yes, we do it in this respectful, careful, and noncontrolling way. Otherwise, why would we bother, right?

You don't really go to work in order to get immersed in your own emotional thing—although it happens.

ANISE: Obviously one of the big risks is that you're seeking your own fulfillment, in some way, in participating in this kind of work. You're seeking your own fulfillment in whatever you're doing, right? If there's nothing in it for you, you're not doing it! So, the extent to which you're getting that, and the ways in which you're getting satisfaction have to be clearly not at the expense of the people you're serving.

So perhaps we are "there" in the work for our own reasons. It may even be true that there are times when we may disclose for our own reasons. Some of the reasoning behind these actions are as complex as those touched on in the interaction in one conversation about the use of disclosure in one-to-one counseling, one context in which the ethics of self-disclosure have been extensively theorized (Brown, 1994; Goldstein, 1997; Heyward, 1993; Miller and Stiver, 1997; Pennebaker, 1990, Peterson, 2002; Simi and Mahalik, 1997). In response to my archeological questioning, Ned shared his belief that an irrelevant disclosure, offered for reasons beyond the present relationship, would have an immediate impact on the connection with the listener, even if the action may have a justifiable intention in the moment.

LZ: Well, this is another meaning of self-disclosure, which is to question, "What is self?"—Is self all the power that allows you to do this, or is self the experience of pain that put you in the position that made you decide you wanted to [do this work]? Usually, when we say "self" disclosure, in the context of this kind of work, we're talking about disclosing the part of the self that's not powerful.

NED: Right.

LZ: Disclosing it to whom? Sometimes we disclose it to the other—and we do that for several purposes, some of which we have talked about. Sometimes we just do it to ourselves.

NED: Yeah. That's when their eyes glaze over.

LZ: Well, maybe. Or is it so that we have a check on our behavior?

NED: But I think that's already [too late], because if we're doing that, then we're not checking our own behavior. We're exploiting them in the moment—for us to self-disclose, for our own particular reasons, so that ain't why I'm there.

LZ: But what if the reason that you're doing it at that point, your own particular reason, is to remind yourself that you actually need to pay attention to the fact that you used to be like this guy?

NED: Then it's very valid.

LZ: And what if it serves a necessary purpose for you: to keep you more present in the relationship? ... Maybe you could shorthand it, maybe we could make it shorter!

NED: Very short—very short.

LZ: What if that's one of the purposes of self-disclosure?

NED: Is to wake myself up? Yeah.

LZ: Yeah. To keep out of the fog of privilege.—To drop yourself out of the sort of golden moment of being God for a second there.

If sometimes a disclosure is a reminder to the speaker, or a way of keeping ourselves accountable to our own reasons for practice, perhaps it also increases our accountability to those who are asked to recognize us as bordered, as like them in important ways. This sensitivity to subtle shifts in the connection supported by the helping relationship is, in other language, one way that experienced practitioners register the kind of consequence that arises out of interpersonal "othering." If self-disclosure can also be seen as a strategy of uncovering the vulnerable self in an effort to avoid othering the client, as a practical, momentary solution to the enduring problem of distance in helping relationships, then paying attention to this sensitivity to connection and disconnection may prove to be one of our strongest ethical guidelines for the practice. The identification with others that resists stereotyping goes beyond empathy, it takes the form of a principle, a strategy, a choice to stay in relation to effect change. One of the ways this has been articulated in the practice of therapy is in the Stone Center conception of relational "mutuality," which

> involves profound mutual respect and mutual openness . . . It does not mean equality—there is a certain, though different, vulnerability for both participants . . . building authentic connection is predicated on tolerating uncertainty, complexity, and the inevitable vulnerability involved in real change. (Miller and Stiver, 1997, p. 3)

> ANISE: Well, what I'm focused on is the ethics of othering. . . . And you know, I think othering is an ethical issue, but it's when . . . we all "other" and there is the Other, but on what basis do we "Other"? And there's inclusionary and exclusionary othering . . . so I'm really talking about the exclusionary kind of othering that draws forth biases and stereotypes and marginalizing acts and that kind of thing. And yet I think that the piece that you're paying attention to is . . . as the agent in that, how do you position yourself and what are you doing? Because a lot of time, I watch people "Othering" as a way of bolstering their own identities, which is fascinating. . . .

> It's interesting to me that people would go, "Okay, violence—that's the thing that the Indians do to each other, and the East Indians do to each other!" But it was also about them when they did that, because if it's them, then it's not me, do you know what I mean?

> LZ: Yeah. Then I'm safe.

> KATE: It's about having a belief in terms of what kind of a society she sees—wanting to live and work for social change. But everything kind of gets reduced to stereotyping in this culture. It's so huge. And not much has changed in twenty-five years around the stigma. And there are so many [of us]—and so much that we're talking about, and yet there's such a lack of awareness about it. But, you know, all the people in your vignettes are all at that place. Challenging the notion that we're either or.

> LZ: Yeah. There are just so many flag-bearers.

> KATE: Well, I mean if someone said, "Okay, how many women have lived through this? Or how many people, this . . . ?" Mental illness, or sexual abuse or whatever. It's everybody almost. We just don't like that "othering."

Beyond these principles and these strategies, beyond whatever personal identification we have with the sources of our own professional interests and our career trajectories, each action of speaking out in this way is the result of a decision taken in a particular moment. Seen in this way, an understanding of the practice requires an answer to this question: how do bordered helpers make the decision to take the risk of talking about our experience, or our histories, in any specific situation? Before any individual performance of a professional self-disclosure can be undertaken as an empowerment practice with some purpose larger than whatever therapeutic value may or may not result for the speaker, we have to take into account several ethical questions. So, having once made the first, principled, decision—that we will carry our histories of marginalization into our work—each of the ethical choices after that must be made in response to the specific conditions of any situation in which we may be in a position to speak from experience.

We need to identify whom we think we are speaking to: Who is listening? What do we know that is relevant to the immediate context, and who do we think needs this information? What parts of the story are safe to tell in the situation? What outcome do we expect to follow our use of the story? In the moment? In a longer-term view? Why my story, rather than someone else's? Are we shutting down another voice by speaking? And finally, how are we going to feel after the story is done? What will be the price for us, when we choose to tell the "truth" about ourselves?

Disclosure for Empowerment

MARY: Empowerment is not something you can give someone else, but you can sure take it away easy.

One of the most familiar contexts where disclosure is encouraged in the name of knowledge production is the classroom, where the desire to allow or to support diversity sets up the possibility/necessity for contributions to the conversation by the subaltern voices present in the group. In "Why Doesn't This Feel Empowering?" Elizabeth Ellsworth's critique of the uses of this conception of voice in liberatory or critical pedagogies is focused mainly on her experience of the formal academic setting, where the knowledge offered by students in the service of empowerment is potentially received, in the same way that other knowledges are taken up in the academic frame, as

the kind of knowing   in which objects, nature, and Others are seen to be known or ultimately knowable, in the sense of being "defined, delineated, captured, understood, explained, and diagnosed" at a level of determination never accorded to the Knower herself or himself. (Ellsworth, 1992, p. 112)

It is perhaps this same concern with how things can be known in that environment, that some of the participants in the study bring to their deliberations about whether or not they should self-disclose as educators in a pedagogical setting. One predictable problem, which often follows any disclosure story in an empowerment context, is the tendency for listeners to want to disclose their own experience in turn, whether or not they have ever spoken about it before. Many practitioners are very conscious of this potential if we create a context where disclosure is possible and hold ourselves responsible for the protection of the space where some speakers may find themselves in danger of disclosure consequences—where stories may emerge that are not "worked out," that are too vulnerable for public presentation.

> LZ: But we create the culture where it's possible or not possible. And it doesn't matter whether we say something different. What we do creates the culture.
>
> ELLEN: So if it begins to look as if folks have got the impression that if they go as deep as I'm going, then they'll somehow be better, then I know I haven't defended the classroom adequately, or as much as I can. And I also know I have to call it. Because that's where disclosure becomes dangerous.

For the bordered educator, this requires a particular ethical engagement with the sometimes contradictory requirements of our professional responsibility to the group and our desire to demonstrate respect for the strength and the agency of the person who wishes to "talk back" (hooks, 1988) with their own story.

> ELLEN: Though I never intentionally made a person disclose, I know I can make somebody do it just by being there and being a mentor, a role model.
>
> LZ: After you "tell," they want to tell you. They want you to hear it. It isn't just that you can say it. It's that they want to share. . . . If part of what we do, when we do this, is reach for connection, we get it.
>
> ELLEN: Yeah.
>
> LZ: That means that they reach back. Right? Whether that's one-to-one, or whether that's a whole group. So when we reach for connection by saying, "I'm powerful over here, but I know the same things you know," maybe first we give the message about "what I know the same as you know," but how can we give the message "you're as powerful as I am," and still take care of them?
>
> ELLEN: Well, that's I think where the contradiction for me comes, with making the intervention—every time I have done that, I've triple-, quadruple-thought myself. Because I know I have a rescue thing that I've got to give up, [but I still want people to be safe]. So that's what I struggle with, it's that if I tell a story, and I don't give ample opportunity for people to come back . . . then the connection has gone only one way. And then if I suddenly said, "Oh, but you know what, you're not really able to tell the story." Well, any kind of message like that says to the listener—"So I've got this awful story that I really need to tell now because she's reminded me of it. It's sitting up here. And now she's telling me—I've got the impression that I'm not supposed to have said it."

Whether or not we are willing to use our own stories in a specific instance, there are many contexts where the professional is in the position of encouraging or supporting the disclosure of another, sometimes by creating the safety of a dialogue in the intimacy of a closed setting but sometimes also by facilitating another's public speaking out. In many of the interviews for the study, I asked a question about how we would know if someone else would be safe to disclose in a public context. This was answered by the participants in a way that addressed both the sense of responsibility for setting up the possibility of a disclosure and the need to avoid a patronizing kind of protectionism that would not allow the individual to make her own risk assessment as a part of deciding whether or not she could undertake to expose herself.

> ANISE: A public disclosure is not a way to get therapy, right? And this particular woman that I referred to [a journalist], she's not going to try to do that. But she's also going to give them enough of a story that it'll be newsworthy, if you get my meaning.
>
> LZ: Right. So she can stay close enough to the intensity of her story to make it a good story.
>
> ANISE: Yeah. But if I pulled apart my reasoning for picking her over a lot of other people that I know, but would never even think to suggest, there are reasons in there that are about what your question is, which is—what are the conditions of a safe disclosure?
>
> LZ: Right.
>
> ANISE: And so, on one hand, I say I'm not being paternalistic, but the fact is that I didn't give the [magazine] reporter ten other names. I am, in a way, I suppose, being paternalistic and protecting those other women, because I don't think that it would work for them.

An expansion on the issue of the conditions for a safe disclosure for others came in response to the question of how we manage the problem of supporting voice with the people for whom we feel a responsibility. In this conversation, Anne makes a clear commitment to informed (conscious) decision making for the speaker, and at the same time she recognizes the need for the helper to demonstrate respect for the person's agency and courage. This interaction also introduces another important theme: if we work toward making a space safe for disclosure, how can we make it safe for an individual to choose *not* to disclose? How can we honor and support an individual's choice of silence, the "silence as a will not to say or a will to unsay and as a language of its own" (Trinh, 1989b, p. 373)?

> ANNE: This is one of those times where I think paternalism, or—that's such an ugly word in the feminist hierarchy and rhetoric. But this is one of those times where there is a continuum of paternalism. And that we need to be really thoughtful about how we ask people to participate in things that make it better for the greater good, because there can be, for this particular person, repercussions down the road. Because it's still her choice whether she actually wants to participate
>
> It's like asking someone who's gone through hell and detox and now life is good and all of those things. Well, life may not be good in a year. . . . We

need to be somewhat paternalistic and blunt and say to her "This is the kind of scenario that may happen." Or say "You could also, in ten years, look back on this as "This is my proudest moment, because I did get through this."

People have to feel like they can say no. Absolutely that they can say no.

In academic or social change environments, the presumption of a liberal or relatively benevolent tolerance for difference operates as a screen that obscures the risks of disclosure for those seen as needing "empowerment" to speak. The assumption that "we" (the educators, the listeners, the members of the class) are not like "them" (the bigots, the abusers, the dangerous people) either makes the choice of silence an insult to the group of listeners or implies helplessness or paranoia on the part of the nonspeaker. In supporting voice or storytelling, safe conditions for disclosure are also dependent on the creation of safe conditions for silence and an explicit recognition of agency in an individual's choice to refuse to speak.

> When we depend on storytelling either to reach each other across differences or to resist patriarchal and racist constructs, we must overcome at least one difficulty: the difference in position between the teller and the listener, between telling the tale and hearing it. (Razack, 1993, p. 101)
>
> LZ: So it's a safe place to disclose?
>
> BETH: It would be, yeah.
>
> LZ: Is it a safe place to not disclose?
>
> BETH: Yeah, maybe that's true, too. I think, though, that my biggest thing with not disclosing was the question I had about whether I had to. I was thinking about going into this program, and I was thinking about being in a group [where] at the very beginning there was this dinner that you were invited to go to with your partners and everybody meet each other and I didn't want to go. But it has to do with the experience of people making assumptions about you by learning something about you.
>
> LZ: So stereotyping again?
>
> BETH: Stereotyping. And it's not fair that there's that judgment about who homosexuals are. And I just didn't want to be a part of it.

Although Ellsworth's effort to expose the "repressive myth of the silent other" (Ellsworth, 1992) calls into question the pedagogical empowerment practice of encouraging voice, particularly from a position of relative power, it does not address the many different reasons that someone would choose to willingly respond to such an invitation, even knowing the variable potentials for her listeners or for herself.

> The problems of voice and identity are packed with internal dilemmas not only for the listeners but also the tellers of the tale. . . . Yet the chance to speak, to enter your reality on the record, as it were, is as irresistible as it is problematic. What kind of tale will I choose to tell, and in what voice? (Razack, 1993, p. 117)

In the interviews with these skilled speakers, some of the reasons for telling, even in difficult circumstances, were clearly articulated.

Connections and Identifications

Many times when someone is presented as a speaker who will tell her own story, the introductory explanation of her motivation for offering a public disclosure of painful experience suggests that she is "speaking out in the hope that others will not have to go through what she went through." This is certainly one of the most compelling arguments for testimony, and it is routinely used to encourage an inexperienced speaker: the idea that our pain could be useful in some way, in that others may benefit from what we have learned. This argument seems to suggest that the content of the story is delivered for the benefit of those listeners for whom these experiences are not familiar. James distinguished these preventative intentions from others that he calls "transformative," within a framework of benefits to culture.

> LZ: You said [in the first interview] that when people talk about this, they are actually working on a benefit for the culture in that they are actually trying to do something for others, by expanding on this knowledge that we got from this hard place.
>
> JAMES: Right . . . yeah. Well I guess if were to think about that again, I would have to say it takes me back to the quote that I was talking about . . . about finding a language for people to talk about these things. So I would say that there's innumerable cultural benefits, but the two, probably most profound ones are preventative—by people knowing about things like this happening before—that other people won't necessarily have to go through the same experiences, or not to the same degree of severity—
>
> LZ: Mmhmm
>
> JAMES: And then the other one is transformative—for people who have been through these experiences, understanding that there's other people out there, that they can relate to their experience, and say, "Wow, I'm not alone."

The preventative intention was not explicitly described as a primary motivation for speaking by any of the other people in this study, except in the sense that speaking out could be seen as an action that could make a difference for people like us, or like we used to be, in the future. Neither were those who spoke to me using their references to experience in the way that stories are used in some contexts where sharing a conventional qualifying story is a requirement for membership. Rather, in the instances when audiences were assumed to include both the marginalized and members of the nonmarginalized population (the dominant), speaking out was framed more directly as a knowledge claim, as the exercise of a particular kind of expertise, as an expansion of the speaker's professional credibility, or even as a moral obligation:

KATALINA: It's a little similar to getting a degree. I mean, what do you go to a school for if you don't get to use what you've learned? It's the same kind of deal.

ANISE: My values are that those of us that have had those kinds of experiences have got to turn them into a silver lining in that it gives you understanding and insight, and it gives you special knowledge so that I think you almost have a moral responsibility [to talk about it].

If the chance to speak out offers us the chance to be seen as a "Knower," to act as an authority in some arena where identifying ourselves could make a difference, and if we feel an obligation to offer that knowledge as part of the service to the communities we work with, then many professionals will continue to respond to the call to tell stories that provide the particulars that prove the truths of painful social consequences arising from abstract categories of difference. In her book of portraits of professionals, Sara Lawrence-Lightfoot writes about Kay, a teacher who uses self-disclosure in her classes, because "stories create intimate conversations across boundaries." She articulates some other reasons for the practice that are also reflected in the comments of this study's participants:

I have thought about, and used, stories in many of the same ways that Kay does: as counterpoint to abstraction, as an opportunity for improvisation, as a way to develop greater symmetry with my students, and as a way to encourage the "meeting of minds and hearts." (Lawrence-Lightfoot, 1999, p. 111)

It is in this meeting that the potential for the "transformative" function of such self-disclosure stories operates. Any public audience is understood by the practitioners in this project to include not only those listeners who need to learn the singular truths of the general idea that terrible or unjust things happen in the world but also the listener who *knows* in her own experience that such things do happen but who also perhaps needs to hear that these things can be survived, talked about, and carried with authority. According to my respondents, the presentation of a knowledge claim in the form of a self-disclosure story is intended to enhance the authenticity and credibility of the worker in the estimation of the marginalized members of an audience, but without losing the authority that is necessary for the speaker to be seen as a professional by members of the dominant group. By far the most commonly expressed motivation is the desire to demonstrate solidarity with the listener who already shares the negative or marginalized experience, not as a warning that "it" might happen again but as validation for the possibility of resistance, power, and voice even when it does.

JAMES: I really feel that speaking out in a very political way, really has immense benefits in the end for other people, because it provides them with someone to identify with, to say, "Okay, I'm not alone. There are other people out there who've gone through this same thing. And look! They're willing to talk about it." And so that private declaration, or that private exposure, opens it up—it's like taking a personal experience and making it into a mural that other people can participate in—or in the construction of. Even if that construction—even if their helping is simply a passive identification.

RENEE: Sometimes it makes a personal connection, but to help women see not only their connection to the person they're talking to, but to women in their situation in general, I think ultimately that's where you're wanting to go.

In this context, rhetorical appeals to identification are initiated, first with the desire to connect or to declare membership with a particular part of the audience, in effect providing both speaker and selected audience members with the message, "You are not alone" and, by example, validating a speaking position for those identified as sharing the story.

KATE: I guess it is about membership. Who you're identifying with is the issue, and what's your primary identification? That is what's going on for me in terms of identity. It's more of a solidarity, and that's been helpful for me as well, in terms of looking at other people. So I do base it in part on my own experience, and what I see modeled, where disclosure maintains that kind of solidarity without pretending to erase the real power differences. People still have different levels of power, but it's within that solidarity.

In the process of supporting solidarity and developing these important connections, self-disclosure of bordered identity is also articulated as intended to operate as a model for a challenge to limiting stereotypes, an example of boundary-breaking, or an encouragement for others with the same experience to include themselves in a larger context. And it is with the recognition of this political intent, with this desire to provide a wider frame for identification and power, that such knowledge production performances can be conceived of as activism.

ANISE: When I stand up in front of a class, they usually know, before I get to the point of disclosing that particular thing to them, they know I'm a fairly healthy, well-balanced person. You know? With at least a little bit of a sense of humor. And so, then when I say that, they go, "Oh, god! Not in a straight-jacket! Isn't that interesting?"

JAMES: Especially with something like mental illness, where there is such a stigma surrounding the development of these illnesses, I think it's extremely important for people to be able to talk about their experience and to do so in a way that will benefit other people who also have the illnesses but may not have a position of power or the eloquence to be able to describe that experience in a way that is readily accessible to the general public.

BETH: There's that part of it in a classroom setting, where people come up with their reactions to me, and will those reactions change once they know that I'm gay? I think that's interesting to explore. In some ways it seems like another form of educating. You know, some of these people that don't know anybody who's gay. And then I'm letting them get to know me before they know who's gay. Right?

It is also within this sense of the political, of an action of solidarity, that the idea of empowerment meets this concept of transformation in practice:

> Unlike resilience, transformation suggests not just a return to a previously existing state but a movement through and beyond stress and suffering into a new and more comprehensive personal and relational integration . . . beyond a notion of recovery from individual pain to a sense of greater integrity and integration into the human community as well. Joining others in mutually supporting and meaningful relationships most clearly allows us to move out of isolation and powerlessness. (Jordan, 2004, p. 42)

As Lawrence-Lightfoot expands on her reasons for the practice of storytelling, her work echoes many of the comments by the participants in my study. The idea of creating connection is not simply strategic for any of us, just as the process is not without risks. The sense of commitment to the promotion of the transformative potential in relationship is described as a clear motivation for using our selves and our stories to connect with others.

> But I also use stories . . . to create deeper connections . . . to reveal universal human themes that we share, and to bridge the realms of thinking and feeling. . . . they begin to see themselves reflected in my experiences, and they respond with feeling and insight, passion and analysis. In these moments of personal revelation they also experience my vulnerability, my trust, and my respect. (Lawrence-Lightfoot, 1999, p. 112)

Many of the informants spoke of their sense of responsibility for mentoring or role-modeling, not simply as powerful, accomplished people in the world but also as individuals who are able to create and sustain significant relationships of compassion and caring. For some, this responsibility is reflected in the choices of what content to include in any storytelling, for others it was more directly articulated:

ALMA: I stand up in front of two hundred people, half of whom are survivors, and I talk about survivors with compassion and love and generosity. And I'm taking on both the subject and the object of that. And I'm taking on being loved that way. Because they are loving me that way. And they are loving themselves and each other that way, when I make words around it. And— I don't know, it's maybe even more or less powerful in that kind of a public environment, because I'm doing it as having this identity. Because the identity isn't just of my own experience of abuse—It's the experience of learning, my experience of knowing so many people who've had that history who were so valuable. So it goes from the individual to the whole group . . . and I think without that, there would be no conversation. There'd be nothing to say. My public statement would not have any power in it.

Speaking Out for Separation

In the conversations with participants, however, one of the motivations for speaking out was not expressed in such a benevolent frame. If one of the aspects of self-identification as an activist is a sense of urgency or a moral imperative to address those for whom the realities of marginalization are not tangible, then to be effective, sometimes we feel obliged to present the information in such a powerful way that it could bring some of the pain of it home to those privileged others. In the responses to some of the vignettes as well as in the longer interviews, participants reported that sometimes, even for educational purposes, a public self-disclosure can be motivated by a desire to make it clear that we are speaking with defiance or resistance or a refusal to be identified with the listener. These messages can be delivered with emotions that are fierce and intentional.

ELLEN: The few times that I've been in a situation as a participant when someone has wielded a story inappropriately, I have brought out the stories that will knock you right against the wall and leave a bloody trail. And I've done it on purpose. You know, "You think you know what you're saying [about us]?" I just—I mean, the aura comes out and—

LZ: You use your power.

ELLEN: I let it go. And I do it to say, "And you think that I'm the only one in here that could do this to you?"

ALMA: One of the benefits for me of self-disclosing early in most engagements is that then I don't have to listen to homophobic jokes, and I don't have to hear any slurs or bad things about certain categories or groups of people that I am a member of. And it kind of flushes out some of the goofs, right? Some of the fools. So it's an intentional thing which is sort of a pre-emptory self-defense! Early . . . so I don't have to respond later. Even if I could pass in lots of cases. And I think that is a choice that's developed over the years. . . . But it may be aggressive.

ANISE: I know that if I'm speaking to thirty [people], I know that half of the women in there have had some kind of violent sexual experience, or abusive experience in their life, and probably some of the men too, and I'm reaching out to them as well. But my intent is more on the shaking up the people in the more dominant positions, yeah, for sure.

LZ: Or do you think, that sometimes it's because you *don't* respect those people that you disclose? Do you think that somewhere there's a kind of long-term resentment of people's prejudice or something. That the desire to shake them up—

ANISE: Oh yeah!

LZ: —has a little anger in it?

ANISE: A little! [*sarcastic*] Oh God. You know, so much. No—no. Don't understate it there. Yeah, I'd completely agree with you. I'm ultimately hostile. . . .

One of the ways that disclosure is used for the benefit of those in the audience who share the marginalized or stigmatized identity is to limit the kinds of hurtful responses that may arise out of any conversation that includes such issues. If we declare our biases in the form of our positioned identity/knowledge, then we are, to some extent, determining the tone of the conversation, even if, by protecting the vulnerable others in the space, we end up by saving face for those who might otherwise expose discriminatory or ignorant attitudes in a way that they could later experience as embarrassing.

LZ: I wonder if it's a defense. . . . It's like not passing, because the passing would be uncomfortable for a different reason. Not because you feel bad that the other person doesn't understand, but that they will somehow expose themselves. It's like face-saving for the other person when you don't pass.

KATALINA: I think that's true, not that you go through all that process before you speak up every time. But I think in retrospect all those things happen.

LZ: Do you think that when you go to speak publicly and it's specifically about the issue that you're disclosing about, when you present yourself right from the beginning as a survivor, does that foreclose some kinds of conversation?

KATALINA: It might. But it's probably the kind of conversation that I don't need to be a part of.

LZ: And that's like when I say, "I don't want to hear anybody tell me that sexual abuse survivors ask for it. We're not going to speculate about that." So it limits the conversation.

KATALINA: Yeah. But then it could be replaced by focus.

In some situations, the use of a self-disclosure is a refusal of the obligation to educate, a resistance to being used for the benefit of others' self-awareness, since by allowing them to expose their ignorance, we refuse to take care of their embarrassment. Anise told a story that even more clearly described the way that we sometimes use the knowledge claim in a disclosure as a way to close down any further connection with a person who is being offensive. In her story, a man was telling a joke in her presence that involved making fun of an incident of child abuse.

ANISE: My job is not to elevate this man or to teach him anything, actually. No. And I just don't want to be around that kind of crap. And if I've got to be around a person that thinks like that, actually I'd prefer him to keep it to himself. So in that case, I turned around and I said to him, "You know, as someone who was a 5-year-old who had to [do that], I really don't appreciate that." And you know, he was mightily embarrassed and got quiet for the rest of the time. But I did it as a complete act of vengeance and to shut him up.

BETH: In this class I'm in, I still haven't come out. And it's fun, because I'm playing with it for the first time ever. I'm thinking, "Well, why should I tell them?" Let somebody put their foot in their mouth and find out later, or something, right? You know, I'm not responsible for them or, I'm not going to come out so that they can sort of edit their responses to things.

LZ: But does that lead you to think that sometimes we disclose those things to protect other people?

BETH: Yeah. And then by extension then, for ourselves, right?

LZ: Well, I know for sure that sometimes I just say it out loud so that I don't have to listen to any of that stuff. I don't care what their attitudes are, but if they're looking at me, they can't say it. So I don't have to deal with it.

Stories as Strategy

For many of the practitioners interviewed for the project, perhaps the most potent reason for using stories, whether in relation to other marginalized individuals or to more privileged listeners, is simply that telling stories "works." For some, adding the personal component is an end in itself, since it allows empathetic listeners to imagine themselves in a similar situation. For others, using our stories allows us to teach by example. For at least one person, telling stories from her own experience is a way to keep the focus of the group on the topics that she is working to teach them.

KATALINA: [I disclose] because then I get 100 percent of the attention, whereas otherwise, if I don't—I don't get 100 percent of the attention—well, okay—100 percent is probably not accurate, but much more than I would have had otherwise, and then people remember what I'm trying to say. Not so much about what happened, but other real information that I'm giving them. Because I put my examples throughout, just when they're starting to fall asleep or whatever. [*laughs*] It brings them back.

LZ: Right! But, okay, so "it works" means that your intention is pedagogy, your intention is teaching? And so you use it as a teaching tool to keep people focused

KATALINA: And for them to remember. I think the impact that I have, using my examples, is very closely related to how much retention they have. Well, that's just my guess. I can't prove it, but if they're there with me they absorb more, and therefore they retain more.

But the reason why I think that is that the people who have attended my presentations, [when I self-disclose] tend to refer me to other places and recommend me at a higher pace than [when I don't].

LZ: So that's like a market analysis? And so you wouldn't say "they like me better," you would say "they believe me better."

BETH: Well, I think that what happens is—stories are powerful in that we'll usually identify with stories. And so it personalizes the situation. I think that often I sort of felt that if I told a story, it wouldn't matter whether I disclosed it was me or not. People would walk away thinking that they now know somebody like this. Right? So, it breaks down those barriers between us and them.

. . . Especially in the 80s, nobody wanted to hear about AIDS. They didn't know why we were doing AIDS education. And if we just walked in and started talking statistics, we would've lost our whole audience. And you walk in and tell a story, and you know, well, it works!

In all these examples, the professional disclosures are intentional, their impact on listeners considered, and possible disclosure consequences for the speaker have been taken into account. In every case, the storyteller is operating as a Knower, with important and relevant information to provide, using some part of an otherwise invisible personal history in a narrative of marginalization, stigmatization, or oppression for a purpose beyond the self. How did we move from silence to this position of authority? And how has the story been changed and polished by our interactions with others along the way?

The moment the story is addressed to someone, it assumes a rhetorical dimension that is not reducible to a narrative function. It presumes that someone, and it seeks to recruit and act upon that someone. Something is being done with language when the account that I give begins: it is invariably interlocutory, ghosted, laden, persuasive, and tactical. It may well seek to communicate a truth, but it can do this, if it can, only by exercising a relational dimension of language. (Cavarero, 2000, p. 63)

CHAPTER 8

Testimony: Performing the Polished Story

RENEE: If it's a situation that she can speak about with confidence that she's not going to be hurt by the reactions of others, and it could be a persuasive story, those are some good reasons to disclose. And it would be very effective if she's saying, "This is where I was and this is where I am now!

The act of witnessing, as a performative act, unsettles established boundaries between writer and reader, (or speaker and audience), between fiction and history, between experience and ideology, even between past and future of memory and desire. The positions of speaker and audience are crucial here, and in fact testimony establishes a contract with its audience different from a literary one. The testimony demands belief (though it may not always get it), though not in the historical accuracy of its story. The testimony is not a recital of history, but it is the creation of a history through an intersubjective process in which both speaker and hearer gain their witnessing subjectivity through the new knowledge of a shared situation. Both subjectivity and knowledge are created in the testimony. Witnessing and testifying are always, in literature as much as in the legal system, performative acts, relying on complex notions of being here and being there. (Davidson, 2003, p. 165)

For a bordered helper, telling a story that is presented as "telling the truth about ourselves" is a performance. And it is more than voice. It is a willing unveiling of both vulnerability and power, a demonstration of the costs of location and positionality, and an appeal for connection. Giving an "account of ourselves" is acting out a model of moral responsibility and ethical engagement with others. It is an offering, by example, of one solution to the domination, alienation, and oppression that is such a painful part of the social world. It provides a dramatization of a hard-won epistemology: a knowledge, rare and precious, not only of how to live but also how to know—how to recognize the world and one another, in all our power and difference, and how to live, knowing. It is an appeal for, and a demonstration of, what Polkinghorne calls phronetic deliberation,[1] which "produces knowledge about practical choices by integrating background understandings, the felt meaning of a situation, imaginative scenarios, prior experiences, and perceptive awareness" (Polkinghorne, 2004, p. 116).

Telling a story of personal travel in the territories between powerlessness and voice is a responsible act of agency by an ethical subject, working to create a bridge of empathy and compassion. It is an act that reaches for the Other, at the same time that it refuses the rounding off of stereotyping and the tyranny of the norm. Using our identities in this way celebrates our separate histories as situated in a larger historical frame and stresses the importance of what is unique and particular in our diversity while holding ourselves open to connection with community. Even in the intimacy of identification, this witnessing action of particularizing our experience operates to avoid the "pathology of recognition, [where] subjectivity is conferred by those in power and on those they deem powerless and disempowered" (Oliver, 2001, p. 24). This is a face-to-face engagement, whether in a one-to-one context or a public presentation, where "the uniqueness of the other is exposed to me, but mine is also exposed to her. This does not mean that we are the same but only that we are bound to one another by what differentiates us, namely, our singularity" (Butler, 2005, p. 34).

It is in our exposure to one another that we subvert the kind of external bestowal of empowerment on the Other that depends on the definition of agency as voice, and on forms of power that sustain hegemonic blindness to difference, rendering unspeakable our knowledge of the forces of dominance and oppression. In fact, it is my belief that carrying our experience into our work in stories is a practice of the relational responsibility described by Levinas, where subjectivity "begins by bearing witness of itself to another" (Levinas, 1991). In Kelly Oliver's explication of this process of becoming,

> Bearing witness, in this context, means not only listening to the other but also telling oneself to the other. It is not the content of its testimony that solidifies the ego; rather it is the bearing witness itself, the relationship of telling oneself to the other, that solidifies the ego. (Oliver, 2001, p. 206)

Telling is therefore a demonstration of finding, and of found, subjectivity, of agency, and of responsibility. Telling identity stories is a strategy for reducing distance while recognizing difference, a commitment to holding one side of a relationship as open and hopeful, an example of a practice that Oliver calls working "Beyond Recognition." Referring to Irigaray, she describes this as

> an alternative nonhierarchical recognition that does not and cannot dominate the other . . . recognition requires two, who are not greater or lesser than each other. Yet these two are also not equivalent: their differences cannot be sublimated in a Hegelian dialectic. They cannot be substituted for each other, or reduced, one to the other. . . . (Oliver, 2001, p. 208)

> NED: If they get your jokes, the odds are they'll get some of the echoes as well, or excitement, or whatever, the mysteries. I don't feel like I have to change my language. I don't feel like I have to keep defining terms. Somebody once described me as being very fluid and very liquid and that I live assuming that other people simply hook on and get it. And these days, they either hook on and get it or they don't. And I'm very aware of it if they don't. And I don't need most of them to get it anymore, so that's fine. I can deal with whatever and share with them at that level. But it's just a feeling of—they get it! They get me. They get you. They get our jokes. I mean, they don't have to like sushi. I don't care!

> LZ: [*laughs*]

> NED: There's kind of an intuitive feeling that the space will hold between the two of us. You know, that the container is made out of the both of us, and I don't have to struggle to get in.

Witnessing—Dangerous Knowledge from Having "Been There"

> As much as anthropologists write about ritual (with its substances, formulas, gestures, acts, embodied symbols) being a partial correction of the "lies" of verbal discourse, so witnessing is a similarly indispensable "referential" activity. The witness's truth hinges on something as trivial as having been there. It is an embodied activity in that one must "see," and "hear" and "smell" what is going on to then "speak" or "write" or "weep" at what one has perceived with one's senses. It is not mere talk in a theatre of language but recounting in the context of bodily presence—having been there to being here now—and intended as a ritualized truth-telling performance. (Zulaika, 2003, p. 96)

Preparing ourselves and readying our stories for such a performance is one part of the ongoing practice of developing what emerges as an identity. Creating a stance, a position from which we make meaning, provides us not only with the tools for understanding the past but also with a framework that will determine our future choices and ethical engagements with others. Learning how to talk about our experience, how to witness to others about what we know, creates a new social role for the individual, a rhetorical identity, a position from which to communicate a new point of view.

LZ: Well, the thing about any of these experiences is that they are profoundly threatening, and some people are broken by them. And some people will never make it back, as you know. But, as the people who are not broken, we have to incorporate an unimaginable, or incommensurate experience, into a thoughtful life.

JAMES: Yes

LZ: And what if "telling" is actually the process of doing that . . . when we talk about it politically?

JAMES: It's almost like you take those aspects of life which are so difficult for society, or for ordinary people, to even admit as a possibility, right? And that's not even to engage with the reality, just to admit that there's a possibility that we could have a comfortable notion of it . . . and then you have an individual who not only has that possibility but goes into the experience as a reality— I think it does open up, for the individual that can make it out alive, new forms of effective communication.

It is in our mastery of the conventions of this kind of storytelling—no matter how much or how little detail is included—that we convert the experiences of harm or loss into a meaningful message for citizens and others. Our capacity to participate in this engagement with authenticity and heart provides an opportunity for learning, for rapprochement and resolution, on the condition that, reflected in the content of the story itself, the disclosure must reassure others that it is possible to survive, to recover, to return to life.

ALMA: If we say that part of the story is making meaning, it's like we have this life-threatening, or life-altering information—knowledge—that such things can happen, and we have to somehow fit that into a world that doesn't recognize it, whether it's victimization, stigmatization, illness, or any of those experiences. And the only way that we can sort of reenter into connection with people is to have a story about it. But the story isn't all cobbled up over here, the story is co-created. Because it's a new story, it's not even just the story that you told, it's the story that was heard, and how it was modified and modulated by the listener's understanding and her acceptance.

Recovery involves learning to tell the story in which the pain is located, recognized and acknowledged in the context of a much larger narrative of a particular life—so that it is no longer a catastrophic breach, but part of an intelligible flux. . . . The particular texture, tenor, tension and pace of the narrative, and most especially its integrative power, depends on what the narrator brings to it—lives can be made intelligible in many ways and it is the individuality of the telling that reveals a personal creative intelligence. (Froggett, 2002, p. 177)

Saying it "Well"—Rhetoric

ALMA: So we say, "Oh, I wouldn't let her out the door with that story because she's too vulnerable," or "I'd really need to know that she was safe with that story before I asked her tell it somewhere else," right? But how do we articulate the difference? Not just in the person and whether the person will say it, or say it well. But in the actual construction of the story. That the story itself has an integrity after a certain number of processes that actually allows it to survive a negative witness. And once the story has that, it can stand—and maybe the person can stand behind it.

As described by the practitioners in this study, performed or political self-disclosure by a bordered professional is consciously rhetorical. It is truly "speech designed to persuade," as defined by Cicero (Burke, 1969, p. 49). In our calls to action, in our motivation to enact both identification and separation, in our desire to have an effect or to influence our audience, our presentations of marginalized identity in these contexts share traditional criteria for a rhetorical stance. However, in these actions, we do not necessarily construct a formal argument based on some external evidence or reference for the purpose of influencing an audience to endorse some abstract policy. Instead, we are using the narrative of the construction of our identities, in the recognizable forms allowed, and from within the limits of varyingly false masks, tropes, or stereotypes; in doing so, we demonstrate by the authenticity of our passion and conviction, the basis for our authority.

> BETH: Well, I think it's practice, too. You practice telling a story—doing it once and seeing how it comes out, and learning from that. You know, having the opportunity to do that. I told stories and when I got so that it didn't matter who I was talking to, whether they were high school students or professionals—doctors, nurses or social workers—service providers—it was the stories that attracted them to become interested, and would make them less defensive.

It is in this, its performative nature as rhetoric, that the action of speaking out can be conceived of as an artistic or creative response—even as a genre with rules and conventions that allow/require us to make a distinction between silence, speaking, and speaking "well." It is also in this sense that we can be said to be offering (or performing) knowledge.

> It is the performance of testimony, not merely what is said, that makes it effective in bringing to life a repetition of an event, not the repetition of the facts of an event, or the structure of the event, but the silences and the blindness inherent in the event that, at bottom, also make eyewitness testimony impossible. . . . what makes testimony powerful is its dramatization of the impossibility of testifying to the event. What makes witnessing possible is its performance of the impossibility of testifying to the event. (Oliver, 2001, p. 86)

Obviously a large part of any attempt at knowledge production is framed as the presentation of logos: an appeal to reason in the form of a logical argument. Yet a significant part of the creativity and power of the kind of speaking out that forms our rhetorical identities is in the skill with which the speaker uses the two other forms of persuasive appeal identified in the classical liberal arts definitions of rhetoric: ethos and pathos.

> Aristotle calls these "artistic" or "intrinsic" proofs—those that could be found by means of the art of rhetoric—in contrast to "nonartistic" or "extrinsic" proofs. . . . Ethos names the persuasive appeal of one's character, especially how this character is established by means of the speech or discourse. Aristotle claimed that one needs to appear both knowledgeable about one's subject and benevolent. . . . Pathos names the appeal to emotion. Criticism of rhetoric tends to focus on the overemphasis of pathos, emotion, at the expense of logos, the message. (http://humanities.byu.edu/rhetoric/silva.htm)

The traditional use of the terminology of pathos describes both "techniques of stirring emotion . . . and for the emotions themselves . . . both the emotions the speaker feels in himself, and those he seeks to invoke in others" (Lanham, 1991, p. 111). The skillful management of this relationship in storytelling practice is illustrated in my second interview with Ellen, during which she describes the way she uses her own emotion as a part of the knowledge that she is enacting as a component of the story.

ELLEN: If I'm using a story—using a story that I have a handle on—I mean, literally, I can carry it like a plaque, what I feel is, it's almost like the hair rising on the back of my neck. The hair rises from the back of my neck and then it goes down again. So I get close to the experience that I'm talking about. But I don't relive it. I just remember it. And yes, sometimes I'm sad.

LZ: You bring the emotions of it?

ELLEN: Yes. And so I will often mimic those in the process of telling the story. But it's like opening the doorway and looking into a room, as opposed to finding myself in a room and not being able to get out.

LZ: But isn't that emotional content part of the color of the story?

ELLEN: Yes, it is. And so—I have no reluctance to do that. I have no difficulty expressing sorrow, which is usually the context. Or crying, if I've made that decision. I've got no problem feeling—anger, shame, whatever . . . mercy—whatever the emotion is, that comes from the story. But I'm not re-experiencing it as if it had happened for the first time.

LZ: Right.

ELLEN: That kind of numbness . . . and so when I use that notion of opening the door, I open the door so that I can reflect the emotion.

LZ: But also so that the listeners can feel it.

ELLEN: Yes. Yes.

LZ: Because you can make it safe for the whole room to feel it, when you can hold it?

ELLEN: That's right. And that's where I believe my great strength and skill is. It's that I can—that I am able to hold it, to bear it.

In another second interview, as part of a conversation about the actual mechanics of the practice of public self-disclosure, Katalina explains something about our measurement of our own success in these terms. In her description of what it takes to do this kind of presentation—what she calls "energy"—she identifies two of the important costs for rhetorical performers: first, the ongoing daily price of the effort involved in bringing oneself to the situation with enough presence to do the performance, and then the additional price we may pay in emotional currency, if we feel we that we have failed in our efforts to move the audience.

> KATALINA: There are times when I'm just not on—I don't have enough energy. See that's another thing. It's not so much about disclosure, but when I do my presentations, if I know that the audience includes a lot of people who have had similar experiences, one of the things I try to do is that I try to raise the amount of energy in the room by the time I end. And it takes a lot of my energy to do that. And I can't really tell you exactly this is Step #1 and Step #2. I just strive for that, and I can only tell if it works or if it doesn't work. So a couple of weeks ago when I was very tired, I couldn't do it. I knew that it was a room full of people like that. And because there was such a big number too, instead of the usual number that I would talk to, I just couldn't raise it. And when I tried and I couldn't, it made me feel even worse. . . . Afterwards I kept sighing, because I was so tired and because I couldn't do it.

It is exactly this kind of ineffable raising the energy of a group that the transformative function of rhetorical performance depends upon. Being moved in this way is being changed, not simply as an effect of artistry but being changed with a liberatory intention. It is our hope, in these engagements, that being changed is being moved to do something about the problem we are describing. It is our loss, if the performance is reduced to simple spectacle. Kenneth Burke makes a distinction between the related arts of poetry and rhetoric: "between persuasion to feel, and persuasion to do, between attitude and act. An antislavery poem leads us to commiserate with slaves; an antislavery rhetoric leads us to free them" (quoted in Lanham, 1991, p. 132).

Further, Burke connects "form" and "acts" as components of rhetoric and, using Aristotle's definitions of tragedy as a way to talk about rhetoric as drama, he makes a case for "how close the realms of knowledge and action are . . . a closeness also suggested in the expressions "knowledge of" and "knowledge how" (Burke, 2001, p. 36):

> Aristotle observes that the word "drama" was derived from a word meaning "to do." . . . the Dramatistic grammar in general gets to knowledge by a dialectical route whereby a character, having acted, suffers the consequences of his act and thereby learns from his sufferings (with the audience poignantly participating in the disclosures). (Burke, 2001, p. 36)

It is this engagement of the audience, their "poignant participation," that the energy in the room reflects. I believe that it is the artistry in our selection of details, and our management of the conventions and language available for ritual truth-telling, as well as the emotional truth of the presentation, that make a disclosure a "good telling."

> There is an interpersonal dimension—a "call and response" exchange—to the telling of an arousing story. The art of storytelling is based not merely on the chronicling a sequence of facts but in the artful juxtaposition of dramatic elements. The power of the story to stir others, to communicate shared tribulations and victorious moments, depends on its felt truth and plausibility rather than on its mere facticity. (Haakon, 1999, p. 23)

However, for the felt truth of a story to be accepted as grounds for validity, the teller must be seen in a particular context. A contemporary interest in storytelling in pedagogical situations has led many to attempt to theorize the use of narrative as an educational tool. An understanding of the complexity of this practice is illustrated in a comment by Ellen, an experienced educator and storyteller. Her experience with the formal conventions of Elder storytelling in aboriginal communities has led her to believe in the power of stories, both positive and negative.

> ELLEN: And I've learned through the stories all elders tell in aboriginal communities. I've watched elders tell stories, and I just think, "Anybody who thinks this is a manageable tool for teaching—It's plain that you're in real trouble!" So I think this is my epistemology. It's my identity. I think all of those things are together. And for me they are an imperative to do well. Because this isn't neutral—teaching isn't neutral.

A "good telling" illustrates Aristotle's description of a story, "the imitation of an action that is serious, complete, and of a certain magnitude" (Turner, 1981, p. 149). In such a story, the beginning, the middle, and the satisfactory end—embodied in the physical presence of a storyteller who relates her own (past) experience—provide the listener with a dramatic form, as a way of teaching the "knowledge how." But it is actually in the performance itself, in the telling, that the central meaning of the story is found, that the "knowledge of" is conveyed. This is why the story must be told over and over, in person, by someone who "was there":

> the kind of "learning" that goes with an audience's engrossed participation in the successive disclosures of a plot may be more directly explainable as a sympathetic delight in the perfect unfolding of a form, with its "natural" order of attitudes, somewhat as though we were to call it a matter of "learning" when we watch with delight a motion picture that shows the gradual bursting of a blossom, thereby enabling us as onlookers to unfold with it. We do unquestionably 'discover' things, when contemplating such a series of

"disclosures"; but there is also the satisfaction of the development as such, of graduated movements in which we "empathically" participate. (Burke, 2001, p. 38)

It is also in telling "well" that, if we are successful, we create/enact the ethos that supports the story, that establishes the credibility of the speaker; it illustrates the persuasive appeal of one's character, based on the believability of the identity delivered in the telling. We introduce ourselves first, as direct Knowers, and then prove that identity in the course of the story, not only by how well we know the specifics of it but also by how well we read and respond to the needs and tolerance of the audience.

> Aristotle claimed that one needs to appear both knowledgeable about one's subject and benevolent. Cicero said that in classical oratory the initial portion of a speech (its exordium or introduction) was the place to establish one's credibility with the audience. (http://humanities.byu.edu/rhetoric/silva.htm)
>
> LZ: So once again, if the measure of that story is the impact, is the measure of the authenticity based in whether or not somebody buys it?
>
> ELLEN: I don't think so. I think the authenticity comes from the person's own—my owned experience.
>
> LZ: And presence in the story.
>
> ELLEN: Yeah. I can tell a good story badly, and it's still effective. I just— sometimes the way it'll come out, I'll think, "Well, that wasn't very elegant or effective or using more teaching language and rhetoric language, but it's done exactly what I hoped it would do. Because it's had the desired effect." So there is a studied quality too—but I think it's retroactively studied.

We need to prepare both the story and ourselves for this ritual performance in order to establish our believability, our ethos. This preparation is an intentional action arising from the double consciousness of a bordered location. It involves doing our own translation, and providing the expert commentary to our own authenticity, by presenting the knowledge / information in a form which proves our familiarity with both the realities of the margin and the requirements of the dominant listener. We prepare a rhetorical space for ourselves, in the form of an identifiable persona, in a process that Gloria Anzaldúa calls "making face":

> Marginalized rhetors rarely can speak out of their authentic experiences in the dominant culture; to be credible in that culture, they must present falsehoods and "make faces" that are appropriate for and adjusted to those in control. Ethos, then, involves a splitting and compartmentalizing of the self, constructing a mask to accommodate the dominant culture, and hiding one's true face behind that mask. *Haciendo caras* [making face] is Anzaldúa's shorthand description for developing credibility. It involves constructing an appropriate face but also contains other possibilities for facework—making a

face, making one's own face, or constructing one's own agency. (Foss et al., 1999, p. 22)

ANISE: Sometimes, self-disclosing, you actually in fact overwhelm your audience. You overwhelm them to the point where they can't hear you. And that can happen in so many ways. You can overshadow their story. You can overshadow the story they've gotten going on in their mind.

You have to assume, unless they've indicated otherwise, that the listener cannot bear to hear the pain. And that is often true. Like people can watch all kinds of murder and mayhem on the television, but you tell them a story of true pain and suffering, and they actually can't handle it. They don't want to hear. And so sometimes you can see, if you go too far with your story, people just glaze over and they just—they're overwhelmed by it.

It is during this task of translation that the speaker pays another significant price for the privilege of telling the truth about herself. If we go too far, the opportunity to be heard is lost, but if we find a story that can be heard, then we are simultaneously aware of how much of our experience of the margin is missing from the account. In a study of the positioning of tellers of traumatic events as "self-defining memories," researchers Avril Thorne and Kate McLean identified three "positions" or emotional stances that were used in the telling narratives of a group of college students. These were described as: "I was tough"; "I was concerned for others"; or "I was vulnerable" (Thorne and McLean, 2003, p. 175). Their findings appear to be consistent with Aristotle's need for rhetoric to display both knowledge and benevolence, and also with the experience of the participants in my study, in that, to be heard, the content of a telling must be framed or positioned in a way that does not place a burden on the listener.

> Vulnerable narratives were more often rejected than accepted by listeners, who preferred vulnerability to be interlaced with concern for others, or to be dismissed altogether in lieu of an action-packed plot. Tough and empathetic positions seemed to place less burden on listeners because the teller seemed to have resolved the crisis more successfully. Some communities seem to recognize the burden of vulnerability and have developed specialized agents, such as priests and psychotherapists, to handle it. (Thorne and McLean, 2003, p. 183)

Those of us who are the specialists, who in our professional roles handle every day the burden of hearing or witnessing others, must understand the difference between telling "Vulnerability" and telling as the Knower. To speak as a Knower is to choose how far to go, and that choice consigns some parts of the story to the unspeakable. We need to recognize the difference between this choice and secrets (in our own stories, and in those of others) if we want to contribute to creating conditions for safe disclosure within the structures of speaking out for social change.

In storytelling, then, while asking ourselves what we can know and not know is important in terms of listening to others and then deciding how to act in a particular situation, I think there is a more basic task at hand. This is the task of calling into question knowledge and being of both the teller and the listener, and struggling for ways to take this out of abstraction and into political action. (Razack, 1993, p. 118)

So What Is the Story?

There's godlike

And warlike

And strong

    Like only some show

And there's madlike

And sadlike

And had

    Like we know

(Testimony, © Ferron, Nemesis Publishing)

It is part of our knowledge as bordered speakers, that we need to have done our own work before we can take our stories into these arenas. In this light, having done our work means that we are positioned as people who do not need anything from the audience for ourselves. Our benevolence is established with our agency, proved by the way we tell for a broader purpose.

> JAMES: So, I sort of started with my friends, and it was a very selective telling, and then it basically just developed into almost a professional sort of thing where I could say, "Yes, I have a mental illness, and, and sure, occasionally it affects me, but you know, it's my life, and it's really nothing to dwell on."
>
> LZ: Right. So it's just a part of your identity
>
> JAMES: It is a part of my identity. And as such, I feel like I need to be clear that it is, with some people—not everybody. At the same time, there are times in my professional life where it's come up, and I feel it's important . . . for people to know. But then that also leads into a whole other thing, which is, trying to be political about it.

One of the ways this is demonstrated, over and over again, is in the trajectory of the tellable story, the form that allows us to relate what we can of the statable truth. We are always already perceived as safe, if we are in a position of telling. We are back from whatever scary or shameful place we have been visiting, or we would not be here to talk about it. A successful story, then, must reflect our present safety. If we get caught in the middle without an analysis, without a resolution, without an end to the tension of the story, we are no longer speaking as a Knower. If we need to be saved, it will be the responsibility of the interlocutor to help us—if not in need of immediate rescue, we will at the very least need to be translated, or to be empowered from the outside.

> ALMA: If she loses it, if she does a disclosure that ends up looking pathetic, because she doesn't have enough self-control, or because she hasn't thought it through enough, then not only the people who have ideas about what is adequate behavior and all that, are going to categorize her, but so are the people she's trying to represent. Her ability to hold herself in some stance that actually allows her some dignity will be the thing that makes a difference for whether or not it's successful.

I therefore believe that many of our stories not only assume a presently safe position for the speaker, as well as serving as a guarantee of the speaker's benevolence toward the listener, but also, at least in spirit, provide a narrative convention or shape that I will call the "Amazing Grace Trajectory." In the successful performance of a Dangerous Knowledge story, such a plot unfolds as follows:

I once was lost (Abject: outside, unacceptable)

> I was down (helpless, victimized—it was not my fault), or

> I was bad (I couldn't make decisions, or I made bad ones)

Then I found

> God

> A therapist

> An education

> A community

> Love

> Myself

> Meaning

Any or all of the above in any order

Now I'm found (powerful, speaking, valid, trustworthy: a Subject in good standing)

LZ: So when you speak, you speak from that position of having moved on, and using the experience as authority. Is it the experience of victimization or the experience of survival that you use as authority?

ANNE: Hmm . . . . I guess that that makes me very thoughtful, because I think that sometimes that victimization stuff is—although I've obviously never felt everything that everybody else [has], . . . but there have been times in my life where I've been completely without power, and—where I can relate on so many levels to what somebody is going through. And I think sometimes we can go there with people and that can be really helpful. I think our job, as therapists or counselors or nurses or whatever, wherever our work is, is to help people move to the journey to survivorship. I think some people do it really quickly. And others get really stuck in victimization. And I think that it can sometimes be helpful to talk about being stuck. And, in terms of sharing my own experiences, that it was many years before I got to the point where I could acknowledge or talk about what had happened, because I was so deeply ashamed of me. And I'm not anymore.

LZ: And that's part of what you mean by stuck?

ANNE: That's right! And I'm not any more. I'm just not.

It is in this form that "what we know" can be communicated, that we can position ourselves as full participants in the commonality of regimes of meaning, as having subjectivity, competence and important information to share. As in singing with a choir, each of us brings our singular voice to the harmony of a familiar refrain, contributing to an ever-new rendition of a powerful expression of agency, survival, and hope. The use of these stories as re-enactments, I believe, represents the kind of ritual process described by Kenneth Burke as "dramas of living," or by Victor Turner as the "social drama":

> Although it may be argued that the social drama is a story. . . in that it has discernible inaugural, transitional, and terminal motifs, that is, a beginning, a middle, and an end, my observations convince me that it is, indeed, a spontaneous unit of social process and a fact of everyone's experience in every human society . . . [and] can be aptly studied as having four phases. These I label breach, crisis, redress, and either reintegration or recognition of schism. (Turner, 1981, p. 145)

In the same way that the participants in this study understand their disclosure stories as counterhegemonic challenges or political actions, Turner suggests that "social dramas are in large measure political processes, that is, they involve competition for scarce ends—power, dignity, prestige, honor, purity . . ." (1981, p. 149) and that when a member of a given society wishes to use these processes "to provoke a breach or to claim that some party has crucially disturbed the placid social order, they have a frame available to 'inaugurate' a social drama, with a repertoire of 'transitional' and 'ending' motifs to continue the framing process and channel the subsequent agonistic developments" (Turner, 1981, p. 149). What if what we consider to be activist speaking out is a response to a social breach in his sense? That a report of oppression, marginalization, or stigmatization is a demand from the margin for social repair, not simply for an individual, or a particular group, but for the community as a whole, both citizens and Others?

If this analogy holds, then the requirement for ethos—the need for speakers to represent themselves/ourselves as high-status enough to be heard—follows another logic. And the trajectory of the story also has a more significant importance, not just for the speaker, who needs to be heard, but for the hearers—the community that needs rapprochement and recovery. Is it possible that by operating as performances of a kind of ritual of accountability to community, our stories first identify and then reconcile the breaches, the strains, the differences that only the marginal can name? If there is a social benefit to this practice, could it be that the repetition of the telling, like theater, provides an opportunity for the move to connection that we all desire, if only for the moment of the performance? And perhaps even if we are unsuccessful in "raising the energy," in achieving even momentary "reintegration," we have still accomplished an important function for the larger group, if we have, as Turner suggested, provided a "recognition of the schism" that requires social change.

> The realization of the narrative is the precondition of an emancipatory impulse. For stigmatized groups who have been in receipt of much negative projection it allows for retrieval of past humiliations and response under conditions which make them amenable to reworking. (Froggett, 2002, p. 175)
>
> LZ: It's also how you carry yourself in the world. And so teaching is a role that you use in order to do this rhetoric. Right?
>
> ELLEN: Yes. That's right.
>
> LZ: And it's a mission! It's not just meaning-making for myself. Right? *It is* the meaning.
>
> ELLEN: Yeah. And I think the word mission is an important one. Because I do know I have a mission. We all do. Everybody does. Nothing that we do in the world is neutral. You know, our interactions with people in the parking lot is—you know, all of those things have consequences. All of those things have rhetorical consequences. All of those things have possibilities for the good as well as possibilities for the bad. So I don't worry about the word "mission" any more than I worry about all those other words.

It is precisely in order to support the creation of social conditions that can make past humiliations amenable to change that the story has to be told in a way that guarantees the status of both the speaking individual and the group represented by identification. For Turner, that means that the "actors" in such social dramas, like the aboriginal Elder story-tellers that Ellen knows, are members of what he calls a "star group"[2]:

> The political aspect of social dramas is dominated by star groupers; they are the main protagonists, the leaders of factions, the defenders of the faith, the revolutionary vanguard, the arch-reformers. They are the ones who develop to an art the rhetoric of persuasion and influence, who know how and when to apply pressure and force, and who are most sensitive to the factors of legitimacy. (Turner, 1981, p. 148)
>
> JAMES: I think maybe what you got at when we talked about the experiences that are so incommensurate to ordinary experience—it seems like we're bringing something from outside the social fold, into the realms of society. And that's bound to make people uncomfortable, because (a) they don't want to think about it, and (b) they don't want to deal with it.

LZ: But, then, people do it all the time, right?

JAMES: People *do* do it all the time.

If we are responding to a social need that is more universal when we create a breach by complaining or identifying an injustice in a personal story, we are carrying a flag that requires us to legitimize, in our own experience, our right to complain, to speak for others. When we are successful at "healing" the breach, creating coherence, rapprochement or even the momentary recovery of a sense of community, we do it at the cost of speaking through a mask, enacting a predetermined resolution that we may not always feel. What if speaking out is not a new revolutionary activism but one that has always existed in a shape as old as art, with new terminologies, new specifics, and the same old risks to the person creating an awareness of the breach— back on the knife-edge of the apparent choice between "playing" the Victim or "playing" the Hero? No matter how much we know about the process, it is a risk that many must be willing to take, in order to have an effect, in order to participate in social change.

> LZ: I think that actually understanding that it's one of the risks of power— that the more powerful you are rhetorically, the more likely you are to have someone misread or be affected in some way that you couldn't predict. And in the end, we still choose the power, right? Not only for ourselves, but for the people who can use it. But it's part of the price, isn't it?
>
> ELLEN: I think so. To me, the alternative is to be ineffective. And I would rather be effective, which has negative and positive connotations. I would rather be effective. I would prefer—I choose to be effective. Does that mean that sometimes I'm effective in ways I don't anticipate or wish for? Yes. My task is to reduce the number of times that happens.

What "We" Know

> ELLEN: A really tightly knit, no edges, polished, not really the "true" story.
>
> There is not, outside of human discourse itself, a level of social facticity that can guarantee the truth of this or that representation, given that the facts of memory are not essences prior to representation, but rather themselves a consequence of struggles to represent and over representation. . . . even the memory of the past is conjunctural, relative, perishable. Testimonio is both an art and a strategy of subaltern memory. (Beverley, 1999, p. 79)

Subaltern memory produces the Dangerous Knowledge that we carry in our stories. It is the absolute, embodied knowledge that terrible things can happen with no reason, no warning, no recourse. That in spite of all our actuarial metaphysics—all our careful research, our endless striving for an accurate calculation of risk factors and the possible rewards of available "lifestyle choices"—people can be struck down by disease or accident

or natural disaster in a moment. Humans, both adults and children, can
be abused, maimed or killed in war, or at home, by family members, by
strangers, because of their skin color, body shape, or religious identification,
or by some simple, unexpected, easy act of random violence that changes
everything. Adults can give up—can passively watch while their own lives
and those around them are destroyed by social upheaval, violence, addiction,
helplessness, and mental illness. People can die of sadness and the despair
engendered by oppression.

But is this the knowledge that bordered professionals are willing to
endanger our professional credibility trying to impart? Is the narrative only
a reiteration of the painful facts of injustice, violence, and vulnerability, the
evidence that proves that the world is not safe?

> Speech addressed to the other, not sinful speech but the speech of faith, is
> pain; this is what locates the act of true communication, the act of avowal,
> within the register of persecution and victimization. Communication brings
> my most intimate subjectivity into being for the other; and this act of judgment
> and supreme freedom, if it authenticates me, also delivers me over to death.
> (Kristeva, 1982, p. 129)

As professionals who are also survivors of the fact that the world is
not safe, we carry in our bodies, in our lives at work and at home, the
knowledge of illness, of injustice, of racism, of homophobia and oppression,
of humanity compromised, and violence intended, but we STILL LIVE.
"We," speaking, are the evidence that it is possible to live, to contribute, and
to speak, no matter what trauma, what stigma, what discrimination we have
been subjected to. But first, we are the proof that the pain is real. It is this
knowing that we speak out about; this subjectivity, this model of survival that
we disclose as professionals, showing that it is possible to have been marked
as Abject, and still BE credible, "professional," valued for our expertise and
experience. It is the process of developing an account for ourselves, polishing
the story of how we got here from there, that requires us to articulate our
understanding of causality, power, and difference, sharing an epistemology
in the form of a narrative, in which "actively revealing oneself to others . . .
grants a plural space and therefore a political space to identity" (Cavarero,
2000, p. 22).

> ALMA: But even that, as a decision about how to live, involves the act of
> self-disclosure. It involves doubt. It involves pain. You know, it involves not
> knowing. But it's a kind of knowing. It's knowing how to live without knowing
> for sure. It's knowing how to live without certainty.
>   I mean, if you think about what we model, we don't just model that you
> were hurt and now you're fine. . . . That's not it! We could get X rays for that.
> [*laughs*] What we're modeling is an on-going day-to-day, "how do you live
> knowing this?"

Telling stories when we know that we could be discredited or not believed—whether they are stories of marginalization, victimization, or stigmatization; stories that illustrate our knowledge that the world is not safe; stories that demonstrate the knowledge that comes from moving out of a personal experience of powerlessness: all of these are articulations of epistemology. But they are not just stories about how dangerous the world is. These stories offer a hard-won "knowledge how," about how we live, knowing how dangerous the world is. And we tell these stories, even in a single word, as a way to go back to those experiences ourselves, in order to answer the question: "How does anyone do that?" Because our experiences mitigate the kind of certainty that comes with privilege, what we construct along with this epistemology is not a solid, unchanging, seamless identity but a practice of accountability and recognition. We build practice as a way to answer our own question of why we practice the way we do. We need the answer not just for the practice of our professional lives but for our practice in the world, in our lives as ethical subjects.

> ANISE: We're also participating in creating a coherence—not just in our own stories, but . . . a coherence within the larger world.

But this claim to the knowledge of how to survive is meaningful only in so far that we describe BOTH our sadness and our strength as parts of a *collective knowledge,* collectively available to those we work to support. For "bordered" professionals, whether we disclose or not, helping others like us, or like we used to be, is a part of that practice. It is, in fact, a way of carrying our stories as a Performance of Dangerous Knowledge. Self-disclosure is only the most obvious demonstration of it. The disclosure itself: the polished story, the one sentence, or simply the use of "we" instead of "I"—is more like a guide for how to live in this space, KNOWING and acting with responsibility to both sides of the bordered space between the dominant and the subordinate, between voice and silence.

> ELLEN: It's making explicit to other people, for our collective benefit, things that I know about myself. It's making explicit the pieces that are usually invisible or implicit. . . . Because this isn't just—you're not living in a vacuum. So when you make a statement with the authority of personal experience, you're talking about possibilities in human behavior, possibilities in humans' minds. And human knowing. If these experiences that I've had can lead to my knowing better, then—and I can show you how I did that—then this may help you to figure some things out, too.

The ritual performance of a life on the border has served a further purpose if it has encouraged the expectation that a professional should work toward some kind of empathetic identification across the boundary of helper/helped. The belief that the development of empathy for others is a necessary component and even a specific pedagogical goal of professional training for work with vulnerable people was expressed directly by at least one educator in the study.

> ANISE: So it's intriguing to think of it as a map for how to dwell in those spaces, because I actually think that people that identify as being firmly embedded in a particular, dichotomized category, ought to live in the spaces as well. Because I think that's where empathy is developed and created for one another.
>
> So the question is how do you move people—for me, for teaching people in a helping profession—how do you move people into those more empathetic places?

Validity, Coherence, and "Truth"

It is in the context of challenges to the truth of the story, that any speaker is vulnerable to the threat of a return to the Abject. Interrogations of the logos, the facts of the story, can invalidate both the ethos and the pathos of a rhetorical stance as well. In this kind of critique or academic debate (Lather, 2000; Roman, 2003; Stoll, 1999), Nobel prize-winner Rigoberta Menchu's believability and even her status as a "native informant" can be challenged by the assertion that she did not actually "see" her brother's death in the way it was reported in her edited account of the oppression of Indigenous communities in Guatemala (Burgos-Debray, 1984). More recently, this critique has taken the form of an extremely public controversy over the necessity for texts represented as nonfiction to be seen as truth. In the clearest example of this, James Frey has been widely characterized as the man who "conned" Oprah,[3] on the basis of a challenge to his book about alcohol recovery (Frey, 2003), after he was discovered to have embellished his story and "lied" about his experience in jail. In an ironic response to such critique, Ryan Knighton begins *Cockeyed*, his memoir of becoming blind as a young man, with this preface:

> This book is a work of memoir. All people, places, events, and neuroses are representations of the facts. That includes encounters with dead philosophers. Should a reader determine that the author is not disabled, please contact the appropriate authorities. He would gladly delete his blindness from any further memoirs. (Knighton, 2006)

If we divide the Dangerous Knowledge story into the components suggested in the Amazing Grace Trajectory, these are forensic challenges to the "I once was lost" part of the story: How lost were you? How bad was it? How many drugs did you take? How many chimneys "really" blew up in the concentration camp? (Felman and Laub, 1992). Even if the original assertions contained in the story are accepted at face value, the following questions return to challenge the credibility of the speaker: Why didn't you tell (Kennedy and Grainger, 2006)? Why didn't you fight back? Why didn't you run away? In this critical thinking paradigm, it follows that if you can't answer those questions adequately (that is, to the questioner's satisfaction), then the original claim cannot be "true."

Challenges to the middle section of the story, the "I found . . . ", are somewhat less personally threatening, although we are always at risk for being seen as naive or foolish for believing in whatever has given us hope. These challenges take the form of questioning the structures or the credibility of the saving grace, sometimes by appeals to science or common sense, but always with an assumption of the listener's superior knowledge of the real world. This can be offered benevolently, as support, as clarification, or even as empowerment, by relieving us of false consciousness (or dependency) by the power of the normative version of the way it is. This is one of the dangers of the demands for testifying, for producing a testimonial, in that the point of the story is to valorize the found element, the grace that saved us. Our claim of knowledge, in this form, rests on the truth of this external body—if it can be found to be untrustworthy, we have been duped again.

> ALMA: You could tell a story of surviving which is actually the piece that we don't usually say out loud, which is, "When I disclose, I don't disclose what happened to me, I disclose what I did about it." . . . Nobody needs to know what happened to me, but people hear what I've done to live. Right? So that's the part of the story that's valuable. And what happened to me is not valuable to anybody. So when someone speaks about this, part of what happened to her is still there like a sign on her door. But what she did about it is also absolutely present. She learned everything she could learn.

The ending of the story, the "now I'm found," may be the most vulnerable part of the interaction, the one that requires the most preparation and the most carefully constructed performance mask. It is the challenge to this part of the story that holds the greatest potential for us to be lost again, and it is here that the temptations of the Heroic are the most seductive. Because, in fact, it is in the truly convincing performance of "foundness," of social membership as a normal person, that we can invalidate the first, or even the second, section of the story. Either what we say happened (who we were) is true, and so we are wounded and different in some important way that makes us unreliable, or who we are now is true, and so we must have been this powerful all along; we could never have been silenced. If that is the case, why are we saying this? What is our (suspect) motivation for telling this story? Once again, we can be discredited, paradoxically, by virtue of our powerful presence; made incoherent, Abject and unintelligible by telling from a powerful position. However, if our performance falters, and we lose it, we are not truly "found," and then what we say happened may be true, but it doesn't help.

Why do we use story as the form for telling about what happens in life and
in our own lives? Why not images, or lists of dates and places and the names
and qualities of our friends and enemies? Why this seemingly innate addiction
to story? Beware an easy answer! Even etymology warns that "to narrate"
derives from both "telling" (narrare) and "knowing in some particular way"
(gnarus)—the two tangled beyond sorting. (Bruner, 2002, p. 27)

What this representation problem demands from speakers is coherence,
not just at the level of the story as a logical narrative but also in the way the
story meets the limitations and the expectations of the audience to which
it is addressed. Speaking from the audience, from the "we" that sets up
the necessity for dangerous knowledge to be presented as coherent, Judith
Butler asserts that WE prefer the story—even though it may be the lack of
coherence that is the mark of the authentic "truth of a person":

If we require that someone be able to tell in story form the reasons why his
or her life has taken the path it has, that is, to be a coherent autobiographer,
we may be preferring the seamlessness of the story to something we might
tentatively call the truth of the person, a truth that, to a certain degree, for
reasons we have already suggested, might well become more clear in moments
of interruption, stoppage, open-endedness—in enigmatic articulations that
cannot easily be translated into narrative form. (Butler, 2005, p. 64)

This does not presume a particularly agonistic relationship with the
citizens for whom such reports are news. But this is the place where the
rubber of the epistemology hits the road. The position of Knower implied in
the intelligent critique that we so value is one based on a particular kind of
logos: knowledge that by definition excludes differences in knowledge and
ways of knowing. This is taken for granted, even within a paradigm that is
intended to be empowering. In fact, it seems to me that it is our awareness
of these gaps or flaws in epistemology that provides the motivation for an
empowerment commitment to rediscover silenced lives and supports the
ideology of speaking out as pedagogy. Is there another way to think about
this? As a direct challenge to some of the foundational assumptions of this
conception of knowledge, Linda Martin Alcoff states that she is "arguing
for the potential of coherentist epistemologies" (Alcoff, 1996, p. 11),
specifically, the potential for these systems to account for or explain "the
way in which beliefs are justified"—or *how* we know. Significantly, for her
description of "Coherentism," it is also important to take into account the
effects of prior beliefs on *what* we can know:

On a coherentist view experience and evidence are recognized as beliefs,
not self-presenting phenomenological states whose meaning is transparent
. . . coherentism starts with a knower who always already has a great many
beliefs, and thus is always already "in the world." Coherentism further
recognizes that these prior beliefs interpret and inform every experience the

knower has. This makes it easier for coherentism to shift from an individualist account of knowing to a collectivist account—a shift long overdue in Western epistemologies—because coherentism posits the knower as always already committed to a variety of beliefs based on the testimony of others. (Alcoff, 1996, p. 10)

In this paradigm, it is relevant to the experience of the subaltern speaker that she is operating in a collective, historical context, where what she knows comes up against what everybody knows. Her need to be believed is greater than the need to prove the exact truth of the facts of her account, although it may, indeed, depend on it. But if we take seriously the implications of the Coherentist view, then the stakes for the listener, too, are very high. If, in order to believe the speaker, the audience or witness must endanger other, personal, precious and long-standing beliefs about the world, or even about individuals in our own communities or our own families, then along with the speaker, the listeners share the risk of a significant loss. If, as the speaker, my testimony constitutes a significant and believable countertestimony, I am asking my audience to be responsible to the ways in which they contribute to the construction, not only of my ethical subjectivity but of truth itself. This is asking a lot.

> If truth is not a representation of the intrinsic features of reality, if it is rather the product of an interaction between reality and human beings, then truth, and not merely justified belief, can be thought of as historical. We need not relinquish our intuition that truth is beyond our subjective control, but we must relinquish the idea that truth is something wholly other to us, intrinsic or inherent to a reality where our input has been erased or discarded. Truth is historically relative, on this view, without being irrational, subjectivist, or ideological. (Alcoff, 1996, p. 229)

So what is Dangerous, about Dangerous Knowledge in this form? It is not necessarily the specific information provided in any of the three sections of the self-disclosure story—beginning, middle, end. It is not even that there may be things we don't understand, or can't imagine. It is not that there are many of them (Others) invisible among us, although that is threatening in itself. What if these simple descriptions of the unthinkable, presented coherently and with authority, open up the beginnings of an ethical, moral questioning about the truths we have grown up with? What if they hold us responsible for self-consciousness, for the double-consciousness of the constructedness of Truth? What if we are responsible for deciding, not discovering, the real?

> Coherentism traditionally holds that beliefs are justified by other beliefs, which means that a correspondence relation between beliefs and an extradiscursive, transcendent reality is not required for knowledge. The experience and empirical evidence that play a determining role in the confirmation of many

beliefs can be acknowledged as themselves the product (at least in part) of interpretation and theoretical commitments. (Alcoff, 1996, p. 10)

If we are to take this seriously we are required to see the speaker, and ourselves, as contributing, in a larger sense, to the coherence of our communities, to the creation of meaning for ourselves and one another. In these stories we are asked, even implored, by ethical subjects to respond as moral agents. We are called on to engage with the problems of pain and power in the world with thoughtfulness and integrity, with our strongest, most courageous, response-ability.

> The intertwining of selves and stories in narrative constructions which locate what is at stake, what is needed, and what is possible is at the heart of moral thinking for many women and feminist writers. The understanding of such stories requires many forms of intelligence; all are at work in the competent moral agent, on this view. (Walker, 1992, p. 168)

The Practice of Ethical Subjectivity

It is with this understanding of the practice of telling the truth about ourselves that I assert that these professional performances are ritual political actions that demonstrate the lived epistemology, the moral philosophy of a group of people who, in their daily responsibility to Others, are working out solutions to ethical and philosophical problems in concrete terms.

> A moral philosophy is a particular rhetoric, sustained and deployed by certain groups of people in certain places; its apparent form may belie its real application and meaning. . . . There are alternatives to the abstract, authoritarian, impersonal, universalist view of moral consciousness. The picture of direct mutual response and responsibility is not a whole ethics, but it is one way of rotating the axis of our investigation around the fixed point of our real need. (Walker, 1992, p. 172)

Using ourselves and our experience in the form of a meaningful narrative changes our struggles for coherence and accountability themselves into the details of the story. As in a traveler's tale, in the tellable, hearable, self-disclosure story the turns and interruptions of a journey out of pain and silence must be presented in a kind of order that allows suffering to be seen to contribute to a reassuring final outcome: a safe homecoming. This reiteration provides reassurance not only for the listener but also for the performer.

> ALMA: Whenever I'm doing this with a group of people, or even one person—because that's what I do all day—whenever this happens, and they go there and they come back, it happens for me too. I get back every time. I get stronger about not being there every time I tell it.

Conclusions/Closing: The Portrait of a Practice

"The portraitist, like the artist, is constructing and communicating her understanding for the reconstruction and reinterpretation of the reader" (Davis, 2003, p. 214). Beginning with my interest in ideas of marginality and "border work," and based on a conception of the border as a space of connection, intersection and inclusion, this project was developed and enacted at every stage as a crossing of various boundaries. In my conversations with individuals who play out their professional roles in several different contexts, and furthered by my reading across many different academic disciplines, the action of boundary-crossing finally culminated in my decision to use the frames and conventions of an arts-based form in order to represent the data developed in the research.

This resulting portrait of our shared work is first offered to other Performers of Dangerous Knowledge who may see themselves in it, with the hope that some part of the picture may ring true to them, but my imagined audience for this work is also made up of people from the many different personal and professional locations where such performances are witnessed. It includes those professionals who work to support the vulnerable: the educators, social workers, health practitioners, and community activists engaged in front line relationships where individual stories may form an important part of communication. However, I also believe that "the act of witnessing begins in a personal raid on the inarticulate and creates a chain of witnesses each of whom receives this newly wrought history, charged with the affect which compels its retelling" (Davidson, 2003, p. 166). Therefore, I am hoping that it could also include those people at a management or policy level who are involved in the funding, support, and supervision of service delivery programs, as well as those working toward the expansion of the theoretical understanding of bordered spaces and Subaltern speech.

In this representation, I have worked to illustrate some of the knowledge of the practitioners who were generous enough to speak with me: something about memory and learning, language and silence, resilience and recovery; something about connections made across the boundaries of experience and location, across a diversity of competencies and orientations, of interests and preoccupations. Some of the language I have used for this portrait is dramatic, or emotional, in the same way that performances of this kind of voice are fueled by passion and pathos. This language, or tone, provides the color saturation for the portrait, it reflects the subject matter and opens up the image to new meanings: "In such testimony the unspeakable is spoken in such a way that the affective clings to the speaking, so that what is given is an ethical and ultimately political imperative toward understanding not just the past, but also the future" (Davidson, 2003, pp. 165/166). This project is, itself, a disclosure for me, a story of discovering, or rediscovering, a community and a commitment to myself and others "like me, or like I used to be."

The emotional appeal of this story is an intentional call for this or any audience to listen to the kinds of stories that constitute speaking out with care and respect for both the vulnerability and the strength of the Other. The urgency in this call is founded on the constructionist (coherentist) understanding that the quality of listening presence can co-create "truth" or "believability," not necessarily for a specific account or testimony, but for the speaker. In asking readers to be responsible for the ways they believe or hear this kind of speech, I am hoping to encourage them to think of these stories in a new way, starting with recognition of their content as a form of dangerous knowledge. I am characterizing it as dangerous for the individual but also for those who bear witness, because what it lets us know is not that by the telling it will never happen again but that by the hearing we must truly accept that there are bad or sad things happening in the world. I am describing it as knowledge because believing that such things happen affects our relationship to everything else we believe or know.

A reconceptualization of disclosure as a practice supported by an epistemology that frames telling and hearing as a kind of relational knowing could change helping practice for both bordered and nonbordered professionals. I can imagine the example of an educator working to address a social justice agenda, who may expect a difficult discussion to lead to the kinds of self-disclosure that Ellsworth (1994), Razack (1993), or Srivastava and Francis (2006) all find troubling. These accounts of similar situations may be useful to her, even to the extent that she could decide to make it safe to *not* disclose; she may decide that limiting or ultimately stopping a student disclosure could be the most ethical thing for her to do in that moment. Or perhaps, by taking into account some of the responses to the vignettes in this study, thinking about the potential consequences for a speaker who is presented as an example of victim voice could make a difference to the ways that fundraising organizations might choose to represent their marginalized client base.

What is offered in this portrait is an ethical approach to considering and witnessing disclosure. The practitioners represented here are suggesting that, as listeners to any given example of this kind of speech, we ask ourselves about what would constitute the conditions for a safe disclosure. Both speakers and listeners are here encouraged to ask themselves, in any circumstance where a disclosure might be called for: "Is this another situation in which speakers will be seen as powerless, tragic, Abject, Other, simply because they are vulnerable? Will they see themselves this way? Have we asked them to expose some part of their experience that they have until now chosen to keep private?" If this effort is truly continuing the conversation about this kind of speech, then it is also an invitation to contribute further to the dialogue, in theory or in person.

In this study, as in my practice, I have operated from the belief that the bordered, the marginalized, even the subaltern, have a right to privacy and enough power to choose it, if only by silence. But for this study I have also explicitly taken the position that we have no reason to be ashamed of the fact that we are constructed in relationship and that we do not need to keep secret the way the negative or patronizing "gaze" of dominant others affects us. In this form I am once again, speaking out: I am breaking the silence about the costs of breaking the silence, but not because I expect myself, or anyone else, to stop this practice, to stop telling about the effects of domination and oppression in individual terms. In fact, it is because I know that this is an important practice, that many more individuals and communities will learn it and perform it in our continuing commitment to social change, and that I think we all need to understand as much as we can about its risks and responsibilities, its ethical and epistemological ground.

Methodological Framing

Different individuals bring different backgrounds and understandings that have an impact on what they see, hear, and make sense of in any setting. . . . On a very basic level, voice is what makes individual researchers see what they see and include or leave out what they choose to in a portrait. Voice necessarily affects observation, understanding, and reportage. Beyond

individual perspectives, however, [researchers] need a set of foundations
and constraints with which responsibly to focus their ultimately indelible
individual voices. (Davis, 2003, p. 206)

For this portrait of a practice, the set of foundations and constraints was,
in fact, almost entirely constructed by my original choice to study something
so close to my own work. My desire to bring to light some of the complexity
and expertise involved in the apparently simple practice of speaking out from
a bordered professional location led me to ask specific questions of a unique
group of people, to direct the research interviews with them in a particular
way, and to make very personal choices for my use of the recorded materials
that we created together. The result of these choices has been the production
of a very particular kind of text.

Once I decided to gather voices as a way to create the outline of this
portrait, I needed to determine the focus of my research interviews. Was
this a description of a certain kind of disclosure? Should it be limited to
people who have shared a similar painful experience, in order to allow me
to generalize about the possible consequences of a disclosure of sexual
victimization, or bullying, or ethnic discrimination? I decided that for this
project it was important for me to concentrate on the act of speaking out
itself and not on whatever content might be revealed in such an action.
This decision widened the field of possible informants, allowing me to cross
some of the boundaries of academic discipline and professional practice and
to talk with people whose life experiences have been very different from my
own. This same decision, however, created what I saw as a need for some
important constraints for the conversations themselves.

I then chose to narrow the frame even further and to focus on some
of the particularities of this practice, including "the price people pay to
tell the truth about themselves." From the beginning of the process, my
concern was that a conversation with me about the negative experience
of "Disclosure Consequences" could itself hold the potential for painful
feelings for the participants. This led me to impose two important
constraints on my interviews: first, that I would seek out people who
identified themselves as already having had a more or less public experience
of speaking out as a part of a successful helping practice; and second, that
I would need to find a structure that would limit our conversations to the
practice of speaking out in order to reduce the potential for the recording
of the actual contents of such disclosures. Both of these constraints
contributed to my choice of the vignette methodology for the interviews
in the first stage, and influenced my construction of the scenarios.
In particular, this consideration informed my choice to use the kinds
of hypothetical professional situations that perhaps only an experienced
bordered practitioner might have encountered, as a way to identify the
ethical and practical deliberation required of people like them, as they

choose how and when to use the personal authority that accompanies the authenticity of "having been there."

The use of vignette methodology gave the "portrait" some background, filling in some of the texture of the preoccupations and considerations of those professionals who inhabit "bordered" spaces. The structuring of responses as "hypothetical" allowed me to speculate, along with these expert practitioners, about some of the external conditions that could influence a particular helping relationship and to imagine the internal processes that might affect decision making in any given situation in which self-disclosure may be an option for a helper. The scenarios engaged the participants in an examination of the reflexivity of helpers who, like them, construct ethical connections for a purpose, positioning them as mentors to others who may be less experienced in the practice. It also provided them with the opportunity to declare their political investments in relation to the people that they serve, demonstrating in practical terms their compassion for, and commitment to, social justice for vulnerable others. These exercises also documented their awareness that some vulnerable people may also be engaged in professional work, that "they" can be "us."

For the second stage interviews, the need for speaking in hypothetical terms was dropped, but my commitment to limit disclosure was maintained. The people who met with me for the second time, therefore, spoke at length about their own experiences of disclosure; managing, as a rule, to avoid any direct reference to the content of those disclosures. It was in the process of negotiating this in conversation that I began thinking of the actions involved in self-disclosure explicitly as practice. These extended interviews were, in many cases, deeply personal discussions in which we explored ideas of identity, purpose, and meaning; sharing much laughter and some tears. This part of the study produced some of the most beautiful articulations of the bordered self, exposing the caring and respect for others, as well as the critical power and determined resistance of these eloquent and resilient individuals. Along with many important moments of connection and understanding in the initial interviews, this series of conversations provided me, personally, with a profound sense of meaning and membership and left me with a renewed sense of pride in and commitment to our shared work in social justice. These conversations strengthened my voice.

However, the constraints I imposed on the content of our talks have also resulted in certain absences in the data. There are no detailed individual accounts of the terrible feelings of abjection, since, for this project, no one I spoke with was currently suffering, either from the extreme deprivations of marginalization, stigmatization, or oppression or from any recent humiliating disclosure of their experience of such things. Therefore, any description of the Abject is abstracted and moved into distancing language, but not because I think that these things are all in the past for any of us. For this portrait I made a choice and created a process that would support that choice, in the way that we can sometimes choose to *almost* not listen to the voices reporting a war we know about, on a television that has been turned down in another room. This choice, of course, has had implications for what is represented. Acting either as a speaker or as a researcher, my refusal to provide an individual report of violence or suffering requires the audience to understand and take for granted that "such things happen" in the world. This is a portrait created against a social backdrop of separations and "borders," where war, exploitation, abuse, racism, homophobia, poverty, and illness are assumed without question to endure, as present pains, in the lives of many individuals and groups.

In the introduction to this work, I presented three stories as references: reports of suicide, desperation, and the pain of abjection. I made the assertion that these accounts could be understood as examples of the existence of an emotional economy that I called "Disclosure Consequences." This hypothesis is not supported in the study by any first-person story of individual suffering—which does not mean that there were no stories that these participants could have told, but it has created an intentional absence. Because of my choice of this strategy of silence, support for my original hypothesis must come from other evidence in the material. To understand the connection between "speaking out" and the stories of abjection that opened this conversation, therefore, the reader must look to the ways these expert practitioners have learned to keep themselves safe in the practice of self-disclosure and to the strategies they have employed for preventing or reducing the doubt and despair that can result from "speaking in the wrong voice at the wrong time." The participants in this study have provided ample evidence of this dynamic in the descriptions of their efforts to avoid it—in the importance of the risk assessment before entering possible situations for "speaking out" and in the protective measures that we learn to take, for ourselves and for others.

The precautionary voices in this conversation have offered warnings and expert suggestions to those who wish to use this tool for the empowerment of themselves and others. They have articulated the dangers of a "runaway story," for both tellers and hearers, while emphasizing the need for a speaker to have the control over content or details that comes from the preparation of the "polished story." They have spoken against certain kinds of coercion and certain uses of the witnessing story as testimonial, while encouraging the speaker to be aware of her need for ongoing control over the contexts that her story will enter, and they have offered many suggestions for working to ensure the conditions for safe disclosure.

The Practice of "Telling"

How can talking about stories be a portrait of a practice? Portraiture is an attempt to communicate, whether in words or by a visual image. If the portrait actually communicates something about the artist's response to the subject, the content of the representation still must hold some recognizable relationship to what observers might agree could be the subject. In a picture of a person, there must be a nose somewhat like other noses. How unique can a nose be? How particular an eye? In a portrait of a practice, some characteristics must be recognizable as pertaining to practices in general. It must be a type of "thing" that can be described to others. So, like a portrait of an individual who may be shorter than some, and taller than others like her, a practice can be seen as existing on a continuum of practices, rough or refined, casual or formal. In both these cases, the relative height or refinement is illustrated by elements in the background, but the implications of this comparison can be understood only by reference to the environment in which the recognizable differences can be identified.

Any given practice is a series of actions taken in particular contexts, for specific reasons, and the skills required are developed and transferred in certain ways. Any given practice involves a process of study and repetition that incrementally increases the practitioner's competence in performing the gestures, the stances, and the manipulation of materials that define the practice. For the practice of "telling," of Performing Dangerous Knowledge, the materials are our selves, our experiences, and our relationships with those who witness our knowing. This is a practice that creates and sustains both connection and identity—"It is in and through practice that many of our human potentia are realized, potentials whose realization are themselves indispensable to the subsequent emergence of those higher strata, the individual with strict personal identity, who is also a social Agent and Actor" (Archer, 2000, p. 190). Language is the observable "stuff" that makes up the material that is manipulated, but this practice is beyond language.

This particular practice uses the vulnerability of a precarious social location to illustrate itself. The use of a singular voice to speak of an experience outside of normal imagining is a demonstration of the moral of the story it tells, and the content of this kind of story is itself a report of developing the practice of using "voice." The practice of "telling" is an action, a tool to use in teaching about using voice in this way. It is an action that people undertake, but the subject of this portrait is not a person, any more than it is a report of an individual experience of the pains of marginalization or subalternity. Rather, this is an attempt to portray an invisible move in a series of movements that make up an intentional and meaningful practice. Spivak refers to the difficulty of separating the practice from the person in terms that recognize some of the ways that this move is rendered "unseeable":

> Quite often what happens is also that the remarkable organic intellectuals who become spokespersons for subalternity are taken as token subalterns. This reception is a feature of our desire to fixate on individuals. The effort

involved in those singular figures becoming organic intellectuals is completely
undone in their positioning as "the" subaltern. . . . The effort required for the
subaltern to enter into organic intellectuality is ignored by our desire to have
our cake and eat it too: that we can continue to be as we are, and yet be in
touch with the speaking subaltern. (Spivak, 1996, p. 292)

One way to acknowledge this effort is to see the actions of these
"singular figures" as part of an ongoing practice. For example, we can be
given a still portrait of a particular dance, an image that allows us to feel the
artistry or *duende*[1] ("spirit") recognizable as flamenco, or to read the grace
of a dancer en point as ballet, without making it possible to identify the
individual dancer. These are portraits of one aspect of the practice of dance.
What remains unseen and unrepresented, and what can be only implied
from a knowledgeable reading of the image, are the years of preparation, the
physical effort, the injuries, the pain, and the determination of the dancer
who has endured to arrive at the perfect moment of the performance where
the image is captured.

These elements make up another picture of the practice that is seen, or
needs to be seen, by a developing dancer, or by the teacher (or parent, or
supporter, or lover) of a dancer. These costs and commitments are a part of
the performance, but rendered invisible in the moment of performance—and
the more skillful the performer, the more invisible they are. In "practice"
portraits of the dancer, however, some of the power and the beauty of that
effort, even of the pain of inevitable injury, illustrate and dignify the back-
stage hours and weeks that make possible a moment of powerful performance.
It is this picture, the description of the costs and pains of the practice of
"speaking out," that is the subject of this particular practice portrait.

Telling Matters

The content of this portrait is the first-hand knowledge of committed and
experienced practitioners, providing the kinds of description and advice
available only to someone familiar with the back-stage world behind a
particular kind of performance of "bordered self." Profound articulations
of ethical deliberation, of compassionate care for others, and pragmatic
solutions to relational struggles are represented here in the words of these
remarkable people. Their shared experience of the preparation of the story
for presentation and their clear communication about the ongoing need
for risk assessment and control for the performance of the "polished story"
were a welcome, if unexpected, validation of my own experience as a "teller."
Their unanimous and heartfelt demand for careful "listening" to such stories
was, however, precisely what I had anticipated from them, and it provided
an eloquent illustration of the integrity, empathy, and identification with
which they engage the Others who depend on their help.

In many of these conversations, we spoke about the conditions that might cause some people to fall into the worst of the "Disclosure Consequences" as I described them, to find themselves reliving their pain, or reinscribed into an Abject position. The hurt persons described in these discussions were not judged harshly or blamed for their own suffering. In fact, several respondents explicitly stated that feeling this pain would not be evidence that a person should not be acting in a helping role. Rather, these helpers were characterized as "needing support" or "needing to work it out," the latter phrase perhaps meaning that they needed more control in polishing the story or in managing the context of speaking in order to protect themselves. "Telling well" was not represented as a competitive endeavor but measured partly by how much impact the story had on its particular audience and partly by how intact the teller might feel after telling. I read the absence of this critical judgment as evidence of recognition that, as truly bordered, no matter how "practiced" or how "professional" we are, we live precariously close to the vulnerability we allude to in our stories. The participants' attention to risk as a way of deciding when or whether to speak about our knowledge of a world beyond the norm, implies a shared awareness of a very real and continuing danger for any who work on the margins and illustrates an enduring sense of solidarity and responsibility to each other.

Following this thread of solidarity in my analysis of the material led to the construction of theoretical explanations for the uses of "first-person plural" as a description of bordered subjectivity in these accounts. Although I had not directly addressed this in conversations with the informants as an issue of language, I found many examples of their use of "we" in descriptions of actions or intentions. I also discovered in the data several practice-oriented suggestions for this use of an inclusive pronoun as a kind of shorthand to safely communicate membership without the details of a narrative. I am intrigued with the implications of this for some kind of future study. It would be very interesting to engage a wider sample of bordered speakers in an examination of this kind of language in particular, as a way to understand more about the kinds of temporary or intentional definitions of community that are created in just this way. Would the ideology of empowerment be a factor here? Could a study determine if this tendency (or rhetorical strategy) is limited to "social drama" situations, or if it is used more generally, perhaps even by individuals who see themselves as always already in the mainstream? I am also interested in a deeper theoretical investigation into "voice" and individual subjectivity, but that also is work for another time, some other project.

The Product of the Practice: Subjectivity

A compelling part of my agenda was, and is, a desire to represent this practice as grounded in, as supporting, or even as constructing the powerful ethical subjectivity of those who act in this way. Once again, in relation to this agenda, my choices have affected the outcome. My first step in this direction was to examine what I believed to be the founding epistemology of "speaking out": the ideology of empowerment. My own reservations and my critiques of this ideology threatened to flood the background of the portrait with a color that could have affected not only my ongoing identity as a helper but also my self-perception as a researcher, and might have profoundly changed my relationship to the subjects and the subject matter of the study. At the end of that exploratory process, however, I was able to come to terms with some of the limitations of the ideology and to recommit to a shared belief in the relevance of "bordered" participation in social justice activism for what may be called "empowerment," even if the individual action does not always end with the experience of any liberation, or even any measurable success. This allowed me to engage with the informants with an assumption of shared goals and expectations and to analyze the material after the fact without critiquing the basic motivations of those who spoke with me.

Making this choice also left another kind of absence in the data. I did not involve anyone in a process of challenging her own political commitments. The only critique of empowerment in the text is presented in my own words, and once again, except for my own expressions of trepidation, it is abstract and theoretical. This does not assume for a moment that any of those people who spoke with me could not address an eloquent challenge to the ideology, and it would be an interesting project to engage these same people on those issues, but that would be a very different study from this one. In this case, by choosing not to shake the ground under the practice, I was able to observe and record some of the ways that moral reasoning and practical, ethical decisions can follow from committed "empowerment" positions on social justice.

One of the ways that we can seek to describe a practice is perhaps by deciding on a measure that could evaluate its value in application. One question may be this: "Does it meet its declared goal?" If that is a relevant question in this case, then how can we conceive of the goal or the intent for the political practice of "speaking out"? What does this practice work to produce? In the language of empowerment, the "voice" of the subaltern produces, or constitutes, a kind of power that can contribute to social change. In this study, both the responses to the vignettes and the longer conversations provided ample evidence that this ideology not only supports the practice of "speaking out" but also becomes a central theme in the choice of "stories" that can be seen to be constructive or politically justified. In the end, what this practice produces is a valid "speaker," a "Knower," or even the "organic intellectual" that Spivak refers to. Learning the practice, "speaking out" with intention, creates the Activist and encourages the development of activism in others. It supports and sustains respect for diversity and the recognition of agency in the vulnerable members of a community. Speaking from the border opens up, for those who live in the dominant, a view across, but it also provides those who live as Other a map of the space between— how we get here from there.

The Product of the Practice: The Story of Change

This portrait of the practice of "speaking out" rests on a solid ground of reverence for the most important product of the many unseeable stages or processes involved in the preparation for "telling." This product is the story itself. In the story of "how I got here from there," the expressions of pain and power, of hopelessness and courage; of our struggles with the decision to live and our singular choices about how to live, are all recorded in the multiple forms of human narrative: in art, music, dance, and drama; in words spoken, performed, and written down for permanence. These stories are precious, not only to those who make or co-create them, like those "tellers," helpers, and activists who agreed to be held still for a moment in the making of this portrait, but also to us all. These particular stories help all of us to understand ourselves, they give us the courage to face the unbearable, and they allow us to hope for change.

> The border between abjection and the sacred, between desire and knowledge, between death and society, can be faced squarely, uttered without sham innocence or modest self-effacement, providing one sees in it an incident of man's particularity as mortal and speaking. "There is an abject" is henceforth stated as, "I am abject, that is, mortal and speaking." Incompleteness and dependency on the Other, . . . allow [us] only to make [our] dramatic splitting transmittable . . . Our eyes can remain open provided we recognize ourselves as always already altered by the symbolic—by language. (Kristeva, 1982, p. 88)

For me, one of the most important findings of this project is the articulation of how important to the teller is the story of "being there, and being here." I believe that it is, in fact, the preciousness of the story (as the product of this practice) that makes us sometimes unexpectedly vulnerable to the negative experiences that make up "Disclosure Consequences," because this kind of story lives only in the relational spaces between teller and hearer. If this kind of story describes and enacts a strategy for connection, for community, for change in the conditions of dominance and violence, if its performance by a present "Knower" allows us to believe in those possibilities, then its power relies on the creation of a "we"—the reunion between "us" and "them" that is accomplished in witnessing.

It is in the fragility of holding Kristeva's "mortal and speaking" position as "knowledge" that we maintain a precarious balance, the loss of which has the consequence of abjection. When the story is not heard or misheard; when its meanings are distorted, used against us, or turned back on us, we are altered in our own perception, sometimes beyond tolerance or resilience. If, speaking, we are pushed back to the subaltern, translated, re-inscribed, then the precious story is not lost, but it can't be "true." If we are Subaltern, we are not heard; if we are not heard, we are Subaltern, Abject. But if our stories of Dangerous Knowledge can be heard or witnessed as one dance in a multitude of dances, as one movement in a practice of self and responsibility, then we are, to ourselves and one another, made visible as ethical subjects, participants in a changing social world. In this kind of witnessing, both speakers and hearers contribute to the creation and maintenance of connection and inclusion, of empowerment and meaning-making, enabling us to live, knowing, in a world where such things happen.

The project has not directly recorded any stories that are themselves examples of "speaking out." It is presented with the expectation that any audience it might find will be familiar with at least some of the conventions of such storytelling and the hope that they may perhaps recognize the outlines described here in future efforts to witness others, and that some of the information in this portrait will contribute to a wider conversation on the meanings and significance of "speaking out." It is, in itself, a story, told to encourage a reconsideration of bordered spaces and a reimagining of the act of witnessing as a context where the openness of allowing for the singular subjectivity of the Other is different from learning a skill for eliciting a "full" disclosure, different even from developing techniques for listening to one.

This portrait of a practice is an appeal for respect—respect for the risks of taking the position of "teller" and respect for the story itself. It is directed not just to the potential listener/witness but also to those who may be asked, or who may choose, to "speak out," to use their story for a purpose outside themselves. As speakers, we need to give ourselves credit for having both good judgment and benevolence, for knowing how to decide when and how and how much to say. As people who encourage this kind of speech, we need to honor the strength and the decisions of the speaker. We need to identify and value the teller's focused action of connecting to the audience and the sensitivity involved in the continual monitoring that works to maintain the connection across the inevitable line created by difference. This project is a request to take this powerful practice seriously, because any expression of marginalized "voice" carries a potential for both positive and negative consequences. For the construction or continuation of community identity, and for the very life of the "bordered" speaker, some of these consequences have been, and will continue to be, world-changing.

Notes

Chapter 1

1. Lyotardian Paralogy/Neopragmatic Validity, as described in Lather, 1994, Fertile obsession: Validity after poststructuralism, *Power and Method: Political Activism and Educational Research,* A. D. Gitlin (ed.). New York, London: Routledge, p. 43: a "model of legitimation [where the] goal is to foster differences and let contradictions remain in tension. . . . "Rather than evoking a world we already seem to know (verisimilitude) in a story offered as transparent, the move is toward 'attempts to create indeterminate space for the enactment of human imagination'" (Lubiano, 1991, Shuckin' off the African-American native other: What's Pomo got to do with it? *Cultural Critique* 18, p. 177). "Paralogy legitimates via fostering heterogeneity, refusing closure." It entails "knowledge of language games as such and the decision to assume responsibility for their rules and effects" (Lyotard, 1984, *The Postmodern Condition: A Report on Knowledge.* Minneapolis, University of Minnesota Press, p. 66).

Chapter 8

1. Polkinghorne argues for recognition for a more experience-based (or practitioner-judgment based) practice in "care" fields. He outlines the technification of "evidence-based," research-driven responses to the

limits of service and health-care funding, and he looks at practice and practice theory, using Aristotle and Gadamer: "Unlike theoria, the purpose of which was to produce knowledge about the realm of the unchanging, techne and phronesis are types of practical reasoning used to produce practical knowledge about carrying out activity in the realm of the changing. Techne is the reasoning used in making or producing (poiesis) things and art. Phronesis is the reasoning used to deliberate about good actions (praxis)."

reasoning	activities	outcomes
Techni—planning how to make something (reproduction)	Poiesis—producing, making	Artifacts
Phronesis—deliberating on activities for the Good	Praxis—acting, doing the Good (in a particular situation)	Good Action

(Polkinghorne, 2004, p. 114)

2. The people Turner calls "star-groupers" are described as those who are important to the group in a particular way: "Social dramas occur within groups of persons who share values and interests and who have a real or alleged common history. The main actors are persons for whom the group has a high value priority. Most of us have what I call our 'star' group or groups to which we owe our deepest loyalty and whose fate is for us the deepest personal concern. It is the one with which the person identifies most deeply and in which he finds fulfillment of his major social and personal desires" (Turner, 1981, Social dramas and stories about them, *On Narrative*, W. J. T. Mitchell (ed.). Chicago and London, University of Chicago Press, p. 145).

3. References to the James Frey/Oprah controversy can be found on the web at www.thesmokinggun.com/archive/0104061jamesfrey1.html.

Chapter 9

1. Federico Garcia Lorca, in a famous lecture on *La Teoria y Juego del Duende* "(The Theory and Function of Duende)": "All through Andalusia . . . people speak constantly of *duende* and recognize it with unfailing instinct when it appears. The wonderful flamenco singer El Lebrijano said: 'When I sing with *duende*, no one can equal me.' . . . Manuel Torres, a man with more culture in his veins than anybody I have known, when listening to Falla play his own 'Nocturno del Genaralife,'

made his splendid pronouncement: 'All that has dark sounds has *duende*.' And there is no greater truth. These dark sounds are the mystery, the roots thrusting into the fertile loam known to all of us, ignored by all of us, but from which we get what is real in art. Thus *duende* is a power and not a behavior, it is a struggle and not a concept. I have heard an old master guitarist say: '*Duende* is not in the throat; *duende* surges up from the soles of the feet.' Which means it is not a matter of ability but of real live form; of blood; of ancient culture; of creative action" (www. duendedrama.com/duendees.htm).

References

Abu-Lughod, L. 1993. *Writing Women's Worlds: Bedouin Stories*. Berkeley and Los Angeles, University of California Press.

Adorno, T. W. 1985. Commitment. *The Essential Frankfurt School Reader*, A. Arato and E. Gebhardt (eds.). New York, Continuum.

Ahmed, S., and J. Stacey. 2001. Testimonial cultures: An introduction, *Cultural Values* 5(1): 1–6.

Alcoff, L. 1991. The problem of speaking for others, *Cultured Critique*, L. Alcoff (ed.). New York: Telos Press, 5–32.

——. 1996. *Real Knowing: New Versions of the Coherence Theory*. Ithaca, NY: Cornell University Press.

——. 2000. Who's afraid of identity politics? *Reclaiming Identity: Realist Theory and the Predicament of Postmodernism*, P. M. L. Moya and M. R. Hames-Garcia (eds.). Berkeley and Los Angeles: University of California Press, 312–344.

Alcoff, L., and L. Gray. 1993. Survivor discourse: Transgression or recuperation? *Signs* 18(2): 260–290.

Allison, D. 1994. *Skin: Talking about Sex, Class, and Literature*. Ithaca, NY: Firebrand.

——. 1995. *Two or Three Things I know for Sure*. New York: Plume/Penguin.

Alvesson, M., and K. Skoldberg. 2000. *Reflexive Methodology: New Vistas for Qualitative Research*. Thousand Oaks, CA: Sage Publications.

Anderson, K., and D. C. Jack. 1991. Learning to listen: Interview techniques and analyses, *Women's Words: The Feminist Practice of Oral History*, S. B. Gluck and D. Patai (eds.). London: Routledge, 11–26.

Anzaldúa, G. E. 1987. *Borderlands/La Frontera*. San Francisco: Spinsters/Aunt Lute.

Archer, M. S. 2000. *Being Human: The Problem of Agency*. Cambridge: University of Cambridge.

Baistow, K. 1994/1995. Liberation and regulation: Some paradoxes of empowerment, *Critical Social Policy* 14(3): 34–46.

Benmayor, R. 1991. Testimony, action research, and empowerment: Puerto Rican women and popular education. *Women's Words: The Feminist Practice of Oral History*, S. B. Gluck and D. Patai (eds.). London: Routledge, 159–174.

Berlant, L. 2001a. The subject of true feeling: Pain, privacy, and politics. *Feminist Consequences: Theory for the New Century*, E. Bronfen and M. Kavka (eds.). New York: Columbia University Press, 126–160.

——. 2001b. Trauma and ineloquence, *Cultural Values* 5(1): 41–58.

Bernstein, M. A. 1992. *Bitter Carnival: Ressentiment and the Abject Hero*. Princeton, NJ: Princeton University Press.

Beverley, J. 1992. The margin at the center: On testimonio (testimonial narrative), *De/Colonizing the Subject: The Politics of Gender in Women's Autobiography*, S. Smith and J. Watson (eds.). Minneapolis: University of Minnesota Press.

——. 1999. *Subalternity and Representation: Arguments in Cultural Theory*. Durham. NC: Duke University Press.

——. 2004. *Testimonio: On the Politics of Truth*. Minneapolis: University of Minnesota Press.

Bickford, S. 1996. *The Dissonance of Democracy: Listening, Conflict, and Citizenship*. Ithaca, NY: Cornell University Press.

Borland, K. 1991. "That's Not What I Said": Interpretive conflict in oral narrative research, *Women's Words: The Feminist Practice of Oral History*, S. B. Gluck and D. Patai (eds.). London: Routledge, 63–76.

Braidotti, R. 1998. Sexual difference theory, *A Companion to Feminist Philosophy*, A. M. Jaggar and I. M. Young (eds.). Malden: Blackwell Publishers, 298–306.

Brookfield, S. 1983. *Adult Learners, Adult Education and the Community*. New York: Teachers College Press.

Brown, L. S. 1994. *Subversive Dialogues: Theory in Feminist Therapy*. New York: Basic Books.

Bruner, J. 2002. *Making Stories: Law, Literature, Life*. Cambridge, MA: Harvard University Press.

Budick, S., and W. Iser (eds.). 1989. *Languages of the Unsayable: The Play of Negativity in Literature and Literary Theory*. New York: Columbia University Press.

Bugental, J. F. T. 1992. *The Art of the Psychotherapist: How to Develop the Skills That Take Psychotherapy Beyond Science*. New York: W.W. Norton.

Burgos-Debray, E. (ed.). 1984. *I, Rigoberta Menchu: An Indian Woman in Guatemala*. London: Verso.

Burke, K. 1969. *A Rhetoric of Motives*. Berkeley and Los Angeles, University of California Press.

Burke, K. 2001. Watchful of hermetics, to be strong in hermeneutics: Selections from "Poetics, Dramatically Considered," *Unending Conversations: New Writings by and about Kenneth Burke*, G. Henderson and D. C. Williams (eds.). Carbondale: Southern Illinois University Press, 35–80.

Butler, J. 1993. *Bodies That Matter: On the Discursive Limits of "Sex"*. New York, London: Routledge.

——. 1997a. *Excitable Speech: A Politics of the Performative*. London: Routledge.

Butler, J. 1997b. *The Psychic Life of Power: Theories in Subjection.* Stanford, CA: Stanford University Press.

———. 2005. *Giving an Account of Oneself.* New York: Fordham University Press.

Butterwick, S. 2002. Your story/my story/our story: Performing interpretation in participatory theatre, *Alberta Journal of Educational Research* XLVIII(3): 240–253.

Campbell, S. 1997. Women, "false" memory, and personal identity, *Hypatia* 12(2): 51–82.

Cavarero, A. 2000. *Relating Narratives: Storytelling and Selfhood.* London: Routledge.

Chanfrault-Duchet, M.-F. 1991. Narrative structures, social models, and symbolic representation in the life story, *Women's Words: The Feminist Practice of Oral History,* S. B. Gluck and D. Patai (eds.). London: Routledge, 77–92.

Chaudhry, L. N. 1997. Researching "My People," researching myself: Fragments of a reflexive tale, *Qualitative Studies in Education* 10: 441–453.

Clair, R. P. 1998. *Organizing Silence: A World of Possibilities.* Albany: State University of New York Press.

Code, L. 1995. *Rhetorical Spaces: Essays on Gendered Locations.* London: Routledge.

Cohen, S. 2001. *States of Denial: Knowing about Atrocities and Suffering.* Cambridge: Polity Press.

Cohler, B. J., and P. L. Hammack. 2006. Making a gay identity: Life story and the construction of a coherent self. Identity and Story: Creating Self in Narrative. D. P. McAdams, R. Josselson, and A. Lieblich (eds.). Washington, D.C.: American Psychological Association, 151–172.

Cottle, T. J. 2002. On narratives and the sense of self, *Qualitative Inquiry* 8(5): 535–549.

Cruikshank, J. A. 1994. The will to empower, *Socialist Review* 23(4): 29–55.

Daly, B. 2004. When the daughter tells her story: Rhetorical challenges of disclosing father-daughter incest, *Survivor Rhetoric: Negotiations and Narrativity in Abused Women's Language,* C. Shearer-Cremean and C. L. Winkelman (eds.). Toronto: University of Toronto Press, 139–165.

Davidson, H. 2003. Poetry, witness, feminism. *Witness and Memory: The Discourse of Trauma,* A. Douglass and T. A. Vogler (eds.). London: Routledge, 153–172.

Davis, J. H. 2003. Balancing the whole: Portraiture as methodology, *Qualitative Research in Psychology: Expanding Perspectives in Methodology and Design,* P. M. Camic, J. E. Rhodes, and L. Yardley (eds.). Washington, D.C.: American Psychological Association, 199–217.

Delbridge, R., P. Turnbull, et al. 1996. Pushing back the frontiers: Management control and work intensification under JIT/TQM management regimes, *New Technology, Work, and Employment* 11(2): 97–106.

Denzin, N. K. 2000. The practices and politics of interpretation, *The Handbook of Qualitative Research,* N. K. Denzin and Y. S. Lincoln (eds.). Thousand Oaks, CA: Sage Publications, 897–922.

———. 2001. The reflexive interview and a performative social science, *Qualitative Research* 1(1): 23–46.

Deshler, D., and D. Selener. 1991. Transformative research: In search of a definition, *Convergence* 24(3): 9–22.

Douglass, A. 2003. The Menchu effect: Strategic lies and approximate truths in texts of witness, *Witness & Memory: The Discourse of Trauma*, A. Douglass and T. A. Vogler (eds.). London: Routledge, 55–84.

Du Bois, W. E. B. 1903. *The Souls of Black Folk*. Chicago: A.C. McLurg.

Egan, J. 2001. Insider out: An activist's journey from grassroots to academe, 31st Annual Standing Conference on University Teaching and Research in the Education of Adults, SCUTREA, City of London, United Kingdom, July 2001, 99–102.

Ellsworth, E. 1992. Why doesn't this feel empowering? Working through the repressive myths of critical pedagogy, *Feminisms and Critical Pedagogy*, C. Luke and J. Gore (eds.). London, Routledge, 90–119.

——. 1994. Representation, self-representation, and the meanings of difference, *Inside/Out: Contemporary Critical Perspectives in Education*, R. A. Martusewicz and W. M. Reynolds (eds.). New York: St. Martin's Press.

——. 1997. *Teaching Positions: Difference, Pedagogy, and the Power of Address*. New York: Teachers College Press.

Fallot, R. D., and M. Harris. 2002. The trauma recovery and empowerment model (TREM): Conceptual and practical issues in a group intervention for women, *Community Mental Health Journal* 38(6): 475–485.

Fanon, F. 1967. *Black Skin, White Masks*. New York: Grove Press.

Felman, S., and D. Laub. 1992. *Testimony: Crises of Witnessing in Literature, Psychoanalysis, and History*. London: Routledge.

Finch, J. 1987. Research note: The vignette technique in survey research, *Sociology* 21(1): 105–114.

Fine, M. 1994a. Working the hyphens: Reinventing self and other in qualitative research, *Handbook of Qualitative Research*, N. K. Denzin and Y. S. Lincoln (eds.). Thousand Oaks, CA: Sage Publications, 70–82.

——. 1994b. Dis-tance and other stances: Negotiations of power inside feminist research, *Power and Method*, A. D. Gitlin (ed.). London: Routledge, 13–35.

Fine, M., L. Weis, et al. 2000. For whom? Qualitative research, representations, and social responsibilities, *Handbook of Qualitative Research*, N. K. Denzin and Y. S. Lincoln (eds.). Thousand Oaks, CA: Sage Publications, 107–132.

Foss, K. A., S. K. Foss, et al. 1999. *Feminist Rhetorical Theories*. Thousand Oaks, CA: Sage Publications.

Foucault, M. 1977. *Language, Counter-Memory, Practice*. Ithaca, NY: Cornell University Press.

——. 1982. The subject and power, *Michel Foucault: Beyond Structuralism and Hermeneutics*, H. Dreyfus and P. Rabinow (eds.). Brighton: Harvester.

——. 1990. *The History of Sexuality: An Introduction*, Vol. 1. New York: Vintage Books.

Fraser, N. 1989. *Unruly Practices: Power, Discourse and Gender in Contemporary Social Theory*. Minneapolis: University of Minnesota Press.

Fredriksson, L., and K. Eriksson. 2003. The ethics of the caring conversation, *Nursing Ethics* 10(2): 138–148.

Freire, P. 1999. *Pedagogy of the Oppressed*. New York: Continuum.

Frey, J. 2003. *A Million Little Pieces*. New York, Doubleday.

Fritzman, J. M. 1990. Lyotard's parology and Rorty's pluralism: Their differences and pedagogical implications, *Educational Theory* 40(3): 371–380.

REFERENCES   197

Froggett, L. 2002. *Love, Hate, and Welfare: Psychosocial Approaches to Policy and Practice*. Bristol: The Policy Press.

Furrow, D. 2005. *Ethics: Key Concepts in Philosophy*. New York: Continuum.

Gardner, G. 2001. Unreliable memories and other contingencies: Problems with biographical knowledge, *Qualitative Research* 1(2): 185–204.

Gardner, H. 1986. *Art Through the Ages*. New York: Jovanovich.

Geertz, C. 1973. Thick description: Toward an interpretive theory of culture, *The Interpretation of Cultures*, C. Geertz (ed.). New York: Basic Books, 3–29.

Gergen, K. J. 1994. *Realities and Relationships: Soundings in Social Construction*. Cambridge, MA: Harvard University Press.

——. 1999. *An Invitation to Social Construction*. Thousand Oaks, CA: Sage Publications.

Giddens, A. 1993. *New Rules of Sociological Method*. Stanford, CA: Stanford University Press.

Gilligan, C., A. G. Rogers, et al. (eds.). 1991. *Women, Girls, and Psychotherapy: Reframing Resistance*. New York: Harrington Park Press.

Giroux, H. A. 1992. *Border Crossings: Cultural Workers and the Politics of Education*. London: Routledge.

Gitlin, A. (ed.). 1994. *Power and Method: Political Activism and Educational Research*. Critical Social Thought. London: Routledge.

Goldstein, E. G. 1997. To tell or not to tell: The disclosure of events in the therapist's life to the patient, *Clinical Social Work Journal* 25(1): 41–58.

Gramsci, A. 1971. *Selections from the Prison Notebooks*. New York: International.

Gugelberger, G. M. 1996. Introduction: Institutionalization of transgression—testimonial discourse and beyond, *The Real Thing: Testimonial Discourse and Latin America*, G. M. Gugelberger (ed.). Durham, NC: Duke University Press, 1–19.

Haakon, J. 1998. *Pillar of Salt: Gender, Memory, and the Perils of Looking Back*. New Brunswick, NJ: Rutgers University Press.

——. 1999. Heretical texts: The courage to heal and the incest survivor movement. *New Versions of Victims: Feminist Struggle with the Concept*, S. Lamb (ed.). New York: New York University Press, 13–41.

Habermas, J. 1989. Justice and solidarity: On the discussion concerning "Stage 6," *The Philosophical Forum* 31(Fall/Winter).

Haig-Brown, C. 1992. Choosing border work, *Canadian Journal of Native Education* 19(1): 96–116.

——. 2003. Creating spaces: Testimonio, impossible knowledge, and academe, *Qualitative Studies in Education* 16(3): 415–433.

Hendley, S. 2000. *From Communicative Action to the Face of the Other: Levinas and Habermas on Language, Obligation, and Community*. Lanham, MD: Lexington Books.

Herman, J. 1992. *Trauma and Recovery: The Aftermath of Violence—From Domestic Abuse to Political Terror*. New York: Basic Books.

Hermans, H. J. M. 2001. The dialogical self: Toward a theory of personal and cultural positioning, *Culture and Psychology* 7(3): 243–281.

Heyward, C. 1993. *When Boundaries Betray Us: Beyond Illusions of What Is Ethical in Therapy and in Life*. San Francisco: Harper Collins.

Hollway, W., and T. Jefferson. 2000. *Doing Qualitative Research Differently: Free Association, Narrative, and the Interview Method*. Thousand Oaks, CA: Sage Publications.

hooks, b. 1988. *Talking Back: Thinking Feminist, Thinking Black*. Toronto: Between the Lines.

Horsman, J. 1999. *Too Scared to Learn: Women, Violence, and Education*. Toronto: McGilligan.

Hughes, R. 1998. Considering the vignette technique and its application to a study of drug injecting and HIV risk and safer behavior, *Sociology of Health and Illness* 20(3): 381–400.

James, W. 1978. *The Varieties of Religious Experience: Being the Gifford Lectures on Natural Religion Delivered at Edinburgh in 1901–1902*. New York: Image Books (Doubleday).

Jordan, J. V. 2004. Relational resilience, *The Complexity of Connection: Writings from the Stone Center's Jean Baker Miller Training Institute*, J. V. Jordan, M. Walker, and L. M. Hartling (eds.). New York: Guilford Press, 28–46.

Kennedy, S., and J. Grainger. 2006. *Why I Didn't Tell Anybody: The Sheldon Kennedy Story*. Toronto: Insomniac Press.

Khanna, R. 2001. Ethical ambiguities and spectres of colonialism: Futures of transnational feminism, *Feminist Consequences: Theory for a New Century*, E. Bronfen and M. Kavka (eds.). New York: Columbia University Press, 101–125.

Kieran, E. 2002. Portfolio assessment in language education: A theoretical justification and the results of a classroom-based research project, *Empowerment of the Learner: Changes and Challenges*, R. Kupetz (ed.). Frankfurt am Main: Peter Lang GmbH, 57–84.

Kittay, E. F. 1997. Human dependency and Rawlsian equality, *Feminists Rethink the Self*, D. T. Meyers (ed.). Boulder, CO: Westview Press, 210–266.

Knighton, R. 2006. *Cockeyed*. Toronto; Penguin Canada.

Kosko, B. 1993. *Fuzzy Thinking: The New Science of Fuzzy Logic*. New York: Hyperion.

Kristeva, J. 1982. *Powers of Horror: Essays in Abjection*. New York: Columbia University Press.

——. 2001. *Hannah Arendt: Life Is a Narrative*. Toronto: University of Toronto Press.

Kvale, S. 1996. *InterViews: An Introduction to Qualitative Research Interviewing*. Thousand Oaks, CA: Sage Publications.

Lamb, S. 1999. Constructing the victim: Popular images and lasting labels, *New Versions of Victims: Feminist Struggle with the Concept*, S. Lamb (ed.). New York: New York University Press, 108–138.

Lanham, R. A. 1991. *A Handlist of Rhetorical Terms*. Berkeley and Los Angeles: University of California Press.

Lather, P. 1992. Post-critical pedagogies: A feminist reading, *Feminisms and Critical Pedagogy*, C. Luke and J. Gore (eds.). London: Routledge.

——. 1994. Fertile obsession: Validity after poststructuralism, *Power and Method: Political Activism and Educational Research*. A. D. Gitlin (ed.). New York, London: Routledge, 36–60.

——. 2000. Reading the image of Rigoberta Menchu: Undecidability and language lessons, *Qualitative Studies in Education* 13(2): 153–162.

Lawless, E. J. 2001. *Women Escaping Violence: Empowerment through Narrative*, Columbia: University of Missouri Press.

Lawrence-Lightfoot, S. 1999. *Respect: An Exploration*. Reading, MA: Perseus Books.

Lawrence-Lightfoot, S., and J. H. Davis. 1997. *The Art and Science of Portraiture*. San Francisco: Jossey-Bass.

LeCompte, M. D. 1993. A framework for hearing silence: What does telling stories mean when we are supposed to be doing science? *Naming Silenced Lives and the Process of Educational Change*, D. McLaughlin and W. G. Tierney (eds.). London: Routledge.

Levinas, E. 1969. *Totality and Infinity*. Pittsburgh, PA: Duquesne University Press.

——. 1985. *Ethics and Infinity*. Pittsburgh, PA: Duquesne University Press.

——. 1991. *Otherwise Than Being*. Boston: Nijoff.

Lincoln, Y. S. 1993. I and Thou: Method, voice, and roles in research with the silenced, *Naming Silenced Lives: Personal Narratives and the Process of Educational Change*, D. McLaughlin and W. G. Tierney (eds.). London: Routledge, 29–47.

Lorde, A. 1980. An interview with Karla Hammond, *American Poetry Review* March/April: 19.

Lubiano, W. 1991. Shuckin' off the African-American Native Other: What's Pomo got to do with it? *Cultural Critique* 18: 149–186.

Lyotard, F. 1984. *The Postmodern Condition: A Report on Knowledge*. Minneapolis: University of Minnesota Press.

Marecek, J. 1999. Trauma talk in feminist clinical practice, *New Versions of Victims: Feminist Struggle with the Concept*, S. Lamb (ed.). New York: New York University Press, 158–182.

Martin, J. R. 1996. Aerial distance, esotericism, and other closely related traps, *Signs* 21: 584–614.

McKeganey, N., M. Abel, et al. 1995. The preparedness to share injecting equipment: An analysis using vignettes, *Addiction* 90: 1253–1260.

McLaren, P., and J. Pinkney Pastrana. 2000. The search for the complicit native: Violence, historical amnesia, and the anthropologist as ideologue of empire, *Qualitative Studies in Education* 13(2): 163–184.

Meiners, E. R. 2001. Exhibiting authentic ethnicities? The complexities of identity, experience, and audience in (educational) qualitative research, *Race Ethnicity and Education* 4(3): 109–127.

Miller, J. B., and I. P. Stiver. 1997. *The Healing Connection: How Women Form Relationships in Therapy and in Life*. Boston: Beacon Press.

Mohanty, C. T. 1991. Under Western eyes: Feminist scholarship and colonial discourses, *Third World Women and the Politics of Feminism*, A. Russo and L. Torres (ed.). Indianapolis: Indiana University Press, 51–80.

Naples, N. A. 2003a. Deconstructing and locating survivor discourse: Dynamics of narrative, empowerment, and resistance, *Signs: Journal of Women in Cultural and Society* 28(4): 1151–1184.

——. 2003b. *Feminism and Method: Ethnography, Discourse Analysis, and Activist Research*. London: Routledge.

Narayan, K. 1993. How native is a "Native" anthropologist?" *American Anthropologist* 95(3): 671–686.

Nelson, H. L. 2001. *Damaged Identities Narrative Repair*. Ithaca, NY: Cornell University Press.

Oakley, A. 2000. *Experiments in Knowing: Gender and Method in the Social Sciences*. Cambridge: Polity Press.

Oliver, K. 2001. *Witnessing: Beyond Recognition*. Minneapolis, University of Minnesota.

Oliver, K. (ed.). 2002. *The Portable Kristeva*, European Perspectives: A Series in Social Thought and Cultural Criticism. New York: Columbia University Press.

Parpart, J. L., S. M. Rai, et al. (eds.). 2002. *Rethinking Empowerment: Gender and Development in a Global/local World*, Routledge/Warwick Studies in Globalisation. London: Routledge.

Pease, B. 2002. Rethinking empowerment: A postmodern reappraisal for emancipatory practice, *British Journal of Social Work* 32(2): 135–147.

Pennebaker, J. W. 1990. *Opening Up: The Healing Power of Expressing Emotions*. New York: The Guilford Press.

Perrault, J. 1998. Autography/Transformation/Assymetry (1995). *Autobiography, Women, Theory*, S. Smith and J. Watson (eds.). Madison: University of Wisconsin Press, 190–196.

Peterson, Z. D. 2002. More than a mirror: The ethics of therapist self-disclosure, *Psychotherapy: Theory/Research/Practice/Training* 39(1): 21–31.

Pickering, M. 2001. *Stereotyping: The Politics of Representation*. Basingstoke: Palgrave.

Polkinghorne, D. E. 2004. *Practice and the Human Sciences: The Case for a Judgment-Based Practice of Care*. New York: State University of New York Press.

Raggat, P. T. F. 2006. Multiplicity and conflict in the dialogical self: A life-narrative approach, *Identity and Story: Creating Self in Narrative*, D. P. McAdams, R. Josselson, and A. Leiblich (eds.). Washington, D.C.: American Psychological Association, 15–36.

Razack, S. 1993a. Storytelling for social change, *Gender and Education* 5(1): 55–71.

——. 1993b. Storytelling for social change, *Returning the Gaze: Essays on Racism, Feminism and Politics*, H. Bannerji (ed.). Toronto: Sister Vision Press, 100–122.

——. 2000. Your place or mine? Transnational feminist collaboration, *Anti-Racist Feminism*, A. Calliste and G. Dei (eds.). Halifax: Fernwood, 39–53.

Richey, L. A. 2002. Development, demographic, feminist agendas: Depoliticizing empowerment in a Tanzanian family planning project, *Rethinking Empowerment: Gender and Development in a Global/Local World*, J. L. Parpart, S. M. Rai, and K. Staudt (eds.). London: Routledge, 199–217.

Rifkin, S. B., and P. Pridmore. 2001. *Partners in Planning: Information, Participation, and Empowerment*. London: Macmillan Education Ltd.

Ristock, J. L., and J. Pennell. 1996. *Community Research as Empowerment: Feminist Links, Postmodern Interruptions*. Oxford: Oxford University Press.

Rogers, A. G., M. E. Casey, et al. 1999. An interpretive poetics of languages of the unsayable, *Making Meaning of Narratives*, R. Josselson and A. Lieblich (eds.). Thousand Oaks, CA: Sage Publications, 77–106.

Roman, L. 2003. Conditions, contexts and controversies of truth-making: Rigoberta Menchu and the perils of everyday witnessing and testimonial work, *Qualitative Studies in Education* 16(3): 275–286.

Ronai, C. R. 1999. In the line of sight at *Public Eye*: In search of a victim, *New Versions of Victims: Feminist Struggle with the Concept*, S. Lamb (ed.). New York: New York University Press, 139–157.

Said, E. W. 1993. *Culture and Imperialism*. New York: Alfred A. Knopf.

Sandell, J. 1996. Adjusting to oppression: The rise of therapeutic feminism in the United States, *In "Bad girls"/"Good girls": Women, Sex and Power in the Nineties*, N. B. Maglin and D. Perry (eds.). New Brunswick, NJ: Rutgers University Press, 21–35.

Shearer-Cremean, C., and C. L. Winkelman (eds). 2004. *Survivor Rhetoric: Negotiations and Narrativity in Abused Women's Language*. Toronto: University of Toronto Press.

Shotter, J. 1997. The social construction of our "inner lives," *Journal of Constructivist Psychology*, www.massey.ac.nz/~alock//virtual/inner.htm: 1–12.

Simi, N. L. and J. Mahalik. 1997. Comparison of feminist versus psychoanalytic/ dynamic and other therapists on self-disclosure, *Psychology of Women Quarterly* 21: 465–483.

Smothers, R. 2003. Outspoken victim of abuse by priest kills himself, *The New York Times*, Metro Section, October 14, 2003, p. B1.

Sommer, D. 1998. Sacred secrets: A strategy for survival. 1993. *Women, Autobiography, Theory*, S. Smith and J. Watson (eds.). Madison: University of Wisconsin Press, 197–207.

Sontag, S. 2003. *Regarding the Pain of Others*. New York: Picador.

Spivak, G. 1987. *In Other Worlds: Essays in Cultural Politics*. New York: Methuen.

——. 1993. *Outside in the Teaching Machine*. New York and London, Routledge.

——. 1994. In a word. Interview, *The Essential Difference*, N. Schor and E. Weed (eds.). Bloomington: Indiana University Press, 151–184.

——. 1996. Subaltern talk: Interview with the editors, *The Spivak Reader*, D. Landry and G. McLean (eds.). London: Routledge, 287–308.

Srivastava, S., and M. Francis. 2006. The problem of "authentic" storytelling in anti-racist and anti-homophobic education, *Critical Sociology* 32(2-3): 275–307.

Stewart, A. 2001. *Theories of Power and Domination: The Politics of Empowerment in Late Modernity*. Thousand Oaks, CA: Sage Publications.

Stoll, D. 1999. *The Story of Rigoberta Menchu and All Poor Guatemalans*. Boulder, CO: Westview Press.

Stolte, J. F. 1994. The context of satisficing in vignette research, *Journal of Social Psychology* 134(6): 727–734.

Stromquist, N. P. 2002. Education as a means for empowering women, *Rethinking Empowerment: Gender and Development in a Global/local World*, J. L. Parpart, S. M. Rai, and K. Staudt (eds.). London: Routledge, 250.

Styhre, A. 2001. Kaizen, ethics, and care of the operations: Management after empowerment, *Journal of Management Studies* 38(6): 795–810.

Thorne, A., and K. McLean. 2003. Telling traumatic events in adolescence: A study of master narrative positioning, *Autobiographical Memory and the Construction of a Narrative Self*, R. Fivush and C. A. Haden (eds.). Mahwah, NJ: Erlbaum Associates, 169–185.

Tierney, W. G. 2000. Beyond translation: Truth and Rigoberta Menchu, *Qualitative Studies in Education* 13(2): 103–113.

——. 2002. Get real: representing reality, *International Journal of Qualitative Studies in Education* 15(4): 385–398.

Tom, A. 1997. The deliberate relationship: A frame for talking about faculty-student relationships, *The Alberta Journal of Educational Research* XLIII(1): 3–21.

Trinh, M.-H. 1989a. *Woman, Native, Other: Writing Post-Coloniality and Feminism*. Indianapolis: Indiana University Press.

——. 1989b. Not you/like you: Post-colonial women and the interlocking questions of identity and difference, *Making Face, Making Soul*, G. E. Anzaldúa (ed.). San Francisco: Aunt Lute Foundation Books, 371–375.

——. 1991. *When the Moon Waxes Red: Representation, Gender, and Cultural Politics*. London: Routledge.

Tronto, J. C. 2006. Vicious circles of privatized caring, *Socializing Care: Feminist Ethics and Public Issues,* M. Hamington and D. C. Miller (eds.). Lanham, MD: Rowman and Littlefield Publishers, 3–26.

Turner, C. S. V. 2002. Women of color in academe: Living with multiple marginality, *Journal of Higher Education* 73(1).

Turner, V. 1981. Social dramas and stories about them, *On Narrative,* W. J. T. Mitchell (eds.). Chicago: University of Chicago Press, 137–163.

van der Kolk, B. A., A. C. McFarlane, et al. 1996. *Traumatic Stress: the Effects of Overwhelming Experience on Mind, Body, and Society,* New York: Guildford Press.

Walker, M. U. 1992. Moral understandings: Alternative "epistemology" for a feminist ethics, *Explorations in Feminist Ethics: Theory and Practice.* E. B. Cole and S. Coultrap-McQuin. Bloomington: Indiana University Press, 165–175.

——. 1997. Picking up the pieces: Lives, stories, and integrity, *Feminists Rethink the Self,* D. T. Meyers (ed.). Boulder, CO: Westview Press, 62–84.

Walkerdine, V. 1992. Progressive pedagogy and political struggle, *Feminisms and Critical Pedagogy,* C. Luke and J. Gore (eds.). London: Routledge, 15–24.

Weis, L., and M. Fine. 2000. *Speed Bumps: A Student-Friendly Guide to Qualitative Research.* New York: Teacher's College, Columbia University.

Wendt, R. F. 2001. *The Paradox of Empowerment: Suspended Power and the Possibility of Resistance.* Santa Barbara, CA: Preager.

Wenger, E. 1998. Learning, meaning, and identity, *Communities of Practice,* R. Pea, J. S. Brown, and J. Hawkins (eds.). Cambridge: Cambridge University Press, 145–173.

Weseen, S., and L. M. Wong. 2000. Qualitative research, representations, and social responsibilities, *Speed Bumps: A Student-Friendly Guide to Qualitative Research,* L. Weis and M. Fine (eds.). New York: Teacher's College, Columbia University, 32–66.

Young, I. M. 1990. *Justice and the Politics of Difference.* Princeton, NJ: Princeton University Press.

——. 1997. Asymmetrical reciprocity: On moral respect, wonder, and enlarged thought, *Intersecting Voices: Dilemmas of Gender, Political Philosophy, and Policy.* Princeton, NJ: Princeton University Press.

Zimmerman, M. 1996. *Testimonio* in Guatamala: Payeras, Rigoberta, and beyond, *The Real Thing: Testimonial Discourse and Latin America,* G. Gugelberger (ed.). Durham, NC: Duke University Press.

Zulaika, J. 2003. Excessive witnessing: The ethical as temptation, *Witness & Memory: The Discourse of Trauma,* A. Douglass and T. A. Vogler (eds.). London: Routledge, 89–108.

INDEX

About the Author

Linde Zingaro lives in Vancouver, B.C., where she has led a varied work and academic life since arriving at 17 to go to the Vancouver School of Art. She has been a press operator, a cook, a darkroom technician, the Executive Director of two nonprofit agencies serving adolescents at risk, and the owner of an art gallery. Since 1985, she has maintained a private counseling and consulting practice, providing direct support to individuals and skills training for staff groups or classes working in community service delivery. She has also traveled extensively in Japan, working with women's groups and agencies in the expansion of services to vulnerable groups in that country.

She is truly a life-long learner, having completed the Ph.D. for which the original version of this text was written when she was sixty years old.

Breinigsville, PA USA
27 September 2009
224828BV00003B/1/P